Natasla æt 2003

How do gender and race become objects of intellectual inquiry? What happens to marginal discourses when they are taken up by or participate in these processes of scrutiny and evaluation? In *Women Intellectuals, Modernism, and Difference*, Alice Gambrell attempts to answer these questions by examining the careers of a group of women intellectuals – Leonora Carrington, Ella Deloria, H. D., Zora Neale Hurston, and Frida Kahlo – whose recent scholarly rediscovery coincided with the rise of feminist and minority discourse studies in the contemporary academy. Gambrell explores their affiliations with and activities within a range of metropolitan projects during the years between the two World Wars – including Surrealism, Anthropology, and Psychoanalysis – in order to map the shifting contours of the institutional settings within which these women worked and were appraised. She examines the exhibitions, memoirs, poems, ethnographies, and personal correspondences that these women produced, combining concrete local observation with contemporary theoretical perspectives on race and gender. Through a highly original and provocative mixture of empirical detail and theoretical speculation, Gambrell offers new ways of thinking about the relationships between cultural studies, feminist studies, and minority discourse analysis within the ongoing reassessment of Modernism.

C000162292

Cultural Margins 4

Women intellectuals, modernism, and difference

Cultural Margins

General editors

Timothy Brennan
Departmentof English,
State University of New York at Stony Brook

Abdul JanMohamed
Department of English, University of California, Berkeley

The series **Cultural Margins** originated in response to the rapidly increasing interest in postcolonial and minority discourses among literary and humanist scholars in the US, Europe, and elsewhere. The aim of the series is to present books (both contributory and by single author) which investigate the complex cultural zone within and through which dominant and minority societies interact and negotiate their differences.

Studies published in the series range from examinations of the debilitating effects of cultural marginalisation, to analyses of the forms of power found at the margins of culture, to books which map the varied and complex components involved in the relations of domination and subversion. The books engage with expressions of cultural marginalisation which might be literary (e.g. the novels of African or Caribbean or native American writers within a postcolonial context); or textual in a broader sense (e.g. legal or cultural documents relating to the subordination of groups under categories such as race and gender); or dramatic (e.g. subversive performance art by minority groups such as gays and lesbians); or in the sphere of popular culture (e.g. film, video, TV).

This is an international series, addressing questions crucial to the deconstruction and reconstruction of cultural identity in the late twentieth-century world.

Titles published

1. Anna Marie Smith *New Right discourse on race and sexuality: Britain, 1968–1990*
2. David Richards *Masks of difference: cultural representations in literature, anthropology and art*
3. Vincent J. Cheng *Joyce, race, and empire*

Women intellectuals, modernism, and difference
Transatlantic culture
1919–1945

Alice Gambrell
University of Southern California

CAMBRIDGE
UNIVERSITY PRESS

Published by the Press Syndicate of the University of Cambridge
The Pitt Building, Trumpington Street, Cambridge CB2 1RP

Cambridge University Press
The Edinburgh Building, Cambridge CB2 2RU, United Kingdom
40 West 20th Street, New York, NY 10011–4211, USA
10 Stamford Road, Oakleigh, Melbourne 3166, Australia

© Cambridge University Press, 1997

This book is in copyright. Subject to statutory exception
and to the provisions of relevant collective licensing agreements,
no reproduction of any part may take place without
the written permission of Cambridge University Press.

First published 1997

Printed in the United Kingdom at the University Press, Cambridge

A catalogue record for this book is available from the British Library

Library of Congress cataloguing in publication data
Gambrell, Alice.
Women intellectuals, modernism, and difference: transatlantic
culture, 1919–1945 / Alice Gambrell.
    p.   cm. – (Cultural margins: 4)
Includes bibliographical references and index.
ISBN 0 521 55341 5 (hardback). – ISBN 0 521 55688 0 (paperback)
1. Modernism (Literature)   2. Feminism and literature.
3. Literature – Women authors – History and criticism.
I. Title.   II. Series.
PN56.M54G36   1997
809'.91–dc20   96–36666   CIP

ISBN 0 521 55341 5 hardback
ISBN 0 521 55688 0 paperback

CE

Contents

Illustrations

Paintings by Frida Kahlo are reproduced by the authorization of the Instituto Nacional de Bellas Artes, Mexico City.

Acknowledgments

Grateful acknowledgment to the following friends, colleagues, teachers, and press readers for careful (and sometimes contentious) contributions to all or to parts of this project, at various points during its long process of development: Esme Bhan, Joseph Boone, Paul Cantor, Ralph Cohen, Vincent Cheng, Gary Dunham, Mark Edmundson, Patricia Gill, Barbara Green, Richard Handler, Michael Levenson, Deborah McDowell, Teresa McKenna, Katherine Mills, Tania Modleski, Carolyn Porter, Mary Rolinson, Meg Russett, Ray Ryan, Hilary Schor, Brenda Silver, and Kevin Taylor. The learnedness, intellectual generosity, and feminist wit of an anonymous press reader guided my revision process from start to finish, and I give her my sincerest thanks for being able to envision a book in the fragmentary manuscript that she originally read. Perhaps most important, Holly Laird's sympathetic criticism enabled me to start working on this project, and Abdul JanMohamed's enabled me to stop.

Passages from the correspondence of Ella Deloria and Ruth Benedict are reproduced by permission of the Special Collections of the Vassar College Library, Poughkeepsie, New York; special thanks to Vine Deloria, Jr., executor of the Ella Deloria Papers, and Mary Catherine Bateson and Rhoda Métraux, executors of the Ruth Benedict Papers. Passages from H.D.'s *Tribute to Freud* (copyright Norman Holmes Pearson, 1956 and 1974) and *Helen in Egypt* (copyright Norman Holmes Pearson, 1961) are reproduced by permission of the New Directions Publishing Corporation and Carcanet Press. Finally, my thanks to the University of Southern California for financial support in the form of a 1993 Junior Faculty research grant.

Introduction

Cultural histories of academic feminism have only recently begun to be written, and this volume is intended (albeit largely in indirect ways) as a contribution to that ongoing effort. It contains analyses of responses by a diverse range of interwar women intellectuals to major early twentieth-century conceptions of difference and alterity – responses that, in recent years, have repeatedly been cited by academic feminists as precursors to contemporary critical practice.[1] Through the course of separate chapters on Leonora Carrington, Ella Deloria, H. D. (Hilda Doolittle), Zora Neale Hurston, and Frida Kahlo, I will develop a series of analytical procedures meant to encourage a varied and unsettled understanding not only of these earlier figures and their work, but also, more provisionally, of how women intellectuals in recent years have created and disseminated new academic-feminist methodologies through a process of reading, writing, and (in Teresa de Lauretis's phrase[2]) *"thinking within and against"* dominant theoretical vocabularies within which questions of "difference" are, as is now largely understood, insufficiently problematized.

The narrow purpose of the project is to address the question of what it meant, during the 1930s and early 1940s, for women to work within the boundaries of schools, movements, or disciplines in which, under more usual circumstances, they would have occupied the position of "Other": the object of investigation, the eroticized source of inspiration, the respondent in – though rarely the initiator of – an interlocutionary exchange. Within the purview of the project, I include texts by women anthropologists who did fieldwork in their "home" communities (Hurston and Deloria); women who played the peculiar dual role of student–analysand to Freud as he

1

was struggling to solve the "riddle" of femininity (H. D., as well as other women students of Freud to whom she responded); and women publicly associated with the brand of Surrealism set forth in the late thirties by André Breton, who throughout his career had been fascinated by marginalized forms of knowledge (Carrington and Kahlo). Prized in their own time – though in troubling and paradoxical ways – for the experiential immediacy that they would supposedly contribute to a series of cultural practices within which the pure value of "experience" was itself being regarded with increasing skepticism, all of these women engaged in difficult, charged intellectual exchanges whose valences I will go on to measure in the following chapters. I refer to this brand of intellectual affiliation as "insider-outsider" activity, borrowing (for reasons that I will explain in chapter 1) from ongoing social-scientific arguments about the many philosophical and political ramifications of texts produced by credentialized investigators who travel to sites more or less familiar to them in order to perform their professional research.

Many commentators, of course, have addressed these and related issues in the context of *contemporary* cultural life. Examples can be located across a range of fields: de Lauretis's and Gayatri Spivak's mid-eighties writings on the conflictual relationship between the hypothesis of "woman" and the activities of women within the practices of psychoanalysis and deconstruction; Kirin Narayan's complex early nineties answers to her crucial question "How Native is a 'Native' Anthropologist?"; and many others. Recent forms of insider-outsider activity, I would argue, have in fact dominated academic feminist work during the last decade-and-a-half, in the widespread practice of "talking back" (bell hooks's phrase[3]) to prominent male, euroethnic theorists whose conceptions of "difference," as feminists across a range of positions have repeatedly demonstrated, require strenuous and ongoing interrogation. I have noticed again and again, however, that the characteristic debates embedded within contemporary versions of feminist insider-outsider activity – which themselves encompass shifting valuations of theory and experience, simulation and authenticity, philosophical negation and practical affirmation – are typically marked off as "new" or "emergent" or peculiarly "postmodern," when in fact they have a long, fraught history. Tracing out one part of that varied history is the broader purpose of this volume.

I focus, in these pages, on work by five interwar women who ascended from obscurity to heightened visibility during the mid-eighties – the banner years of academic-feminist back-talk – and whose privileged status during that period suggests a partial histor-iographical frame through which recent critical practices and methods might be contextualized and comprehended. The interwar period comprises a transitional phase during which many of these more recent discussions were beginning to assume (but had not yet solidified) their now-distinct contours. We can observe this process in miniature by looking briefly at Walter Benjamin's 1936 essay "The Storyteller," a touchstone in many recent debates about the meanings of "modernism."[4] There, describing the aftermath of World War I, Benjamin mourned the widespread postwar "[de]valu[ation]" of "experience" – a condition whose most catastrophic consequence, he argued, was a sudden "[in]ability to exchange experiences" in the form of storytelling.[5] The raw material of storytelling consisted, for Benjamin, of "[e]xperience which is passed on from mouth to mouth"; he suggested that in the wake of the war, an unmediated faith in the truth of "experience" was abandoned on the battlefields of Europe, which young soldiers left behind equipped with a keen and entirely new sense of their own vulnerability to violent, all-encompassing, and mostly invisible forces that operated far beyond the scope of their control. Interwar insider-outsider activity, as I will go on to argue, prompted a peculiar reengagement of the newly devalued phenomenon of "experience" – one that both accepted and interrogated the terms of the devaluative process that Benjamin in many respects accurately describes.

Benjamin's, of course, was an early formulation of one of the key tenets of many more recent descriptions of conventionally "moder-nist" practice, which tend to feature (here, I quote from Eugene Lunn's oft-cited 1985 itinerary) the condition of "*'Dehumanization' and the Demise of the Integrated Subject or Personality.*"[6] It is significant, I think, that Benjamin locates a version of this *"Demise"* in the figure of the young European soldier, for whom the "full corporeality" of "experience" has given way to a more skeptical sense that "experi-ence" is always shaped and mediated by determinants far larger and more powerful than his "tiny, fragile human body."[7] For during the last decade many more critics working to reassess these conventional definitions of "modernism," following Nancy Hartsock's much-admired 1987 account of "Minority vs. Majority Theories" of moder-nity, have argued that losses suffered by those at the centers of metropolitan cultural life – represented in this instance by Benjamin's homeward-bound soldiers – were matched and perhaps determined by new gains made by those previously silenced and relegated to the margins: "Why is it," Hartsock famously asked, that "exactly at the moment when so many of us who have been silenced begin to demand the right to name ourselves, to act as subjects rather than objects of history, that just then the concept of subjecthood becomes 'problematic?'"[8] The significance of Benjamin's remarks, in light of Hartsock's analysis, might better be taken as local and specific, rather than as more broadly generalizable to the "modernist" condition.

The women whose work I will go on to discuss, however, cannot be situated comfortably within either Lunn's account of the pervasive disillusionment at modernism's center, or within Hartsock's description of the newfound empowerment of those on the margins: their varied intellectual affiliations caused them to vacillate between those two poles. As I will go on to argue in fuller detail in the following chapters, their articulation into interwar metropolitan intellectual life was in large part premised upon the expectation that they would serve as containers, transmitters, or translators of the very forms of experiential immediacy whose purported loss Benjamin mourns; the texts that they produced, however, often worked in subtle ways to undermine that expectation.

In one of the most difficult and suggestive passages in Benjamin's essay, these sorts of tensions are precisely evoked; Benjamin argues that "the storyteller" might best be imagined not as a unified type, but as a composite of two opposed, exemplary figures from the prewar past – the homebody, on one hand, and the wanderer, on the other – who contribute to the storytelling process forms of knowledge that are both familiar and strange, domestic and exotic. Benjamin's privileged example of conditions that enable the "interpenetration of these two archaic types" lies in the "trade structure" of the Middle Ages, where the "resident master craftsman" and the "traveling journeymen worked together in the same rooms."[9] Benjamin might productively have looked somewhat closer to home, as the "interpenetrat[ing]" activity that he describes quite precisely evokes the situation of the insider-outsider:

> "When someone goes on a trip, he has something to tell about," goes the German saying, and people imagine the storyteller as someone who has come from afar. But they enjoy no less listening to the man who has stayed at home, making an honest living, and who knows the local tales and traditions.[10]

Insider-outsider intellectuals, whose value consisted in their simultaneous distance from and intimacy with the subjects of their own inquiry – in "stay[ing] at home" *and* in " 'go[ing] on a trip' " – thus enacted a version of Benjamin's lost art of "storytelling" that was in part simply compensatory, in part highly complex, and in the process performed their work atop one of the most volatile philosophical faultlines within present-day remappings of the field of "modernism."

Surrealists, ethnographers, and psychoanalysts all trafficked in "experience "passed on from mouth to mouth" – in other words, in the collection and dissemination of testimony about the lived immediacy of those on the peripheries of metropolitan cultural life: hysterics, nonwestern peoples, children, the masses, those who comprised the now-familiar litany of "Modernism's Other[s]."[11] Although Kahlo, Carrington, *et al.* were important agents in this process, what they brought to it was not an uncritical engagement, but rather a methodological skepticism borne out of their awareness that their task was to supply frequently romanticized, purportedly authentic vestiges of a form of experiential immediacy that was, in Benjamin's terms, newly devalued within the very institutional contexts in which they worked, even as it was ardently sought after as a compensation for the widespread postwar sense of loss.

As such, interwar insider-outsider activity was inevitably fraught with ambiguity – philosophical, political, and otherwise – which partly explains why recent critical arguments about Kahlo, Carrington, *et al.* have vacillated so sharply between polarized claims that their work was either resistant or collaborative, subversive or complicitous. I will show in the following chapters how these contemporary debates, while never fully resolvable, can at the very least be clarified by much closer attention to the shifting disciplinary contexts within which these women's work was performed. Central to my own analysis will be a consideration, mapped in much fuller detail in chapter 1, of the problem of female intellectual affiliation; this emphasis is meant to enable, most crucially, a tracing out of the "latent self-presentation" (the phrase is Chandra Talpade Mohanty's[12]) that appears in these women's works as a critical countercurrent to the more clearly legible, more easily recuperable aspects of their "storytelling" practice.

Historian E. H. Carr, writing in the early sixties, argued that "the function of the historian is neither to love the past nor to emancipate himself from the past," but instead, to put the past to work in the services of "understanding the present."[13] This volume, from its beginnings, has been motivated by the concerns of the present time;

its execution, moreover, has been framed by two distinct moments in the development of academic feminism. I began working on the earliest version of this project in graduate school during the mid-eighties, at a time when the most influential feminist commentators were largely preoccupied with the manner in which questions of gender and race were elided within the dominant theoretical vocabularies of the time: primarily those of Derrida, Foucault, Freud, and Lacan. "Theory," as Deborah McDowell recently put it, had come to constitute itself in *"a very particular practice"* (emphasis added).[14] The following chapters began, as such, as a historically displaced effort to comprehend the attraction felt by the most influential feminist theorists of that period to particular analytical paradigms within which, in de Lauretis's oft-quoted words, the position of woman is "vacant," and "cannot be claimed by women."[15] The project developed over time into a more sustained and systematic effort to provide a partial critical genealogy of the kinds of debates over the competing values of "experience" and "theory" that have framed academic feminism during the last fifteen years; this is an opposition that has its own lengthy and entangled history – a history that has both enabled and excluded certain kinds of discussion, and that needs to be examined concretely and in its own right.[16] I complete this book, finally, in the wake of at least one influential call for an end to one of the major forms of theoretical engagement that inspired my own retrospective examination of these issues: philosopher Elizabeth Grosz's 1994 critique of de Lauretis's oppositional reengagement of psychoanalysis in the 1994 volume *The Practice of Love.*

Using psychoanalysis as her test case, Grosz asks more broadly in her essay whether persistent feminist and lesbian interest in "extend[ing] one model of power, particularly a masculinist text, so that it covers domains and objects hitherto left out or unthought," might still serve some useful purpose, or whether, to the contrary, such interest might in fact serve primarily in order to "shore up and support a discourse whose time has come ... to resurrect a theoretical paradigm facing its limits."[17] In her published response to Grosz, de Lauretis argues in detail, to the contrary, that psychoanalysis is still necessary and useful, if only when read in stringent and subtle ways against its own grain. In this important exchange, neither of these two major theorists, both of them operating at the top of their form, succeed in persuading me that these fraught questions have yet been answered. Grosz's terminal declaration of the "limits" of the psychoanalytic paradigm, while powerful and provocative, nonetheless fails to account for the long history of intellectual and political innovations made by women who deployed a particular practice or technique whose usefulness was largely perceived as being spent. De Lauretis, on the other hand, provides a strong and witty defense of her own reengagement of psychoanalysis; to Grosz's broader questions, however, she responds in notably distanced ways, filtering brief but pivotal portions of her argument through quotations from reviews of *The Practice of Love* published by other feminist writers.[18]

At the same time, however, both Grosz and de Lauretis offer hints of a way beyond this apparent impasse, some of which I will pursue in the following chapters. Most importantly, while Grosz makes the crucial point that reading psychoanalysis against its own grain often serves to create a specious homogenization of the irreducibly diverse category of "women," de Lauretis responds that her own work engages in dialogue not only with psychoanalysis, but also with

> works by other lesbians and feminists ... be they theorists or poets, novelists or critics – [which] constitute the epistemo-logical terrain of [her] own thinking no less than do the more prestigious writings of Freud, Lacan, or Foucault.[19]

De Lauretis's contemporary version of insider-outsider practice, in other words, affiliates itself in *multiple* ways – not simply with psychoanalysis – a condition, I will go on to argue in the next chapter, that has been crucial to the development of insider-outsider activity throughout this century; to read her work (as Grosz does, in this instance) solely as an oppositional encounter with a dominant "masculinist" paradigm is thus to overlook one of her central procedural complexities. In light of the irresolution of the Grosz/de Lauretis debate, however, I suspect that during the next few years the questions raised within it will themselves loom large in academic feminist discussion. Eventually, perhaps, they will also serve to generate new forms of feminist-theoretical activity, along with a newly configured canon of feminist-intellectual precursors far different from the one I will go on to investigate in the following chapters. In large part, then, I offer the following analyses as an alternative to the opposed options set forth by Grosz and de Lauretis: I will suggest, instead, that a series of local, specific, and historically informed considerations of the ways in which insider-outsider debates emerged during the interwar period – only to mutate, eventually, into the forms within which feminist-theoretical analysis is now habitually practiced – might contribute in clear ways to an understanding of where we came from, and also, albeit in much more tentative ways, of where we might go from here.

"Familiar strangeness": women intellectuals, modernism, and difference

> It was bad enough for white people, but when one of your own color could be so different it put you on a wonder. It was like seeing your sister turn into a 'gator. A familiar strangeness. You keep seeing your sister in the 'gator and the 'gator in your sister, and you'd rather not.
>
> Zora Neale Hurston, *Their Eyes Were Watching God* (1937)[1]

Repeatedly throughout her career, Zora Neale Hurston used this startling trope – a perfectly ordinary person, metamorphosing quite suddenly into an alligator – in order to call attention to the irreducible complexity of African–American cultural identity. In the passage that appears as my epigraph, Hurston's narrator describes the attitudes of the people of Eatonville, Florida towards their new mayor and his wife, Joe and Janie Starks. With their freshly painted two-story house, complete with his and her spittoons, the Starks display an abundance of "power and property"[2] previously unknown to any among Joe's largely working-class constituency. In Janie's case, this sense of uncanniness is heightened by the fact that she is a woman; while Janie, like Joe, is separated economically from the broader community, the narrator claims specifically that it is "any *man* who walks in the way of power and property [who] is bound to meet hate," leaving her position rather more ambiguous than her husband's.[3] Janie and Joe – both of them familiar to the community by virtue of being "one of your own color" – are nonetheless estranged from it by virtue of their relative wealth; they embody a disruptive paradox – what Hurston calls a "familiar strangeness."

Hurston wrote *Their Eyes Were Watching God* during a respite between the composition of two book-length ethnographies: *Mules and Men* (1935), comprised mostly of a study of rural African–American oral traditions, and *Tell My Horse* (1938), an extended scholarly treatment of "Voodoo and Life" in mid-thirties Jamaica and Haiti. An African–American woman raised in the postreconstruction South, who was trained in literature and anthropology at Howard, Barnard, and Columbia, and who performed social-scientific research on a variety of western-hemispheric black traditions, Hurston was constantly aware of and attentive to the mixture of "familiar[ity]" and "strangeness" that marked her real and imagined encounters with the subjects of her nonfiction research, as well as those of her fictional writings. Working part-time in a discipline that stressed the importance of the "native point of view," Hurston nonetheless produced a series of books and essays that called into question the possibility of rendering that other perspective in any singular, monolithic way. Despite this, however, Hurston was routinely praised by contemporaneous academic authorities, reductively and with palpable condescension, for the experiential immediacy of her writings – for their "intimate," "true," and "revealing" qualities.[4] Her complex scholarly and fictional formulations were oftentimes received as representative truths, spoken by an insider.

For entirely different reasons, Hurston went on to achieve in the late seventies another form of representative status – as an intellectual heroine, a foremother, and (in both quotidian and otherworldly senses) a "familiar."[5] Not without reason, Hurston's concerns – as a scholar working within the boundaries of an academic institution that othered her – remained significant long after her death in 1960, seeming closely akin to those of a diverse range of women intellectuals who came of age during the mid to late seventies, and who turned increasingly during the last two decades towards critical reexamination of dominant theoretical paradigms for the analysis of "difference." Since the time of her scholarly reclamation, critical reassessments of Hurston's ethnographies have revolved around the question of the extent to which Hurston either complied with or managed to resist the institutional imperatives that supported anthropological research performed in the United States during the thirties. In the decade and a half since Hurston's work came back into print, the tone of those reassessments has turned increasingly pessimistic: Hurston's reevaluation began with a chorus of critical praise for her brilliant subversions of conventional ethnographic practice; it then shifted into a second phase of cautious reconsideration; in the third and most recent phase, finally, many of Hurston's readers have begun closely to consider Hurston's implicatedness in some of the more politically troubling aspects of interwar ethnographic practice.[6]

There are many reasons for these shifting emphases, reasons having as much to do with the exigencies of the present moment (and especially of Hurston's skyrocketing fame) as they do with those of Hurston's own; recent reception studies by Hazel Carby, Ann Ducille, Michele Wallace, and Mary Helen Washington have painted a series of richly detailed pictures, where I have merely provided the barest outlines.[7] By sketching those outlines in such a cursory way, however, my intention is not to dismiss the critical importance of ongoing arguments about Hurston's intellectual resistance or compliance: those shifting (and occasionally overlapping) discussions register clearly the persistence of a variety of pressures still felt by women in the academy, to which many in recent years have responded, in historically displaced ways, via analyses of Hurston's work. Instead, what I mean here to map out is a particular argumentative trajectory that has marked not only Hurston's recent reception history, but also those of many other interwar women intellectuals whose works, largely ignored for nearly fifty years, regained the critical spotlight during the last two decades: among these, I include poet H.D. (Hilda Doolittle) and painter Frida Kahlo, as well as the lesser-known Leonora Carrington, a British painter and writer most often associated with late-thirties Surrealism, and Ella Deloria, a Yankton Sioux anthropologist, linguist, and novelist who performed field research in South Dakota during the thirties and forties.[8] Celebrated initially – even treated (as Michele Wallace has noted with regard to recent Hurston criticism) as "role model[s]" *in absentia* to a later generation of women scholars who had few women teachers of their own[9] – their works now constitute (in Kamala Visweswaran's phrase) an "alternate ... canon," which carries with it many of the problems conventionally associated with *non*-alternate canonicity.[10] As such, they are currently being reinterrogated in respectful but profoundly serious and skeptical ways.

Although my own project takes part in this ongoing process of reassessment, in it I attempt to engage these women's works in a way that operates in excess of the polarized notions of compliance and resistance that I have just described. My own sense is that the skepticism that is currently being articulated by third-phase reinterrogators – however necessary it may be as a corrective to earlier, more celebratory critical tendencies – is nonetheless moving us steadily toward a critical impasse; in theoretical terms developed during the early nineties by historian Gyan Prakash, such arguments leave these women's works "scorched by the power/knowledge axis, leaving nothing ... except the remains of that which was either appropriated or stood resistant."[11] Their position within late-modernist intellectual life, I will argue, was at once less stable and more multiply resonant than that. Thus, in the chapters that follow, I will locate their works within a more varied discursive field, one that operates beyond the confines of these women's charged, one-on-one encounters with the powerful modernist "formations" (the term is Raymond Williams's[12]) with which they are most often associated. I mean to leave room for acknowledgment of compliance, of resistance, *as well as* of other, less polarized effects – by posing a series of questions that directly confront the relationship between "familiar[ity]" and "[e]strange[ment]" with which this chapter began. By situating detailed textual analyses within a cross-disciplinary examination of a broader milieu, I will show how – on the eve of the Second World War, and in the twilight phase of what we now think of as "Modernism" – these women's works helped to bring to crisis several influential strains of cultural critique that operated throughout the early decades of this century, including Anthropology, Surrealism, and Psychoanalysis.

1

What, I asked in my introduction, does it mean to be affiliated with a school, movement, or discipline in which one would, under more usual circumstances, occupy the position of "Other": the privileged object of investigation, the fantasized source of inspiration, the respondent in (though rarely the initiator of) an interlocutionary exchange? What, moreover, are the consequences of bearing witness to particular ranges of experience in a context in which they have habitually been deemed alien, mysterious, or somehow inaccessible? Finally – given the fact that hegemonic otherings tend to be encrypted with multiple significances, having to do not only with gender, but also with race, nation, class, and sexuality – how do these issues impinge in specific ways upon the careers of *women* intellectuals? In the chapters that follow I will take these questions up in the context of interwar cultural life, by examining in detail texts by women intellectuals who were affiliated in this peculiarly ambiguous way with a range of metropolitan formations that includes

Bretonian Surrealism, Psychoanalysis under Freud, and Franz Boas's Anthropology program at Columbia University.

Social scientists sometimes place these issues under the heading of what they call the "insider/outsider debate" – here, referring to the long history of challenges posed by scientific observers who have performed field research – as Hurston did – in their own home communities.[13] In an early-1980s discussion of the contemporary significance of insider-outsider activity, sociologist Peter Rose noted that

> [t]he insider/outsider debate is complex but far from esoteric. Everyone, it seems, has gotten into it. It reaches far beyond the groves of academe, although it is on the campuses where some of the fiercest arguments and confrontations about "who speaks for whom – and who can?" have taken place.[14]

In ways that I described in my introductory remarks, the reverberations of what Rose calls the "insider/outsider debate" are currently being felt across a range of discursive fields both inside and outside the academy. Thus, although my working home is in a department of "English" literature, I have borrowed this radiantly suggestive (if admittedly awkward) hyphenate in order to mark out a broader range of activity that similarly calls into question the hierarchy implicit in relations between a credentialized observer and her or his subjects: when Hurston played the dual role of observer and informant, for example, she occupied an anthropological border area in which constitutive distinctions between the familiar and the strange, the domestic and the alien, became crossed and blurred.

The category shares much in common with Abdul JanMohamed's recent definition of the "specular border intellectual" – a category within which he includes Hurston herself – who is, in JanMohamed's words, "caught between several cultures or groups, none of which are deemed sufficiently enabling or productive." The "specular border intellectual," according to JanMohamed, then proceeds by "utiliz[ing] his or her interstitial cultural space as a vantage point."[15] As will become clear in the chapters that follow, however, the "border[s]" that mark the divisions within the intellectual practices of these women cannot be defined wholly – though they can be in part – as "cultural" borders. The category of the "insider-outsider" shares at least as much in common – and more distinct verbal echoes – with Teresa de Lauretis's 1987 description of contemporary feminist studies, the field where I have my own, primary affiliation. In the passage to which I here refer, de Lauretis poises recent feminist configurations of the subject against an Althusserian model, in which, as de Lauretis puts it, the subject is "completely 'in' ideology [while believing] himself to be outside and free of it." In much recent feminist debate, to the contrary, de Lauretis notes that "the subject that I see emerging from current writings and debates within feminism is one that is at the same time inside *and* outside the ideology of gender, and conscious of being so, conscious of that twofold pull, of that division, that doubled vision."[16]

Here, de Lauretis assesses the stakes of many recent and specifically feminist versions of insider-outsider activity, which operate, like their interwar predecessors, both *"within and against"* dominant theoretical vocabularies.[17] While maintaining a steady focus upon the crisis-ridden context of metropolitan intellectual life during the twenties, thirties, and forties, I hope to demonstrate historical continuity *and* rupture between works by women intellectuals produced earlier in this century, and those "current" or "emerg[ent]" concerns that de Lauretis has demarcated much more recently.

All of the cases that I will go on to examine are enmeshed within the tense dynamic of insider-outsider activity: Frida Kahlo and Leonora Carrington first came into contact with international audiences under the aegis of late-1930s Bretonian Surrealism, a phase marked by Breton's strenuous efforts to locate disciples who made literal the figurative "Othernesses" that had fascinated him and his cohort for close to two decades; Zora Neale Hurston and Ella Cara Deloria, tenuously affiliated with Columbia's anthropology department during the interwar years, both did major portions of their fieldwork in the communities in which they were born or raised – Hurston in Florida, Deloria in South Dakota; finally, H.D. – one of Freud's final, handpicked student-analysands in Vienna before his exile to Britain towards the end of the thirties – worked with Freud in his late efforts to sort out solutions to the perplexing "riddle" of femininity in the context of speculative anthropological works like *Moses and Monotheism.*

Their very presence within these formations marked a significant turn in the logic of modernist cultural critique: a turn away from abstract hypotheses of difference and alterity, and towards more concrete efforts to make public the voices of those previously relegated to the margins. Within each of these interwar formations (as commentators across a range of disciplines have recently noted) "otherness" was, primarily, a device put to use in the services of self-critique or self-ironization; thus, for example, Franz Boas encouraged his students to produce clear, coherent accounts of cultural alternatives to the euroethnic standard – accounts of African– American story-telling traditions, for example, or of Sioux kinship arrangements – in part in order to shatter that standard's imagined singularity.[18] Clifford Geertz, writing about Ruth Benedict's Columbia-based anthropological research, has referred to this process as "self-nativising," which he defines as a technique for juxtaposing "the all-too-familiar and the wildly exotic in such a way that they change places"[19] – for making the observer seem strange to him- or herself. Most often, this "self-nativising" effect was achieved by approximating as closely as possible the other point of view, using an array of strategies ranging from third-person description (as in empirical ethnographies or psychoanalytic case histories) to first-person ventriloquism (as in Surrealist "simulations" of the voices of madwomen).

For the insider-outsider, however, the process of "self-nativising" would generate strikingly different effects. To implicate Hurston, for example, in a "self-nativising" practice – as her more critical recent commentators, albeit in different terms, have in fact done – would constitute an accusation of nostalgist complicity, rather than a celebration of "proto-pomo" (the term is Gayle Rubin's) resistance.[20] By means of modernist practices of "self-nativising," othered voices were frequently and predictably denied any serious measure of internal complexity or contradictoriness of their own. Within the Boasian milieu, for example, clear, coherent cross-cultural description – even in the services of a politically progressive process of self-critique – tended in practice to present a purified, static, near-fantastical picture of the object under scrutiny, one contradicted in obvious ways by the questions of class and gender that both Hurston and Deloria introduced into their own analyses. Bretonian Surrealism (which valorized the voices of women, of the insane, of cultures designated "primitive") and Freud's brand of psychoanalysis (which remained preoccupied with the pesky "problem" of femininity) deployed parallel self-critical strategies, complete with parallel limitations.[21] And those limits, I will suggest, were troubled and at least partly disclosed as a result of the increasing visibility and audibility, during the interwar years, of insider-outsider intellectuals working within each formation. Serving as the real-life counterpart to rarefied imagings of difference and alterity, the woman insider-outsider could not simply occupy the preexisting space of otherness, but was forced, instead, to make room for complexity by devising an altogether new set of tactics. At the same time, moreover, her work pointed out the shortcomings of self-critical strategies grounded in the hypothesis of a distant, mysterious, but ultimately coherent and fully interpretable other.[22]

Of course, much useful commentary has appeared during the last decade that explores the profoundly troubling nature of these aspects of modernist cultural history: the privileging of particular forms of modernist irony, coupled with the search for purportedly authentic vestiges of difference and alterity. In the pages that follow, I attempt to extend these ongoing discussions by asking – with specific regard to works by women – what kinds of motivations and concerns were obscured or suppressed by the relentless and entirely problematical emphasis that was placed upon the supposedly genuine, unvarnished nature of insider-outsider texts. Moreover, by looking at the strategies with which these women sought to renegotiate, renounce, or (even, on occasion) to redeploy fanciful, more conventional conceptualizations of difference or alterity, I will be making an effort to draw connections across the gulf of what I recognize to be a series of somewhat more tangible differences – differences among the women themselves, among the formations within which they worked, and finally, within those formations, among the shifting valuations attached to "difference" itself. This, I realize, is an effort that entails some risk, in that it involves working my own way between and across several fields whose concerns are not by any means analogous, but which are instead related to each other in complicated and sometimes conflictual ways: on one hand are Feminist, African–American, and Western-Hemispheric Studies, which were constituted within the academy (under different names), during the late sixties, as interdisciplinary "area studies" projects; on the other are a series of more recently initiated attempts (often performed under the banner of Cultural Studies) to transfigure "the Modern" by remapping it across disciplinary lines.

The extensive reach of this project resulted from a determining (and by no means an unusual) lacuna in my own mid-eighties literary training: while we focused our work intently on the theoretical problems generated by the strategically useful but deceptively homogeneous category of *"women* writers," we spent little time thinking about the parallel reductiveness of our emphasis upon "women *writers*." Indeed, many of the women whose works we encountered for the first time in mid-eighties feminist-literary classrooms had careers that called the limited designation of the (presumably literary) "writer" into question, spanning as they did a broad disciplinary range: Hurston's literary and anthropological engagements provide a single and somewhat obvious example, while H.D.'s literary, cinematic, sexological, and psychoanalytic experiments comprise another slightly more varied case. Thus, while the proceeding chapters are not traditionally interdisciplinary in their methods – I do not, for example, poise psychoanalytic and literary-critical strategies against one another in my readings of H.D. – I am quite centrally concerned with the question of why women intellectuals have so often performed their work across disciplinary lines.

This necessary contextual breadth has in turn dictated my decision, enacted in the chapters that follow, to pursue these wide-ranging and internally conflictual issues with some caution and tentativeness, gauging their significances within a series of concrete, limited, and highly specific settings, within which I include detailed analyses of a range of texts including museum displays, experimental ethnographies, memoirs, case histories, and personal correspondences. In addition, my own point of departure is located somewhere within the interstices of the broader contemporary fields that I mapped in the preceding paragraphs: that is, in writings by present-day commentators working within and around contemporary versions of the "insider/outsider debate," including anthropologist Lila Abu-Lughod, poet Nathaniel Mackey, filmmaker Trinh T. Minh-Ha, and theorists Teresa de Lauretis and Gayatri Spivak. Among them, they have raised a series of questions that I have recalibrated and displaced into the interwar context; particular aspects of their arguments will be addressed in the pages that follow. They have demonstrated across the range of their writings how central the issue of insider–outsider activity is to the constitution of knowledge in contemporary academic life, and have begun to create an intellectual context in which hegemonic processes of othering can no longer function with the kind of impunity that marked their operation during the interwar period. Where I diverge from Abu-Lughod *et al.*, however, is in the fact that I will be looking at these issues *retrospectively*, in the particular and in many respects distant setting of metropolitan intellectual life during the years leading up to World War II. The "insider/outsider debate," so crucial to present-day academic (as well as political and popular) discussion, has its own specific histories, one of which I will examine in the chapters that follow.[23]

2

I have noted that my own project negotiates between, on one hand, the kind of contextual particularity often demanded within area studies, and on the other, the broader-based impulse towards demystification that has informed many recent efforts to reconceive the field of "modernism." In order to show how this polarity is itself a lot less clear-cut than it might at first appear to be, and to describe how my own project enacts this negotiation, I will turn to an analysis of a single moment in recent debate: bell hooks's 1990 response, launched from a complex position within the varied field of black feminist studies, to the influential anthology *Writing Culture: the Poetics and Politics of Ethnography*, which was edited by James Clifford and George Marcus and published in 1986. In her response, hooks addresses the better part of her attention to Clifford's introductory essay, which was titled "Partial Truths."

The story of the late-eighties feminist response to Clifford's "Partial Truths" has by now been told several times, most recently in the detailed and fair-minded history given by Ruth Behar in her introduction to the 1995 volume *Women Writing Culture*; the effects of these critiques, moreover, reverberate in important ways in Clifford's own more recent work.[24] I will here recount only as much as is necessary in order to situate hooks's 1990 commentary. Clifford and Marcus's influential volume, now over a decade old, grew out of an American Research Council seminar, and contains essays by anthropologists, historians of anthropology, and literary critics, many of whom present detailed theoretical analyses of what hooks refers to as "old school" ethnographic writings, and all of whom show pointed interest in the postmodern writing experiments which, over the last decade, have flooded the field of anthropology. Among those essays, Clifford's brief introduction has achieved the greatest recent notoriety, much of it the result a few notably ambivalent claims, scattered throughout the essay, about the purported failure of feminist scholars, *circa* 1986, to contribute in any substantial way to the theoretical conversation in which he and his cocontributors were then engaged. Explaining why none of the volume's contributors based their essays in feminist analysis, Clifford wrote that

> [i]n the case of our seminar and volume, by stressing textual form and by privileging textual theory, we focused the topic in ways that excluded certain forms of ethnographic innovation. This fact emerged in the seminar discussions, during which it

became clear that concrete institutional forces – tenure patterns, canons, the influence of disciplinary authorities, global inequities of power – could not be evaded. From this perspective, issues of content in ethnography (the exclusion and inclusion of different experiences in the anthropological archive, the rewriting of established traditions) became directly relevant. And this is where feminist and non-Western writings have made their greatest impact.[25]

During the seminar meetings, as Clifford notes in this oft-cited passage, feminism emerged as a ground upon which he and his colleagues were able to critique their own positions; therefore its implications "could not be evaded." On the other hand, he goes on to claim that feminism's greatest "impact" stands apart from the discussion in which the seminar participants were engaged. Although Clifford qualifies these points in an important (if somewhat self-contradictory) footnote,[26] in the above passage he nonetheless sets forth an exceedingly problematical association between "feminist and non-Western writings" and "content," "experienc[e]," and "archiv[al]" materiality, while associating his own project, to the contrary, with form, abstraction, and self-consciousness.[27]

Clifford's remarks very quickly generated a series of charged responses from feminist anthropologists, literary theorists, and cultural historians whose observations, looked at collectively, have entailed an important critical rethinking of the terms through which feminist intellectual historiography might be understood. From among these responses, I isolate hooks's for close comment because of the subtlety with which she works to force a renegotiation of Clifford's claims about methodological distinctions between his project and the varied projects of area studies. hooks begins by taking care to suggest points of contact between *Writing Culture* and her own training and subsequent work in and across African–American and Feminist Studies. At the same time, however, she makes what I take to be her crucial intervention, early in her essay, during the course of an extended consideration of the ways in which, within the US academy, Cultural Studies rapidly achieved an institutional "legitimacy long denied African–American and Third World studies."[28]

There, noting the symptomatic inattention paid to work by "nonwhite" anthropologists over the course of the *Writing Culture* volume, hooks goes on to pose a series of rhetorical questions – questions that highlight the historical importance of insider–outsider activity:

> Can we believe that no one has considered and/or explored the
> possibility that the experiences of ... non-white scholars may
> have always been radically different in ways from their white
> counterparts and that they possibly had experiences that decon-
> structed much old-school ethnographic practice, perhaps
> reaching conclusions similar to those being "discovered" by
> contemporary white scholars writing on the new ethno-
> graphy?[29]

The implicit response to these questions, of course, is "No": "non-
white" anthropologists – a group including though not exclusively
composed of insider-outsider ethnographers – have already mounted
a series of congruent challenges to the ethnographic status quo. A
Hurston scholar herself, hooks is aware of the broader theoretical
implications of experimental ethnographic practices developed by
Hurston during the thirties and forties; it's no accident that the essay
that follows this one in her 1990 collection contains a reading of
Hurston's work that foregrounds the ways in which Hurston's
writings from the thirties anticipated the postmodern experiments
that are valorized throughout the *Writing Culture* anthology.[30]

At first it appears that hooks is merely playing the part of
"archiv[ist]," filling in a historical gap in Clifford's essay, referring
twice to the question of "experience," pointing to the "content" of
texts that he and his cocontributors fail to consider – in other words,
conforming her analysis precisely to Clifford's own distinctly limited
summary of recent "feminist and non-Western writings." At the
same time, however, an opposed impulse is also in operation in
hooks's essay. Working well within the grain of many of the essays
published in the *Writing Culture* volume itself, hooks also resituates
Clifford's comments within the domain of storytelling, showing how
this moment in his analysis is undergirded by a particular historical
narrative that is (to use her own term) decidedly "old-school": as
hooks implies, Clifford in the above-cited passage conforms to an
extremely traditional historiographical pattern of progression and
uplift. He moves through time to the experimental fullness of the
postmodern moment – in other words, to a conventional happy
ending – while shifting attention away from earlier works by "non-
white" anthropologists that anticipate and/or exceed the current
experimental writings so admired by Clifford and his cocontributors.
Rather than casting Clifford in the role of high-flown theorist to her
own materialist, hooks recombines those roles, performing a formal
analysis that casts Clifford, now looking a bit blinkered and befuddled, back into the archives. Indeed, in his more recent work,

Clifford has returned to the archives, scrutinizing precisely the sorts of historical gaps in his own mid-eighties work that hooks examines in her reading of "Partial Truths": his 1992 essay on "Traveling Cultures," in fact, gives a privileged place to a figure that Clifford calls the "disconcertingly hybrid 'native'" – in other words, to a figure closely akin, in his heterogeneous commitments, to an insider-outsider like Hurston.[31]

My central point, however, is that the distinction between "form" and "content," upon which Clifford insisted in "Partial Truths," is implicitly recast by hooks in terms of a dynamic relation, apparent throughout her own commentary (as well, it should be noted, as throughout much recent work in black feminist studies) between textualist and archivist, theoretical and empirical, activities.[32] Looked at from a slightly different angle, Clifford's more recent work in the field of early twentieth-century studies – collected in his 1988 volume *The Predicament of Culture* and in subsequent essays – represents the first pole in the dynamic that my own project engages: throughout those essays, Clifford makes strong efforts to demonstrate how a major component of modernist intellectual history can be located in the practice of hegemonic self-critique, exemplified by what Clifford calls "ethnographic Surrealist practice" (and in which category I would also include psychoanalysis), a term that has gained in complexity since he first deployed it in 1981. In that phrase, Clifford refers to a process (apparent in some branches of the social sciences as well as of the arts, and closely akin to Geertz's notion of "self-nativising") that systematically "attacks the familiar, *provoking the irruption of otherness – the unexpected.*"[33] He thus presents a partial historiographical frame through which the activities of interwar insider–outsiders can be understood, by carefully mapping out the context within which their work was made public.

hooks's more specific attention to insider–outsider activity – which is apparent in the passage cited above, as well as in Clifford's own more recent work[34] – represents the second. In her remarks about Clifford's "Partial Truths," as well as in her subsequent essay on Hurston, she draws attention to the tensions that arise when what Clifford refers to as "otherness – the unexpected" is ascribed to real people: to insider–outsiders, whose unfortunate duty it was to "irrupt," as it were, on cue. In so doing, hooks points to historiographical gaps and fissures in Clifford's mid-eighties work. At the same time, however, and perhaps more important, she sets down the principles for a theoretical understanding of these same issues.

3

At the base of hooks's queries into the relation between specific area studies and a broader-based cultural history of modernism is the problem of *affiliation*: the claiming of intellectual allegiances, the formation of coteries that are either inclusive or exclusive, and the possibility of forging temporary coalitional relationships among them; these are issues that she engages throughout her review of the *Writing Culture* anthology. I have attempted to show how hooks's essay implicitly calls into question the conventional polarities (content vs. form; affirmation vs. demystification; materiality vs. abstraction; experience vs. theory) that are so often used to distinguish area studies from projects akin to Clifford's broader-based analyses of modernist culture. Part of what hooks accomplishes is to trace the outlines of an intellectual history that gets obscured when those kinds of polarities are put into play: the figure of the insider-outsider – subsumed in part within hooks's category of "non-white scholars" – enables hooks to suggest both points of conflict and of possible connection between her own work and Clifford's.

My own investigation is likewise grounded in affiliative issues: insider-outsider activity is not simply defined by one's identity (which is itself defined by an amalgamation of markers including sex, nation, race, class, and so on), but also, perhaps especially, by the situation in which one produces work and makes that work public. For my purposes, therefore, one of the most useful recent overviews of modernism is one that places the problem of affiliation front and center: Raymond Williams's "Metropolitan Perceptions and the Emergence of Modernism," which was published posthumously in 1989. In that essay, Williams locates the "key cultural factor of the modernist shift" in the more general condition of early twentieth-century immigration to the metropolis. Modernism's well-known preoccupation with formal innovation, according to Williams's now-familiar analysis, took shape as diverse groups of intellectuals began to congregate in major urban centers and to look for points of contact from among their radically different ranges of experience: "the artists and writers and thinkers of this phase," Williams suggests, "found the only community available to them: a community of the medium; of their own practices."[35]

Williams's insights, developed over the course of his career in a sustained emphasis upon intellectual communities, coteries, or (more generally) "formations," have direct bearing on my own field of inquiry: he evokes an atmosphere common to all of the clusters of activity that I will examine, whether they were located in New York or Mexico City, in London or Vienna. During the last decade, however, Williams's observations have been elaborated and complicated by Edward Said, who gleaned from Williams's writings on the modernist formation a more detailed and at times more skeptical emphasis upon the problem of "affiliation." In his early 1980s essay "Secular Criticism," Said chronicles the late nineteenth-century attenuation of the patriarchal nuclear family (theretofore, according to Said, a locus of cultural authority in the West) in terms of a massive shift resulting in the growth of a "compensatory order" manifested in the increasing importance of social bonds that Said describes as "affiliative."[36]

Using terms that are everywhere gendered and obviously suggestive to feminist critics, Said describes how "affiliative" bonds supply "men and women with a new form of relationship," which he elaborates:

> If a filial relationship was held together by natural bonds and natural forms of authority – involving obedience, fear, love, respect, and instinctual conflict – the new affiliative relationship changes these bonds into what seem to be transpersonal forms – such as guild consciousness, consensus, collegiality, professional respect, class, and the hegemony of a dominant culture. The filiative scheme belongs to the realms of nature and of "life," whereas affiliation belongs exclusively to culture and society.[37]

When Said places " 'life' " within inverted commas, he references in tentative ways the problematical nature of the distinction that he is drawing between "natural forms of authority" on one hand, and "culture and society" on the other. Several decades' worth of feminist social science and historiography suggest that it is dangerous to overstress the "natural[ness]" of "filial" bonds; "obedience, fear, love," and the like are indeed forms of authority, but for feminist analysts they appear less "natural" than constructed or more pointedly coercive, serving above all to contain women within the domestic sphere. Historian Lillian Faderman, to give just one example, has argued that as larger numbers of middle-class women gained access to post-secondary education in the early decades of this century, a panic ensued over the putative abandonment by intellectual women of their child-bearing duties. This panic, according to Faderman, was racist, classist, and homophobic in its tone, and ranged in its sources from popular to medical discourse; in

Said's terms, it marked women's persisting containment within the discourse of "filiation."[38] Said's arguments leave open the question of how specifically female forms of "affiliation" might play themselves out in the public sphere; for women, the transition from "filiative" to "affiliative" structures would have been extraordinarily complicated, if in fact it were achieved at all.

Looking critically at the problem of "affiliation," Said goes on to make the (to feminist analysts) very useful point that "this new affiliative structure and its systems of thought more or less directly reproduce the skeleton of family authority supposedly left behind when the family was left behind."[39] Indeed, Nina Miller has more recently noted how even within interwar avant-garde formations that were explicitly engaged in exploding familial–erotic mythologies, women nonetheless found their places to be circumscribed in strangely familiar, wifely or daughterly ways.[40] How, then, did these tensions manifest themselves in the working lives of women intellectuals? We can begin to address this question by positing some basic and admittedly general contrasts between the typical career trajectories of men and women modernists. The career of the euroethnic male intellectual tended to be inextricably connected to a particular formation, or to a series of authochthanous formations – thus, for example, Jung throughout his life was associated with psychoanalysis; even after breaking with Freud, he went on to invent new forms of psychoanalytic theory and practice; Pound, on the other hand, participated in the invention of a whole series of literary isms. For intellectual men who migrated to European urban centers from the peripheries of the empires, as Said points out, affiliative processes were nuanced in other ways; Said describes those processes in terms of the trope of *"the voyage in,"* manifested in their transposition of homegrown oppositional strategies into the new context of the European metropolis.[41] For women intellectuals, I want to suggest that a further level of complexity was added, in the form of *multiple* affiliation: serial or simultaneous connections to more than one formation – and in many cases, to competing formations.

Sandra Gilbert and Susan Gubar have made related observations about modernist forms of female affiliation, describing the process in theoretical terms that they developed in response to Harold Bloom's "anxiety of influence" model. While retaining the psychoanalytic underpinnings of Bloom's literary–historical narrative, Gilbert and Gubar go on to show how women writers, rather than engaging in pitched battle with a mighty (and usually male) antecedent, tend instead to seek out *multiple* intellectual ancestries, patrilineal and matrilineal.[42] While I find their feminist revision of Bloom to be enormously suggestive, my own analysis of multiple affiliation – which is based upon a review of works by dozens of women working specifically in the insider-outsider mode – replaces Gilbert's and Gubar's familial metaphorics with a more empirically minded emphasis upon processes of intellectual mediation; in this, I follow important work by more recent cultural critics and historians, including Susan Stanford Friedman and Deborah Gordon, each of whom has observed (with regard to H.D. and Hurston, respectively) some of the consequences of these women's movements between and among distinct cultural formations.[43] Among the examples with which I am dealing in this present study, I have observed case after case of multiple affiliation: Hurston's simultaneous engagements with the anthropology department at Columbia and within the Harlem Renaissance; H.D.'s serial affiliations with Pound, Lawrence, Havelock Ellis, and Freud; Frida Kahlo's visibility within the Marxist intelligentsia in Mexico City, coupled with her brief involvement with Bretonian Surrealism; Leonora Carrington's constant circulation among discrete Surrealist coteries; and Ella Deloria's intellectual time-splitting between government-sponsored commissions and Columbia-affiliated anthropological research.[44]

Here, however, I swerve in my understanding of the practice of disciplinary mediation from both Gordon's and Friedman's aforementioned work. Gordon, in her 1990 reading of Hurston, understands interwar anthropological disciplinarity in terms of codes, norms, and protocols designed to differentiate, purify, and professionalize; thus, again and again, Hurston is shown by Gordon to violate the authorizing principles of Boasian practice from her position "on the margins of professional ethnography."[45] While Friedman constructs a more flexible disciplinary model in her description of psychoanalysis under Freud, she nonetheless also places H.D. at the margins of the psychoanalytic community, and characterizes her postanalytic writings as interventions into more conventional, rule-governed interwar debates about modes of psychoanalytic self-authorization; H.D.'s work, according to Friedman, "suggests a loop-hole in [Freud's] Oedipal patterns of discipleship."[46] My own understanding of interwar disciplinarity differs in subtle but important ways from Gordon's and Friedman's. I will go on to argue that interwar Surrealism, psychoanalysis, and anthropology were driven during the interwar years by expansive as well as by contractive energies, and defined themselves as much by incorporation as they did by exclusion; in my readings, therefore, these women will be seen to occupy a position akin to those of the "medial women" that Klaus Theweleit described in his brief early nineties history of women in psychoanalysis – women who served, as he puts it, as "helpers in the *expansion* of psychoanalysis" (emphasis added).[47]

Recognizing this, it is possible to understand why women insider-outsiders were at once so marginal and so crucial to the development of metropolitan cultural life. On one hand, being temporary and shifting, their affiliations rarely afforded them the opportunity to ascend to positions of power and influence. On the other, we can also see how they served the important – if deeply politically ambiguous – function of forming links between discrete, and often between competing, formations. Moreover, by noting this, we can also begin to recognize some of the tensions that were contained within their earliest moments of public recognition: as I noted in Hurston's case, despite the complexity and elusiveness of her ethnographic accounts of African–American cultural forms, she was continually touted to the public as a purveyor of authentic truths about black culture. Looked at through the kaleidoscopic perspective of her multiple affiliations, however, we can also see how Hurston brought to the Boasians something else that they needed badly: an intellectual lifeline to the vigorous and in many respects *competing* efforts to codify African–American culture that were being made, just a few blocks to the north, under the aegis of what is now called the Harlem Renaissance. Precisely the same mechanisms were at work in the other very different contexts that I will go on to examine: during H.D.'s training-analysis, for example, Freud seemed at least as interested in her ability to draw connections between psychoanalysis and the literary milieu in which she more commonly worked, as he was in the particularities of her "feminine" perspective. Or in Frida Kahlo's case, to give a third example, her apparent ability to embody the Surrealist hypothesis of exotic femininity comprised only one aspect of her appeal to Breton during the late thirties; the other crucial aspect was her intimate connection to Leon Trotsky and Diego Rivera, through whom Breton hoped to revivify the flagging political energies of the movement that he had helped to found.

To stop here, however, would be to leave these women in a deeply and perhaps irretrievably compromised position – to position them, primarily, as collaborators, or (somewhat more melodramatically) as capitulators to a series of powerful invasive forces, who enabled the leaders of centrist formations to prey upon the margins. Besides misplacing blame, this kind of reading would starkly reduce the extent of their complicated awareness of and commentary on these very issues. In order to begin to suggest some partial avenues of escape, I will turn to a third and explicitly *feminist* discussion of the problem of affiliation: that is Gayle Rubin's mid-seventies work on the "traffic in women," which helps to bring many of these issues together.[48] In Raymond Williams's agenda-setting work, the modernist formation provides a setting in which difference and alienation are transformed into intermittent solidarities, as new expressive technologies are invented. In Said's elaboration, we begin to see more clearly how the formation serves to exclude, as well as to include. In Rubin's analysis, finally, bonds formed between men serve in graphically gendered ways to block out the uninitiated; Rubin argues throughout the course of her long essay that the circulation of women among men – a process so often used in order to solidify men's ties with one another – serves to prevent women from joining together.

While Williams chooses the term "formation" – which though mixed in its intonations, is largely positive, suggesting gradual processes of making or creating – Rubin is more likely to speak, much more unsparingly, of the enforced homogeneity of the "cult," as she does in the following passage:

> there are gender-stratified systems that are not adequately described as patriarchal. Many New Guinea societies (Enga Maring, Bena Bena, Huli, Melpa, Kuma, Gahuku-Gama, Fore, Marind Anim, ad nauseum) are viciously oppressive to women. But the power of males in these groups is founded not on their roles as fathers or patriarchs but on their collective adult maleness, embodied in secret cults, men's houses, warfare, exchange networks, ritual knowledge, and various initiation procedures.[49]

Rubin argues that "patriarchy" (which she defines, strictly, in terms of the institution of fatherhood and of the ability of an individual to wield "absolute power over ... dependents"[50]) does not constitute the only form of male dominance; thus, returning to Said, we can understand how the declining influence of the patriarchal nuclear family, rather than signaling a decline in female subjugation, as one might reasonably expect, might instead generate new strategies for containing women within the metaphorical household. A primary strategy for this, according to Rubin, is the circulation of women among networks that are constituted through the fact of their "collective adult maleness."[51]

Rubin's essay, as one can see in the passage quoted above, tends throughout its length toward a global, transhistorical argumentative logic, and Rubin (along with other critics who have produced related analyses of female exchange) has been roundly and correctly criticized for this.[52] At times, however, as in her own, odd "ad nauseum" that interrupts that passage, Rubin herself seems skeptical of the apparent ability of her formulation to mutate endlessly, and thus to explain just about everything. She poses the question explicitly: "What," she asks at a crucial juncture in her essay, "are we to make of a concept that seems so useful and yet so difficult?"[53] While I agree with recent critics who have called Rubin's universalism into question, I nonetheless believe that she analyzes with great precision a subject that – as a student of feminist theory working in the US academy during the mid-seventies – she would have known a great deal about: that is, the position of women intellectuals struggling to find a place to work within and among traditionally male-governed academic disciplines.

In a recent interview with Judith Butler published in the journal *differences*, Rubin narrates the circumstances leading to the composition of "Traffic," and in the process, gives a classic account of the working conditions of the multiply affiliated woman intellectual, *circa* 1970. Rubin describes how the earliest version of her essay served as an appendix to a coauthored term paper for an undergraduate anthropology course; she later reworked it as part of a senior thesis for a self-directed major. Rubin tells Butler:

> At that time, the University of Michigan allowed students to declare an independent major through the honors program. I had taken advantage of the program to construct a major in Women's Studies in 1969. At that time, there was no Women's Studies program at Michigan, and I was the first Women's Studies major there. The independent major required a senior honors thesis, so I did half on lesbian literature and history, and half on the analysis of psychoanalysis and kindship. I finished the senior thesis in 1972 and kept reworking the "Traffic" part until Rayna Rapp (then Reiter) extracted the final version for *Toward An Anthropology of Women*. A penultimate version was published in an obscure Ann Arbor journal called *Dissemination* in 1974.[54]

Shifting across audiences and venues, and shifting among variant versions of "Traffic," Rubin produced an argument about the exchange of women that masked its own self-reflexiveness behind a feminist universalism that Rubin herself has since denounced: "At the time I wrote 'Traffic,' she remarks in the same interview, "there was a [*sic*] still a kind of naive tendency to make general statements about the human condition that most people, including me, would now try to avoid ... By the time I wrote 'Thinking Sex,' I wanted to make more modest claims."[55] My own sense, however, is that a more "modest" – and in many respects a more trenchant – analysis can be located within Rubin's commentary by reading the universalizing argument of " 'Traffic' " against its own grain, rather than by dismissing it outright – to read it, in other words, as a narrow, local, and highly self-conscious consideration of the situation of feminist intellectuals attempting to do interdisciplinary work in universities that were still, as in some cases they remain, strictly divided into traditional departments. Rubin's negotiations between psychoanalysis and anthropology, between political and literary theory, leave traditional disciplinary distinctions behind, as did much second-wave feminist writing. It might also be recalled here that Rubin's stirring treatment of global sexual politics ends somewhat surprisingly, with a rousing call for, of all things, further interdisciplinary research. (The essay begins, among other modest proposals, with an ironical suggestion that it might be "time for Amazon guerrillas to start training in the Adirondacks.") Thus, even while broader theoretical aspects of "The Traffic in Women" remain influential within contemporary debates about gendered erotic economies – here I'm thinking primarily about Rubin's pivotal and oft-debated treatment of the "sex/gender system" – I would suggest that some of the essay's most useful applications have to do, rather more narrowly, with its sharp metacommentary on the place of the woman intellectual in twentieth-century metropolitan intellectual life.[56]

What I am suggesting here is a shift of emphasis: the resistance-compliance model that has thus far shaped most critical response to work by women insider–outsiders is based upon a polarized dynamic wherein an individual figure wages a winning or losing battle against a larger and much more powerful institution. While in many (or perhaps most) respects this model accurately depicts the power inequities at work in modernist insider–outsider activity, what it fails to account for is the fact that these women rarely stood entirely alone, but that their histories were instead marked by a long series of alternative intellectual engagements that register volatile faultlines within the field of late-modernist cultural history. Thus, for example, while Hurston's ethnographic activity has traditionally been read as the work of a black woman, who attempts from a unique perspective to revise or correct the white epistemologies that she encountered within Boasian method, it might be worthwhile to add yet another level of specificity to this already complicated description; as such, I join more recent critics like Gordon and Hazel Carby in asking how, as a black woman *intellectual*, Hurston negotiated between the neighboring but hardly neighborly communities of Columbia and Harlem, wherein were situated two of the most concentrated, contestatory, and controversial interwar efforts to codify the meanings of African–American culture.[57]

Put in a slightly more schematic way, in order to sharpen the particular foci of the following chapters, I am arguing that while the work of the insider-outsider intellectual tended to be valued as a result of a hegemonic *desire for mimesis* – embodied in her perceived ability to faithfully represent ranges of experience unfamiliar to her colleagues, but intimately familiar to herself – we might also do well to attend to the ways in which her work was also the object of an institutional form of *mimetic desire*: the desire – which is of course central to Rubin's aforementioned analysis of the "traffic in women" – of one man for what another man has. One of the clearest markers of this condition is the regular appearance in texts by interwar women insider-outsiders of the figure of the exchanged woman – the prostitute, the courtesan, the debutante, or perhaps most unsettling, H.D.'s own self-characterization as "a girl between two boys"; I will demonstrate at length in the following chapters how this process of interformational exchange – and the problems that it poses for women – is in fact allegorized throughout work produced by interwar insider-outsiders.[58] Recent theorists, including Tania Modleski and Gayatri Spivak, have begun to reexamine the philosophical and political ramifications of the intertwined problems of "mimesis" and "mimetic desire," showing how the body of the woman intellectual is frequently used to contain tensions generated within postmodern debate by questions of difference and representation.[59] Their observations, grounded firmly in the present moment, are likewise pertinent to the equally fraught but very different context of interwar metropolitan intellectual life. As the twenties gave way to the thirties, it became increasingly clear that hegemonic strategies for self-critique were not operating in isolation, but were instead being met, point for point, by challenges launched from positions outside: the geographical overlap between the competing formations located in Harlem and at Columbia make Hurston's a particularly vivid though not by any means an exceptional case.

Edward Said has recently noted how such "challenges" impinged in specific ways upon the development of modernist literature, and marked out the limits of modernist forms of self-critique:

> In the works of Eliot, Conrad, Mann, Proust, Woolf, Pound, Lawrence, Joyce, Forster, alterity and difference are systematically associated with strangers, who, whether women, natives, or sexual eccentrics, erupt into vision, there to challenge and resist settled metropolitan histories, forms, modes of thought. To this challenge modernism responded with the formal irony of a culture unable either to say yes, we should give up control, or no, we shall hold on regardless ... [60]

In the cases of interwar anthropology, psychoanalysis, and Surrealism, the space between the "yes" and the "no" – as unclear as the geographical boundary separating "Columbia" from "Harlem" – was occupied by the woman insider-outsider, who circulated constantly among male-governed formations. Like other women insider-outsiders, Hurston was always in motion, a condition that manifested itself, in subtle ways, in all of her writings. In part, this kind of mobility marks the limits within which she was forced, by virtue of being multiply marginalized, to operate; in its waning phases, modernism failed to provide her with anything like a stable intellectual home. In part, however, and less pessimistically, this enforced mobility provided her (as, a half-century later, it would provide Gayle Rubin) the occasion for enacting mutual interrogations of the various formations to which she was so tenuously attached. With this more mobile sense of the insider–outsider career in mind, I will turn finally to the question of how multiple affiliation makes itself felt within insider–outsider texts themselves.

4

Frequent movement among formations – the process that I have been examining, via a rereading of Gayle Rubin's mid-seventies writings, in terms of the problem of *multiple affiliation* – had consequences that made themselves felt in a complex series of textual strategies developed by and shared in common among modernist women insider-outsiders. Most prominent among those strategies is the tendency towards constant self-revision, a practice that I will discuss in some detail as I move towards my conclusions.

I noted at the start of this chapter that while Hurston's ethnographies were praised at the time of their publication for their truth-value and intimacy, the texts themselves are highly complex, elusive, and even, at times, self-contradictory. This sort of critical paradox runs throughout the reception histories of modernist women insider–outsiders.

More recent commentators have paid detailed attention to these sorts of interpretive cruxes, noting again and again how the textual elusiveness of Hurston, Kahlo, Carrington, *et al.* might best be read as an effort to renegotiate the terms through which their works were first received by the public. Thus, while insider–outsider texts were often seen by their initial audiences as unselfconscious, spontaneous, and largely confessional presentations of alien or mysterious realms of experience, we can in fact locate within them powerful revisionary responses to precisely these kinds of reductive misreadings. bell hooks's critique of James Clifford's "Partial Truths," cited earlier, contains a clear instance of this argument at work; there, you will recall, hooks suggested that past writings by "non-white" anthropologists, far from serving as transparent, plain-spoken insider's accounts, might well have "deconstructed much old-school ethnographic practice." In terms that hooks goes on to develop in her readings of Hurston, they might have worked deliberately to revise the epistemological assumptions that informed "objective" social-scientific research.

What I have noticed again and again over the course of my research, however, is that the revisionary impulse apparent in many modernist insider–outsider texts was not simply aimed in one direction: that is, *outwards*, towards the institution, the mentor, the dominant configuration of otherness. Also present in these works was a strong impulse towards *self*-revision, which is itself worthy of careful scrutiny. In her use of the trope of the alligator/sister, for example, Zora Neale Hurston does more than revising dominant assumptions about African–American cultural homogeneity; she also revises her own earlier uses of that same trope. Examples of this kind of double revision – directed both outward and inward – are visible throughout the works that I will be considering in the chapters that follow. Insider–outsider texts are comprised of complex accretions of variants: Kahlo's constantly mutating self-portraiture, Leonora Carrington's careful, deliberate revisions of autobiographical writings, H.D.'s frequent reengagement of the core story of her training-analysis with Freud, Deloria's transformation of field notes into fiction. Because of this, they need to be analyzed using methods that enable close attention to the problem of textual variation.

Self-revision is an activity whose significances have been sharply debated by feminist critics in recent years: Susan Stanford Friedman, for example, has underscored the importance of attending to the presence of variants that appear among what she calls textual "clusters" produced by individual writers: "one kind of cluster," Friedman explains, "is made up of what we conventionally consider the 'final' text and its surviving 'draft' or 'drafts.' Another kind is composed of serial texts on related subjects and characters."[61] Also in a context specifically related to feminism and modernism, Brenda R. Silver has recently shown how self-revision by women writers tends to raise a series of questions revolving around the distinction between "self-editing" and "self-censorship."[62] In important ways, both Friedman and Silver use textual variants as markers of the forces that alternately constrain, delimit, and enable women's writing.

Both Silver and Friedman, demonstrating the necessity of attending closely to modernist women's self-revision, refer frequently to Donald Rieman's well-known metaphor of literary "versioning." Via this metaphor, their analyses dovetail with one of the major recent commentaries on insider-outsider practice: Nathaniel Mackey's 1992 article "Other: From Noun to Verb." In that important essay Mackey traces the outlines of a practice of textual variation, apparent within a number of African–American and Afro-Caribbean traditions, where he locates an oppositional activity that he refers to – inverting the conventionally hegemonic associations of the term – as "othering." This activity, according to Mackey, operates primarily by means of improvisatory self-revision; Mackey stresses throughout his analysis "black linguistic and musical practices that accent variance, variability – what reggae musicians call 'versioning.'"[63] Where Mackey's broad-based analysis of diasporic cultural practice crosses most productively with Silver's and Friedman's similarly far-reaching readings of modernist women writers is in Mackey's attention to the profoundly significant gesture of " 'versioning' ": on one hand, according to Mackey, oppositional "othering" is an activity that registers the overbearing presence of powerful determining forces; on the other, however, he shows how " 'versioning' " has an improvisatory component that enables a partial undermining of those same forces. If modernist women "insider–outsiders" were compelled to circulate constantly among discrete intellectual formations, addressing a series of different audiences with different agendas, then frequent self-revision can be read, in part, as a defense, a necessary evasion. At the same time, however, if modernist configurations of otherness tended to be static and coherent, transparently interpretable and putatively authentic, then the process of constant self-revision can also be read, in part, as a strong effort to renegotiate those kinds of misreadings. Mackey's reading of the practice of " 'versioning' " stands out for its refusal of settled notions of collaboration or resistance, demonstrating instead how oppositional "othering" simultaneously references *and* seeks to reconceive the presence of a series of powerful historical determinants that continually impinge upon work produced by insider-outsider intellectuals. The activity of " 'versioning,' " understood by means of Mackey's analysis, also returns me to one of my own points of departure: to de Lauretis's description of a feminist subject that "is at the same time inside *and* outside the ideology of gender" – that at the same time registers and refuses the discursive imperatives that circumscribe it.[64]

5

In each of the cases that I will go on to examine, I focus upon some aspect of the process of " 'versioning' "; in the course of the book as a whole, however, I perform detailed textual and bibliographical analyses in the context of a series of broader queries about women intellectuals, late-modernist culture, and the development of insider-outsider practice. First, in the cases of Kahlo and Carrington, I examine the issue of multiple affiliation by looking closely at their dealings with Bretonian Surrealism just before World War II. In these two chapters, I pay specific attention to the entrepreneurial apparatus that surrounded their introduction to an international public, focusing on the way in which their public images – Kahlo as a kind of courtesan *extraordinaire*, Carrington as a lapsed debutante – served both to occlude and to bring into focus important aspects of their affiliative relationship to Surrealism. Their late-1930s publicity, I will argue, demonstrates clearly the tension, described above, between the desire for mimesis and mimetic desire. I turn next to an analysis of Hurston's work, where I look closely at her uses of variant versions of a single folktale, one that appears in many different forms, over the course of her career, in fictional, ethnographic, and autobiographical writings; I show how her Harlem-based literary experiments were directly pertinent to the mid-thirties activities of the Boasians, and explore the manner in which her vacillation between "Harlem" and "Columbia" impinged upon the development of her own textual strategies, and brought to light her problematical relation to both formations. Finally, in Deloria's and H.D.'s cases, I look at their insider–outsider texts not only as responses to hegemonic otherings, but also (and perhaps more crucially) as strategic efforts to break out of the isolation imposed by their putative exemplarity – efforts grounded in the establishment of conversation and debate *among* insider–outsider intellectuals; I do this by looking at Deloria's intertextual engagement with Hurston, and, more briefly, at H.D.'s with some of Freud's more orthodox followers. In H.D.'s case, I go on to draw together many of the preceding arguments about multiple affiliation by examining her attitudes towards Freud's late methodological experiments with the hybridization of psychoanalysis, literature, and anthropology.

These last two chapters – focused in part on relationships *among* insider-outsider texts – open outward towards the present moment: one of the many important differences between interwar and contemporary insider-outsider work is the clear and palpable contemporary presence of a diverse (and sometimes conflictual) network of intellectuals working on these same issues. Despite, or perhaps because of their wide-ranging affiliations, the women whose texts I will go on to discuss often worked in solitude, a solitude heightened by the fact that their work was so often touted to the public as representative or exemplary. Speaking to interviewer Paul De Angeles in 1990, Leonora Carrington described in spare and moving terms this kind of isolation, explaining to de Angeles how her own work developed

> outside the Surrealists. I think it's true of people like Frida [Kahlo], who connected very little with the Surrealists except when she was in Paris, because in Mexico she worked alone, she was very isolated, Frida, as Remedios [Varo] was, and as I was.[65]

Even as Carrington is pointing up the fact of her own intellectual isolation, however, she does so in a way that gestures towards connections between herself and other women who shared her tenuous and divided relationship to Surrealism. In the present day, the notion that insider–outsider work transpires in a clearly defined dialogue – between an isolated individual and a broader institution that others her – seems not simply narrow, but almost hopelessly limiting. It ignores the wide-ranging, international, and frequently interdisciplinary conversation that has emerged over the last decade among women and men who are seeking publicly to reclaim, repudiate, or relocate the position of the insider-outsider.

6

Lila Abu-Lughod – a Palestinian–American anthropologist based at NYU, who has performed extensive field research on Bedouin women's storytelling traditions – has produced some of the most incisive recent commentary on the political and philosophical questions surrounding present-day versions of insider-outsider practice. Although her theoretical arguments inform many of the chapters that follow, here I wish to conclude by analyzing in tentative ways some of her textual strategies – this, in order to show how her work is both continuous with and distinct from interwar insider-outsider practice.[66]

Abu-Lughod, throughout her career, has carefully resisted claims of 'insider' status: the daughter of a Palestinian father and an American-born mother, raised and educated in the United States and performing fieldwork in Egypt, she calls herself a "halfie," naming herself as someone always multiple and in-between. Her work is energized not by claims of an experiential intimacy with her informants, but by an examination of the tensions emerging from her profoundly ambiguous relation to them. With her gesture of self-naming, for example, Abu-Lughod foregrounds her difference from her Bedouin informants, even as she manages to maintain a focus on their complexities, their differences from each other. At the same time, however, she also marks out delicate, highly provisional continuities between her own experience and that of the people whom she meets in the field. She tells how her "background as the daughter of an Arab and a Muslim had also been significant, compensating for [her] own apparent cultural incompetence."[67]

In order to dramatize this continual shifting between difference and similarity, estrangement and familiarity, theoretical distance and experiential intimacy, Abu-Lughod has begun several of her major publications by telling how her father traveled with her to her research site on two separate occasions, in 1978 and 1989, in order to establish proper continuity between here and there, between work and home; Abu-Lughod notes that as a woman working alone in the field, "part of what had made [her] acceptable . . . was that [her informants] had met [her] family."[68] Part of what Abu-Lughod accomplishes with these anecdotes, as she herself points out, is to participate in the mainstream anthropological tradition by deploying what she calls the conventional "trope of arrival" and the "image of return."[69] I would also suggest, however, that she participates at such moments in a less-visible tradition of writing (across a range of disciplines) by women insider-outsiders, who often foregrounded in their work the image of a woman being exchanged between male authority figures, as a way of allegorizing their institutional situation between male-governed cultural formations.

Abu-Lughod's depictions of her passage from her father's meta-phorical household to her informants' quite literal home are highly complex. She never allows them to pass without feminist commen-tary – wondering at her own ability to play the role of "dutiful daughter" in deference to her father and to her informants.[70] Abu-Lughod uses these scenes as a way of initiating her own explicitly feminist reinterpretations of Bedouin women's cultural work. Where the gesture of being given away by her father begins to resonate in terms of the history of women insider-outsiders, however, is elsewhere in Abu-Lughod's writing: in the context of her complex description of her own place within the contemporary US academy. There, as Abu-Lughod describes the audiences that she means to address in her published writings, her description is marked by a continuous acknowledgment of her constantly shifting position, her ceaseless transit between and among conventionally configured academic disciplines. She notes that her anticipated audiences will be: "coming to the text informed by anthropology (and its current critics), feminism (and its internal dissenters, in-cluding Third World feminists), and Middle East studies (with its awareness of the problems of orientalism)."[71] Constant circulation or exchange among disciplinary formations – an activity that, during the interwar years, was barely acknowledged, a sign of extreme marginality, the product of deeply unstable working conditions – becomes, in Abu-Lughod's work, the condition of possibility for a relentlessly critical (and self-critical) intellectual practice. Each of the audiences that she mentions, it should be noted, has its own internal complexities which she is careful to point out. Moreover, following this litany of potential audiences and partial affiliations, Abu-Lughod notes that she expects all of her audiences to "approach [her] book critically."[72]

In one last point of both connection and conflict with interwar insider-outsiders, Abu-Lughod is also a relentless self-reviser; again unlike the earlier generation, however, she makes the process of self-revision into an explicit, legible aspect of her own practice, constantly noting how, why, and in what circumstances her own interpretive practices have shifted and changed over time, in part as a result of her shifting affiliations. For my own purposes, one of her more significant self-revisions has to do precisely with the intellectual–historiographical issues that concern me here. In 1990, in her essay "Can There Be A Feminist Ethnography?," Abu-Lughod partly concurs with Clifford's comments, cited earlier, about the dearth of textual experimentation by feminist anthropologists; after making tentative observations about possible alternative histories of women's anthropological textualities, she writes:

> If feminist anthropologists have not pushed as hard as they might on epistemological issues nor experimented as much with form, it is perhaps because they preferred to establish their credibility, gain acceptance, and further their intellectual and political aims.[73]

In 1993, however, Abu-Lughod shifts her strategy; there, she writes that

> [i]n his introduction to *Writing Culture*, Clifford (1986a, 19) made the controversial claim that feminist anthropologists had not been involved in textual innovation, a statement that only later gave me pause. At the time, I simply proposed that my project would fill this gap.
> Over the years I became increasingly skeptical of my initial conceptions.[74]

Within this passage there appears an explanatory footnote in which Abu-Lughod acknowledges early responses to Clifford's essay that coincided with her own – including important interventions by Deborah Gordon and Kamala Visweswaran – that both reinforced her tentative critique and, presumably, extended the claims that she was willing to make in her own subsequent work. By the time of the 1993 publication of *Writing Women's Worlds: Bedouin Stories*, Abu--Lughod's own textual experiments had become less cautious and more self-conscious, her self-revisionary practice signaling a profound responsiveness to a volatile and wide-ranging discussion that was transpiring all about her.

While the similarities to interwar texts might suggest increasingly deliberate efforts on Abu-Lughod's part to allude in subtle ways to an earlier tradition of insider-outsider activity, the differences suggest something else altogether. My own sense – which is necessarily speculative and incomplete; I make no claim, even the most provisional, modest, ironical, or problematized to an insider–outsider's position – is that one of the central distinctions between interwar and present-day insider-outsider commentary is the visible (if diverse and sometimes conflictual) presence of a network of intellectuals working on these same issues. No longer isolated figures forced to circulate among more powerful formations, insider-outsider theorists have in recent years – albeit at times, even now, amidst equally harsh exigencies – marked out new, constantly metamorphosing spaces in which to perform their work. Abu–Lughod registers this kind of reconceived intellectual community in one of her own central, oft-repeated critical gestures: naming herself as a "halfie," she notes throughout her published work how that term is not in fact her own, but attributes it instead to one of her peers, anthropologist Kirin Narayan, and tells how the term emerged during the course of correspondence between them.[75] Interwar insider–outsider commentary, as it has become increasingly internally responsive and conflictual, developed from an isolated and isolating activity into a broad-based conversation, setting the stage for a restlessly varied contemporary field, one that currently finds sustenance both from without and from within.

A courtesan's confession: Frida Kahlo and Surrealist entrepreneurship

Frida Kahlo's fleeting affiliation with Bretonian Surrealism during the late thirties and early forties provides an example that is both clear and complicated of the interwar dynamics of insider-outsider activity. A young painter and Marxist political activist married to the internationally known muralist Diego Rivera, Kahlo was seen by André Breton as an embodiment of exotic femininity who practiced an untutored, spontaneous Surrealism. At the time of their 1938 meeting in Mexico, Kahlo had rarely shown her paintings in public, and out of their acquaintance came two gallery shows (in New York and Paris) and an appearance of her work in the International Exhibition of Surrealism in Mexico City in 1940. During this brief episode of international celebrity, Kahlo became known as a kind of courtesan *extraordinaire*. She was depicted in the popular media, as well as among those purportedly in the know, as a dazzling beauty who shared intimate connections with a series of famed male intellectuals, and who then disclosed in her paintings the truth of her own, somewhat sensational experience: her tempestuous affairs; her life-long suffering that resulted from a horrendous streetcar accident during her youth; her repeated efforts to have a child, efforts thwarted by the physical fragility that persisted until her death in the early 1950s. Kahlo both ambivalently engaged in and carefully distanced herself from this kind of celebrity. It was at once reductive and overblown, and it was not, at any rate, to be repeated on such a scale during the course of her lifetime.[1]

André Breton, the chief early theorist and practioner of Surrealism, was also well-known for his ability to create international sensations, and it is to his strategic manipulation of Kahlo's publicity – his spinning of entrepreneurial fictions – that I will devote my attention in this chapter. By means of detailed scrutiny of Kahlo's first one-woman show (its planning, staging, sequencing, and promotional apparatus) I will argue that the version of Kahlo's work set forth in that exhibit served both to obscure and to call attention to many of the historical determinants and consequences of women's insider-outsider activity during the waning years of modernism. Rather than solely asking how Breton's activities impinged upon Kahlo's career, as Kahlo scholars have traditionally done, I will also in this chapter ask the somewhat eccentric question of how her activities impinged upon his. Kahlo's affiliation with Surrealism points up the manner in which women insider-outsiders frequently served as mediators between male-governed cultural formations: in Kahlo's case, between Breton's own, Paris-based coterie, and the Marxist intelligentsia in Mexico City. In particular, I will argue that the form in which Breton cast Kahlo's exhibit – a form that I will go on to describe as a "courtesan's confession" – brings to light the relationship between the hegemonic *desire for mimesis*, and the institutional *mimetic desire* that more broadly characterized interwar women's insider-outsider activity.

1

When Kahlo first came into contact with Breton in 1938, she and her husband were familiar figures in the politically charged intellectual scene then thriving in and around Mexico City, where both a vibrant local community of artists, intellectuals, and activists and a growing number of artists-in-exile from Europe made their home. During his travels through Mexico, Breton set out specifically to meet with Leon Trotsky and with Trotsky's friend Rivera, hoping through his dealings with them to invest his own brand of Surrealism, whose avant-garde influence and force were rapidly waning, with fresh political and intellectual energies. Breton's brief collaboration with the two men resulted in the publication of an important public dialogue in the pages of the *Partisan Review*: the essay "Manifesto: Towards a Free Revolutionary Art," which appeared under Breton's and Rivera's names late in 1938, and Trotsky's letter of response to the "Manifesto" that was published early the following year.[2] A side-effect of Breton's visit to Mexico was his brief professional collaboration with Kahlo.[3]

What I refer to as their "collaboration" – and by this I mean their joint but frequently conflictual effort to consolidate Kahlo's international reputation – presents particular historiographical difficulties that I will go on to discuss in some detail. Until quite recently, histories of Surrealism have been guided by a pair of parallel tendencies. The first, evidenced in work produced during the eighties by feminist and/or postcolonialist scholars working to restore to public attention neglected figures associated with the movement, devoted its attention to the late thirties and early forties; that was the phase during which Breton, hoping to churn up a Surrealist second wave, spent a great deal of time as entrepreneur and patron to a scattered group of younger artists. During that time, Breton showed pointed (and for him unprecedented) interest in work by women (including Leonora Carrington, Leonor Fini, and Gisèle Prassinos), as well as in work by male artists (including Wifredo Lam and Matta) from nations on the periphery of the dying European empires. Fascinated throughout his career by simulations of otherness – the madwoman, the *femme-enfant*, the exotic – and by the destabilizing effects that those simulations might have upon received notions of the real, Breton began in the 1930s quite consciously to seek out and promote work by writers and visual artists who, for him, embodied and made literal those carefully constructed fictions of difference and alterity.[4]

In historical and critical analyses that followed in this first pathway, Breton served as a thoroughly problematical figure: he tended to be portrayed – not, I should add, without reason – as a bad boy who aged gracelessly, his force blunted by increasingly naive and detached politics, his sensibilities bloated by widespread public acceptance and an increasingly strong will to dictate the tendencies of the movement he had helped to found. Many of Kahlo's own remarks – cited over the years by biographers – have helped to bolster this view of late-thirties Surrealism.[5] According to this kind of reading, Breton then went on to burden his protégé(e)s with a troubling set of assumptions which they, almost inevitably, proceeded to resist or to repudiate. In a strong series of critiques, these commentators have argued in a variety of contexts that Breton – here, in the 1995 words of Kahlo scholar Sarah M. Lowe – derived his "inspir[ation]" from "what was alien to the rational world of the white European male – madness, women, the exotic," while, to the contrary, "Kahlo's creative impulse came from her own concrete reality."[6] The relationship between Lowe's remark and Nancy Hartsock's broader commentary on "majority" and "minority" versions of modernity that I cited in my introductory remarks should be clear.

For "Kahlo," moreover, we might here substitute any number of second-wave Surrealist affiliates.

My own readings derive from and share much in common with those produced by these recent interlocutors of Surrealism, especially in the sense, which I share with them, of the limited – and necessarily oppositional – relatedness of Surrealist theory and practice to the methods developed by Breton's late-thirties protégé(e)s. At the same time, however, what concerns me about many of these critiques is the way in which they tend to ground the practice of Kahlo *et al.* in a "concrete reality" (Lowe's phrase) that to my mind, however unwittingly, reinscribes some of the more troubling aspects of Breton's own constructions of marginal authenticity. I will go on to argue that a dynamic philosophical complexity underwrote much of Kahlo's work, one characterized by a constant negotiation between "living immediacy" (Walter Benjamin's phrase), on one hand, and more abstract self-resistance, on the other.

The second tendency within recent Surrealist historiography came from critics interested in Surrealism as a series of radical representational technologies, rather than merely as a movement circumscribed by Breton's own activities. James Clifford, perhaps the most influential of these writers, described Surrealism as an "activity" that operates in many disciplinary guises – most prominently in a cross-cultural, "ethnographic" mode – and that is designed to "attac[k] the familiar, provoking the irruption of otherness – the unexpected."[7] Clifford and his followers admired the disruptive aspects of Breton's early formulations – his embrace of contradiction, his attention to shocking incongruities and strange juxtapositions. However, following the timeline set up in Maurice Nadeau's old-school classic, *The History of Surrealism* (1944), these chroniclers tended to declare Bretonian Surrealism finished by the mid-thirties, drained of its earlier radical potential. They either concluded their stories at this point, as Nadeau himself did, or they left Breton behind, going on to locate further manifestations of or variations on Surrealist activity in later work produced by what Clifford terms "fellow travelers": Marcel Mauss, Michel Leiris, Georges Bataille, and others.

In the first perspective – which includes much Kahlo criticism produced during the eighties – Surrealism was implicitly equated with the admittedly troubling institutional machinations of the late-thirties Breton, when a great deal more could be said about the unruly potential of the representational technologies that he had developed during earlier decades. Moreover, and perhaps more important, in this first perspective the interventions of second-wave practitioners tended to be presented as grounded, concrete responses to Bretonian mystifications of their own lived experience. In the second line of argument, far more problematically, the crucial interventions into Surrealist practice made by members of the second Bretonian generation were often marginalized or largely overlooked, while what might be termed the "concrete reality" of Breton's late-thirties institutional machinations was seen as a slightly embarrassing betrayal, rather than as a logical extension, of Breton's earlier and more radical practice.

Over the last half-decade, however, cultural historians of Surrealism have turned increasingly towards the productive conflict and overlap between the two critical tendencies that I have just traced. Clifford, for example, has in recent years undertaken a severe interrogation of his own earlier account of Surrealism, one that includes far closer attention to the ways in which, as he puts it, "Surrealism traveled, and was changed in travel."[8] Among feminist commentators – including Oriana Baddeley, Valerie Fraser, Susan Suleiman, and also, in a series of important interventions, the above-cited Sarah Lowe – many productive efforts have also been made to move beyond this apparent impasse. My analysis of Kahlo's work likewise looks for possibilities of critical *rapprochement*; my own sense is that many questions still need to be posed, both about certain concrete facets of late-thirties Surrealist institutional "reality," and also about the rather more abstract interventions made into Surrealist practice by Kahlo and by her diverse, scattered cohort. In this context, the most useful description of the movement that I have found is one that appeared in print soon after Kahlo met Breton, in Kenneth Burke's essay "Surrealism," which was published in a *New Directions* annual volume in 1940. Burke's essay contains an overview and critique of Surrealism, which he describes, with great precision, as a "cult of incongruity";[9] Burke sums up in that phrase both the movement's "incongru[ous]," centrifugal energies (the more radical aspects of Surrealist "activity") as well as its homogenizing, "cult[ish]" tendencies (which were so obvious to many of Breton's second-wave protégé[e]s). It is this kind of tension – so subtly evoked by Burke at the very moment of its emergence – that was brought to light in Breton's promotion of work by Kahlo and by other, contemporaneous artists and writers theretofore marginal to the movement itself.

Surrealism, of course, was founded upon a conflictual ideal, a productively unsettled notion of "dialogue" that Breton articulated precisely in his early manifestoes. He wrote, for example, in 1924:

> Poetic Surrealism ... has focused its efforts up to this point on reestablishing dialogue in its absolute truth, by freeing both interlocutors from any obligations of politeness. Each of them simply pursues his soliloquy without trying to derive any special dialectical pleasure from it and without trying to impose anything whatsoever upon his neighbor.[10]

Reading this remark, which posits the ideal of restlessly argumentative, nonhierarchical relations among "neighbor[s]," it is easy to see the radical potential of Surrealist "activity," which aspires to a state of sustained dissonance that refuses to resolve itself by privileging one tone over the other. As such, in recent years, Bretonian Surrealism has at times been described as a kind of protodeconstructive practice, whose methods were inspired in part by the violence of the First World War: thus, for example, we have Sidra Stich's prefatory essay to the 1990 retrospective exhibition "Anxious Visions: Surrealist Art," where Stich writes that "[m]ost significantly, the Surrealists called attention to oppositions while simultaneously breaking the barriers that separate and distinguish them, thereby upsetting the polarizing *we/they* mentality that World War I had promoted, entrenched, and even enobled."[11] It must be noted, however, that in asking his chosen partners to participate in "[im]polite" and paradoxically dual "soliloquy[s]" with him, it is Breton himself who sets the terms of the exchange. His attempt at shattering monolithic notions of truth – at (in Stich's words) "breaking the barriers that separate and distinguish" – depends upon his ability to delimit and delineate those realities that he considers "other." Further, the success of his method is premised upon the willingness of the "soliloqu[izing]" partner to perform spontaneously, sincerely, without self-consciousness, self-censorship, or suspicion. It is precisely this sort of idealized exchange that Edward Said took to task in his late-eighties work on the limits of postmodern ethnographic strategies; there, Said wrote that

> this kind of scrubbed, disinfected interlocutor is a laboratory creation with suppressed, and therefore falsified, connections to the urgent situation of crisis and conflict that brought him or her to attention in the first place. It was only when subaltern figures like women, Orientals, blacks, and other "natives" made enough noise that they were paid attention to, and asked in so to speak.[12]

Perhaps inadvertently, Breton in the late 1930s exposed the limits of

Surrealist self-critique: up to that point, Surrealism had relied for its disruptive force upon the hypostatization of pristine, near-fantastical versions of difference and alterity, rather than upon direct dealings with the messily complex realities of those deemed "other" by himself and his cohort. Breton's own reading of Kahlo's work – which I will go on to discuss – suggests in pointed ways the distance that separates Surrealist simulations from the cultural production of marginalized artists.

2

Shortly after meeting Kahlo, Breton enlisted the support of art dealer Julien Levy in an effort to set up a public exhibition of her paintings. Levy went on to stage the exhibit at his midtown Manhattan gallery later that same year, and in the process, helped to dramatize many of the contradictory impulses that propelled Breton's late-1930s entrepreneurial activities. In the United States, Levy was one of Surrealism's most visible champions; in 1936, he published a book-length anthology, *Surrealism*, that introduced the movement to many US readers.[13] During the late 1930s and early 1940s, his gallery provided the setting for an eclectic series of exhibitions, ranging from a collection of gouaches by Disney cartoonists; to a show devoted to advertising, interior design, and other applied arts; to a grand-scale retrospective, "Documents of Cubism," that included work by influential figures like Picasso, Braque, and Léger. Levy, however, made his reputation as an art dealer by virtue of his energetic promotion of the Surrealists, whom he called "the most enduring artists of the period."[14]

Levy's faith in their powers of "endur[ance]" even inspired him to construct his gallery space in accordance with Surrealist principles; he arranged his showroom in a curving shape that he would go on to describe, several decades later, in his 1977 memoir:

> The curved wall in my first gallery had been merely decorative. I now used the idea for the entire gallery, and the floor plan resembled a painter's palette. One could move along a line of paintings, seeing each one individually while the others were around the curve, instead of lined up regimentally along straight walls.[15]

Levy's showroom architecture allowed him to depart from the "regimentally" linear form of a more traditional gallery display, so that each painting might seem to float freely against the white space of the walls, cut loose from the works that preceded and followed it. As Levy makes plain in his description of the gallery, he was profoundly concerned by the relations between the conditions in which artworks were displayed and the contents of the works themselves. Like the Surrealists – indeed, like modernist artists and writers more generally – Levy expressed a wish to shatter the tyranny of cohesive, linear narrative, and to make room for disruptive, unlikely juxtapositions of image and space. Describing his earliest experiments with curved-wall architecture (in the first incarnation of his gallery, where, he concedes, the architecture was "merely decorative"), Levy noted his showroom's resemblance to an "accidental de Chirico still life. Disparate, incongruous and prophetic collection: T *square*, French *curve*, *cookie* dividers for the future."[16]

In light of Levy's strenuous efforts to establish connections between his display techniques and the artworks themselves, it is rather startling to observe how Levy and Breton plotted Kahlo's own show; in stark contrast to the setting in which the show was presented, "Frida Kahlo de Rivera," as the exhibit was titled, set forth a continuous and in many respects a deeply conservative autobiographical narrative. Kahlo's paintings were accompanied by a catalog complete with a preface by Breton and a numbered list of works on display – a model of linearity and cohesiveness, and merely one among the show's many subtle indications that "Frida Kahlo de Rivera" was meant to play the part of a static, alien presence against which her audience could ironize and complicate its own reality.

The show's sole (and extremely delicate) shiver of incongruity was generated by the fact that while Breton's introductory essay appeared in the catalog in French, Kahlo's titles were in English – many of them either improvised for the occasion, or transformed via translation from their original Spanish. Kahlo objected to the fact that Breton's essay was not put into English as well, claiming that she was afraid that this would seem pretentious to US audiences (indeed, one of the exhibition's major reviews did contain a transparently francophobic reference to Breton's "precious French"[17]). More important, however, is the fact that Breton was allowed the luxury of first-language expression, Kahlo was not, so that in the catalog her titles, though always evocative, were sometimes jagged: *I with My Nurse*, for example, or *My Dress Was There Hanging*.[18] In the context of the catalog, Breton's nuanced French was the language of (Surrealist) aesthetics, Kahlo's blunt English the language of (commercial and political) contingencies, while Spanish – the language of Kahlo's own mastery – served as an unspoken third term. The linguistic coding and implicit stratification apparent in the catalog – which result in a deceptively naive intonation to many of Kahlo's titles, a tone heightened by their juxtaposition with Breton's subtle description of her work – show further how Surrealist-inspired self-scrutiny and self-alienation were in many respects contingent upon the projection of, the fantasy of, an untainted, authentic "other."

Just as Breton's sophisticated commentary framed Kahlo's weirdly childlike titles, the self-reflexive architecture of the gallery also framed Kahlo's paintings in such a way as to highlight their apparently raw, confessional intensity. Of greatest consequence to Kahlo's own nascent artistic reputation was the fact that the sequence of paintings carried within itself an implicit, continuous narrative which told a story of Kahlo's career that became, and in many cases remains, canonical. The pictures in the gallery exhibit were painted between 1931 and 1938; Kahlo worked during those years in a variety of genres, producing a range of portraits, still lives, and political allegories alongside her better-known self-portraits. Despite this variety of subject matter, the exhibition's unavoidable preoccupation was a particular version of Kahlo herself.[19]

Without regard to chronology, the paintings were arranged in such a way as to highlight Kahlo's associations with prominent male intellectuals: the first painting was her 1937 self-portrait for Trotsky, titled *Between the Curtains* for the show, and depicting a formal and fabulously beautiful Kahlo holding a bouquet and a note of dedication to Trotsky, with whom she had had a brief affair; a portrait of her husband Diego Rivera, *Eye* (1937), was paired with a colorful self-portrait, *The Frame* (1938), near the end of the display.[20] The central and most notorious segment of the exhibition included Kahlo's horrific images of physical injury and of miscarriage, many of them produced during the early thirties: these included paintings depicting bodily wounding (*Memory* [1937]), a brief and unprecedentedly graphic sequence on miscarriage and childbirth ("Henry Ford Hospital" [1932] and *My Birth* [1932]), and an image of a dead child prepared for a funeral (*Dressed Up For Paradise* [1937]). Biographer Hayden Herrera, upon whose painstaking reconstruction of the exhibition sequence I rely in these pages, notes that the identity of the show's final painting – entitled *Survivor* in the catalog – is still disputed.[21] Although Kahlo's most recent works in the exhibition were a group of still lives of local flora (including *Pitahayas* [1938],

Tunas [1938], and *Food From The Earth* [1938]) and a series of charged paintings on contemporaneous political themes (notably *Four Inhabitants of Mexico* [1938] and *They Ask For Planes And Only Get Straw Wings* [1938], those pictures were interspersed through the display, staged, it would appear, as momentary relief from the confessional intensity of the birth sequence.

The story that the exhibition emphasized was not one concerned with the time and place in which the pictures were produced, although many of the show's newest paintings most definitely were; instead, the exhibit focused upon private and more conventionally universalizable aspects of Kahlo's work;[22] it told a thoroughly traditional tale about a woman who, in the terms that Breton uses in his preface, was "accustomed to the society of men of genius" and who was willing to serve up for them, with "candour and insolence," the secrets of her "mind's private preserves."[23] In his catalog essay, Breton even went so far as to invoke Caroline Schlegel as a historical point of comparison. Moreover, although the paintings which according to Hayden Herrera were most likely to have concluded the show – *Me And My Doll* or a rarely reproduced version of *Girl With Death Mask* – contain depictions of human figures who are solitary and self-contained, in both cases, the images can be made to function as reminders of all the privacies that Kahlo seems to relinquish in the course of the exhibit: her painterly disclosure of her own personal and bodily experience – the confessions of a courtesan.

In his catalog essay, Breton also develops a rarefied image of Kahlo that rhymes with the jagged expressivity of the titles of her paintings. His most enduring (and in recent years, his most sharply contested) claim is summed up in the following remarks, which appear late in the essay:

> My surprise and joy was unbounded when I discovered, on my arrival in Mexico, that [Kahlo's] work has blossomed forth, in her latest paintings, into pure surreality, despite the fact that it had been conceived without any prior knowledge whatsoever of the ideas motivating the activities of my friends and myself. Yet, at this precise point in the development of Mexican painting, which since the beginning of the nineteenth century has remained largely free from foreign influence and profoundly attached to its own resources, I was witnessing here, at the other end of the earth, a spontaneous outpouring of our own questioning spirit.[24]

Breton sets up his characterization of Kahlo as a "spontaneous" Surrealist by tracing a history of post-eighteenth-century Mexican painting, which, he claims, is "profoundly attached to its own resources." While it is true that many western-hemispheric artistic traditions since the early nineteenth century did develop in self-conscious opposition to the "foreign influence" of European traditions, Breton implies, in his arguments for Kahlo's "spontan[eity]," that they also developed *in ignorance of* those traditions. He uses this argument, quite explicitly, in order to make a case for the universality of the psychological forces that motivate Surrealist activity.

Kahlo's more recent critics have invariably pointed out that as well as being self-serving, such claims are, quite simply, factually incorrect.[25] In Mexico City, popular audiences as well as an art student like Kahlo would of course have had access – through public museums, photographic or painted reproductions, or (in Kahlo's admittedly privileged case) private collections – to European "masterworks"; Breton himself served as an advisor to the International Exhibition of Surrealism, two years later, at the Galería de Arte Mexicano. Nonetheless, his argument depended for its force upon his own (US) audience's ignorance of Mexico City as a cultural crossroads, an important early twentieth-century metropolitan center.

Especially evocative in this passage is Breton's alignment of France with the foreign – a disruptive shifting of the center (the home of "my friends and myself," and thus, of Surrealism) to the margins. This gesture has distinctly progressive aspects, reinforcing early twentieth-century efforts (efforts shared, as Clifford has pointed out, among artists and social scientists[26]) to dislodge prevailing notions of the singularity and centrality of European culture. However, the gesture is also profoundly ambiguous, implying as it does an effort on Breton's part to assume for himself the voice of the foreign, the eccentric – to pose simultaneously as a powerful international tastemaker and an outlawed figure on the margins. Breton assumes the voice of the culturally estranged in an even more complicated way elsewhere in the essay, where he compares one of Kahlo's paintings, *What The Water Gave Me*, to a passage from his own 1928 novel *Nadja*, a first-person fiction that chronicles a man's disturbing and passionate affair with a woman, Nadja, who is on the verge of madness. There, Breton writes that "The painting which Frida Kahlo de Rivera was just completing [when he arrived in Mexico] – *What the Water Yields Me* – illustrated, unbeknownst to her, the phrase I had once heard from the lips of Nadja, 'I am the thought of bathing in the mirrorless room.'"[27] Again, Breton stresses Kahlo's naiveté ("unbeknownst to her"), and in a complicated series of juxtapositions, he transforms her painting into an illustration for his 1928 autobiographical novel *Nadja*, in which he had earlier spoken – via his character Nadja – in the voice of a woman on the margins. In this case, however, Breton is careful to present Nadja's oracular pronouncement not as a quotation from his own text – despite the fact that Breton's passage only makes sense if the reader recognizes it as literary auto-allusion – but as a private memory unmediated by literary invention or intervention. Breton wants his reader to assume that he is quoting a source distinct from himself, a mysterious figure to whom he has privileged access: Nadja, a person, not *Nadja*, Breton's own experimental fiction. In these passages, it is possible to see how Breton's late-1930s efforts to extend the boundaries of his own aesthetic were grounded in an effort – albeit an exceedingly ambiguous one – to claim for himself an estranged speaking position: he needs for his own fictions of alterity to be presented as literal truths, and Kahlo, inadvertently providing an illustration for his own ventriloquistic fiction, is implicated by Breton in this circuitous appropriative process: Kahlo ventriloquizes Breton's own ventriloquism of "Nadja."

In reviews of the Levy Gallery show, finally, the tension between Kahlo's elusive self-image and the broader tendency (apparent in Breton's essay) to see her work in terms of confessional purity also made itself felt. In the November 1938 issue of *Vogue*, for example, art historian Bertram Wolfe set the tone for much subsequent debate about Kahlo's work in an essay titled "Rise of Another Rivera." In that essay, Wolfe argued that "so intimate in their import are [Kahlo's] paintings ... we could easily reconstruct her life and personality from them."[28] Wolfe, a friend and champion of Kahlo's better-known husband, made his arguments persuasively and with assurance, quoting from private correspondence, and punctuating his analysis with amusing personal anecdotes. His brief essay was written from the standpoint of one who seemed to have privileged access not only to Kahlo's paintings, but also, and perhaps more importantly, to Kahlo herself. Wolfe's emphasis was prophetic: up to the present day, as Oriana Baddeley has recently pointed out, many of Kahlo's admirers seem vastly more interested in her personal history – which has come to serve as a kind of multivalent political parable – than they are in the contents of her paintings.[29]

Even in Wolfe's analysis, however, his palpable confidence clashes with the more ambiguous visual evidence proffered by *Vogue*'s editors. Wolfe's assertion of Kahlo's easy knowability is illustrated by three wildly different self-portraits, as well as by a portrait of Rivera. (Kahlo – whose own sharp sense of irony is well known to contemporary scholars – was apparently delighted by the *Vogue* illustrations.[30]) It is also significant that Wolfe's remarks about Kahlo's candid self-disclosure appear in the pages of a fashion magazine, one dedicated to inculcating women readers in the finer points of feminine costume, cosmetics, and other forms of everyday imposture. The illustrations themselves show Kahlo undergoing a series of dramatic transformations: in them, she exhibits different props, different costumes, and entirely different attitudes. Moreover, on the page facing Wolfe's review, there appears a brief notice about Elsa Schiaparelli, a fashion designer familiar to contemporary Kahlo scholars for her creation of a gown – the *"robe Madame Rivera"* – that paid tribute to Kahlo's intensely self-conscious sartorial style.

One of the great paradoxes of the Levy Gallery show, of Wolfe's article, and of much subsequent Kahlo criticism, lies in the fact that while Kahlo painted an extravagant variety of subjects, including a diverse, often contradictory array of self-portraits, many critics continue to insist that her paintings disclose (in Wolfe's words) an "intimate," "spontaneous," and "personal" view of the facts of the painter's own life. Wolfe, perhaps intuiting these kinds of difficulties, goes on in his essay to pursue his reading to its own logical extreme; he argues, "even when she does not herself appear in a canvas, she somehow pervades the picture."[31] Thus, according to this way of thinking, even when we *don't* see Kahlo, we somehow, and somewhat weirdly, *do*. Wolfe's strikingly paradoxical conclusion, in which he suggests that Kahlo's work is at once "instinctively *and* calculatedly well composed," points towards fresh possibilities for rereading his own strictly autobiographical reading.[32]

One way of indexing the constructedness of Kahlo's international image, *circa* 1938, is to reshuffle the protocols of the Levy Gallery show, and to imagine alternative exhibits that would have presented a very different "Frida Kahlo de Rivera" to the US public. A strictly chronological arrangement of the paintings, for example, would have placed the two most notorious birth images – *Henry Ford Hospital* and *My Birth* – very near the start of the show. Painted in 1932, they would have followed her 1931 portrait of Luther Burbank, standing for the earliest phase of her career, a tragic period left behind years before. The self-portrait for Trotsky and the portrait of Rivera, both painted in 1937, would have been buried somewhere in the middle of the sequence. The show would have ended with her 1938 paintings, which are overwhelmingly local in their emphases, and which tend to be outward-looking rather than introspective. Different catalog copy, such as the essay that Diego Rivera would write about Kahlo five years later, in 1943, might have also determined a different way of reading Kahlo's work. There, Rivera (who was, it should be noted, an astute, serious critic of Kahlo's paintings) wrote that Kahlo's work was "collectively individual . . . she paints the exterior, interior, and background of herself and the world at the same time."[33] Rivera, unlike Breton, stressed the interplay between Kahlo's autobiographical and historiographical impulses, the relations between "herself" and "the world," rather than her stark disclosure of intimacies.

I do not mean to suggest that such an alternative exhibition would have granted Kahlo's audiences access to some correct or definitive version of her work; like the Levy Gallery show, which stressed Kahlo's familial–erotic biography, this chronological display would bring to the forefront her professional biography, which makes, in its way, for an equally conventional narrative: the story of the career of the artist. Perhaps more useful would be an exhibition that problematized Kahlo's self-representation much more thoroughly. For, besides directing the viewer's attention towards Kahlo's complicated and often tragic private life and away from her more public concerns, the Levy Gallery show also succeeded in blurring one of the central facts of Kahlo's self-portraiture, a fact so obvious that it frequently escapes critical notice: that is Kahlo's constant variation of her own image.

It is only in some of most recent analyses of Kahlo's work – including studies by Oriana Baddeley and Janis Bergman-Carton[34] – that the particular meanings of Kahlo's shifting self-representation have finally moved to the forefront; both of their analyses, however, are directed towards the contemporary "cult" of Kahlo celebrity, not towards her earlier moment of fame. Baddeley, especially, makes a series of crucial points about the political semiotics of clothing in Kahlo's work, concentrating finally on a 1933 canvas, *My Dress Hangs There* (previously entitled *My Dress Was There Hanging*) that features one of Kahlo's Tehuana costumes suspended on a clothesline above a US cityscape. By looking at the specific meanings of that costume in terms of Mexican cultural history (particularly, in terms of the history of Tehuana women's sharp and sustained resistance to European colonization), what Baddeley suggests is the possibility of a more complicated assessment of the function of costume and disguise – subjects that are central to many of Kahlo's self-portraits, but that tend, rather oddly, to provoke among Kahlo's critics further commentary about candid self-revelation, rather than self-concealment or masquerade. Hayden Herrera, for example, commenting on that same canvas in a 1993 essay, writes that the painting is "too personal to carry much political clout. Appalled by the lavish cocktail parties given by the rich while the poor stood in breadlines, Kahlo showed her disdain for Capitalist society by painting her Tehuana dress hanging above Manhattan without herself in it. She wanted to go home to Mexico."[35] Herrera deserves special consideration here; she is, after all, Kahlo's major biographer, and is thus better qualified than most to produce compressed and highly specific readings of the personal determinants of Kahlo's paintings. Still, it is worth noting that Herrera chooses to interpret a painting whose most startling, vivid aspect is the *absence* of Kahlo's image as yet another self-portrait, and then goes on to argue that the "personal" aspects of the painting (which are themselves, at best, elusive) have a depoliticizing effect.

Baddeley's emphasis upon costume is crucial, in that she explores both the variability and the elusiveness of Kahlo's self-display, and the historical and political meanings of Kahlo's constant self-revision. In the Levy Gallery show, Kahlo's varying self-image serves important critical purposes: in the context of Bretonian fictions of alterity, Kahlo was made to serve as a stable object who could be easily reexamined, renamed, enlisted in the services of Surrealist self-critique, but who was at the same time denied a full measure of internal complexity. Chronicling a constant process of transformation, however, Kahlo's self-portraits depict a self that is constantly in motion, rather than one who serves, as Elspeth Probyn put it in a recent critique of the new ethnography, as a "stationary other."[36] We can therefore productively consider her shifting self-portraiture in terms of Nathaniel Mackey's discussion – described in chapter 1 – of the practice of " 'versioning.' "

Another, slightly less intuitively clear example of " 'versioning' " – the topos of mutability in Kahlo's painting – comes in the form of her recurring images of children, which are also much in evidence, though marginalized, throughout the Levy Gallery show. Thus far, readings of Kahlo's images of children have most often been quite narrowly biographical; those paintings have served for critics as an index of Kahlo's very real private anguish over her failed attempts to have a child during her first marriage to Rivera. Only recently has the question of the maternal in Kahlo begun to generate less intimate commentary: for example, Jean Franco and Claudia Schaefer have both suggested that those images disclose Kahlo's feminist critique of larger cultural processes that work to pathologize the female body.[37] I will go on to suggest that at least as important as Kahlo's painterly dealings with the question of the maternal body – in part, because it will finally return us to the possibility of a critical *re*reading of Surrealism – is her constant transformation of the bodies of children into objects, or occasionally into animals, and then back again into human form.

It is a surprising fact that there are almost as many images of children in the Levy Gallery exhibition as there are images of the adult Kahlo; you'd never know it from her early publicists and reviewers, who were so captivated by Kahlo's adult self-portraits that they tended to ignore anything else that appeared in the exhibit. Some of these pictures of children take the form of retrospective self-portraits, identifiable only by Kahlo's joined eyebrows; some are fetuses; one is dead; others depict small monkeys or baby-dolls or odd bits of machinery, not human. Kahlo was as fascinated by the transformation of self-image through costume as she was by the figure of the child as a locus of transformation. And because the transformations that her children undergo are easily as disturbing and radical as those of her adults – and (arguably) less easily recuperable into a raw, confessional narrative – it might be useful to read these figures as experimental efforts to develop a visual language for the kind of mutability that is apparent, if more understated, throughout her adult self-portraiture.

Barbara Johnson has noted the thematic collusion of autobiography and maternity in women's writing; reading Mary Shelley's *Frankenstein* as a critical examination of the maternal, Johnson notes, with regard to the creation of the monster, that "the desire for resemblance, the desire to create a being like oneself ... is the autobiographical desire par excellence."[38] Bringing Kahlo's portraits of children to the foreground, and noting their vacillation between death and life, the animal and the human, the inorganic and the organic, we can also begin to sense within Kahlo's autobiographical impulse a slightly different effort – one directed towards the creation of "a being [*un*]like oneself," rather than towards a fully knowable, coherent self. As in Orianna Baddeley's reading of Kahlo's costuming, we come away from Kahlo's paintings of children without a solid sense of who Kahlo is – in other words, far from the frank and intimate Kahlo who resided in the Levy Gallery show and its attendant publicity. In this light, rather than being an object available for Breton's theoretical dissection, Kahlo looks more like a self-theorizing subject.

Kahlo's pointedly incomplete intimacy – her refusal, noted recently by Sarah M. Lowe, of "'pure' revelation"[39] – is marked by her fascination with transformation, and marks as well her oppositional engagement to Surrealism. I have attempted to show – with regard to the autobiographical narrative imposed upon Kahlo's paintings during the Levy Gallery show – how Surrealist self-irony, no matter how corrosive and self-resistant, nonetheless requires the presence of a coherent fiction of alterity. As such, the disruptive architecture of Levy's gallery stood in uneasy relation to the exhibition's more conservative narrative emphasis upon Kahlo's purported disclosure of an authentic self. I argued further that by shuffling the protocols of the show – its catalog essay, its titles, its sequencing, its implicit thematics – we end up with a stronger sense of Kahlo as an artist engaged in a complex series of transformations, a forcefully manipulated form of self-display that responds to the forces that circumscribe her newfound status as celebrity–artist. What remains apparently immutable, however, is the gallery space itself; other elements of the show can be recombined, but the room cannot itself be rebuilt. It can, however, be looked at anew, with a skepticism towards Surrealism generated from within Kahlo's own practice.

Levy's gallery, with its curved walls constructed in order deliberately to disrupt the sequence of paintings, is meant to allude in sophisticated ways to Surrealism's attack on received notions of the real, including the possibility of a coherent and knowable self. Here, Eugene Lunn's well-known catalog of "modernist" aesthetic strategies, which includes "*Simultaneity, Juxtaposition, or 'Montage'*," is once again useful: Lunn observes that "in much modernist art, narrative or temporal structure is weakened, or even disappears, in favor of an aesthetic ordering based on synchronicity, the logic or metaphor, or what is sometimes referred to as 'spatial form.'"[40] With this in mind, it is fascinating to note that contemporaneous photographs and drawings of Levy's gallery space in fact disclose a much less disruptive architectural arrangement than the one that Levy describes in his 1977 memoir. Hardly the roller-coaster ride that Levy evokes, the curvature of the walls is harmonious, soothing, and actually quite beautiful. When the gallery reopened on West 57th Street, in fact, an anonymous writer for international purveyors of beauty *Harper's Bazaar* described it in this way: "The light along [the wall] is softened, and as people pass by, the pictures seem to present themselves one by one *in a continuous succession* rather than with the collective impact that results in seeing them stiffly regimented against a straight wall."[41] Its effects, in other words, are quite different from those described by Levy: contrary to his claims, the curves do in fact allow the viewer to see more than one painting at a time, and their gentle slopes serve in many respects to underscore, rather than to disrupt, the "continuous succession" of the images.

In this light, it is important to note that Levy himself – in a manner oddly and indirectly akin to Kahlo – occupied an important position *vis-à-vis* the rapidly dispersing movement that Breton had founded: like Kahlo, whose paintings served as a point of contact between Breton, on one hand, and Rivera and Trotsky on the other, Levy through his curatorial activities worked to mediate the heightened tensions among warring Surrealist factions, as well as between what Mark Polizzotti describes as "the organized movement that Breton labored to maintain, and ... the much more amorphous, public tendency that threatened always to elude his control."[42] Polizzotti continues his commentary, noting that Levy's highly visible position as dealer and anthologist led to the formation in North America of a "sense of the movement" that was "dependent less on the daily loyalties played out in Breton's favorite café than on the spirit that emanated from certain artworks, whether or not they were by Surrealists in good standing. It was, then, a less sectarian, and in many ways purer, vision that Levy was able to present in [the 1936 volume *Surrealism*], a timeless Surrealism."[43] What these negotiations entailed, as I have sought to indicate, was the construction of a "less sectarian, and in many ways purer, vision" of Kahlo's decidedly impure work, a "timeless" Frida Kahlo whose universalized image superceded the specific places and times that most concerned her, and whose appeal has persisted up to the present day among a variety of audiences.[44] Looking again at Levy's gallery and its broader function within late-thirties Surrealism, it is useful to think once more of Kenneth Burke's notion of Surrealism as a "cult of incongruity," an aesthetic practice that sought to contain conflicting impulses towards consolidation and dispersal: under scrutiny, the jagged edges of the movement's most apparently subversive structures often appear a bit smoother than they did before.

This shift of emphasis – away from a stable, biographical Kahlo and towards her mutability – enables us to look back at her exhibition from a slightly different angle. As Kahlo begins to look more elusive and self-contradictory, then Breton, by contrast, begins to appear oddly exposed and raw, himself lacking in self-consciousness: his effort to attribute his own words to "Nadja" and then to Kahlo – through multiple ventriloquisms that can be read, finally, as confession – exemplifies this tendency. Breton's purportedly radical gestures of self-critique, seen in light of his promotion of Kahlo, begin to look like ingenious techniques for containing Kahlo's disorderly presence, and the effects that that presence might have upon public perceptions of Surrealism, a movement increasingly fragmentary and divisive.

In this same spirit of reevaluation, however, I would like to turn back briefly to the problem of the "courtesan's confession," in order to suggest – against the grain of my own preceding analysis – that the stories that Breton told about Kahlo did in fact reveal something important about her career, not just about his own. For the courtesan is herself an exceedingly tricky figure, with a history in many ways pertinent to the reading of Kahlo that I am tracing out here. The courtesan is on the one hand a powerful manipulator of her own image, whose skill is measured by her aptitude for various forms of dissimulation. On the other hand, however, her movements are always circumscribed by her connections to more powerful men; mediating between them – as Kahlo did, however unwittingly, between Bretonian Surrealism and the Marxist intelligentsia in Mexico City – she enabled their power to be temporarily consolidated, at the expense of her own. It is to these kinds of contradictions, embedded within the figure of the Kahlo-as-courtesan, that I will now turn.

3

In September 1937, one year prior to the Levy Gallery show, Kahlo contributed a genealogical family portrait to a group exhibition of paintings by Mexican artists sponsored by the Department of Social Action Art Gallery, which had just opened at the National Autonomous University of Mexico. Salvador Azuela presented a public lecture to accompany the exhibition, in which he made efforts to map out space – in the border areas separating socialist realism from crudely commodified art – for the development of a politically charged national tradition. Azuela stated that he wished on that occasion to pay homage to the most respectable kind of artist: to the outlawed, unadaptable, persecuted, the one who fails to understand his art as dispossessed of transcendental permanence, the one who declines to play the role of courtesan in a poor attitude of flattery to the powerful by tying his work to immediate success.[45]

In Azuela's formulation, the artist intervenes courageously in the social real, and defines himself by means of a series of sharp refusals and negations and separations: he "declines"; he deliberately "fails to understand"; he is "outlawed." Azuela goes on in his lecture to supply equally disruptive commentary upon the idea of artistic "universality": he states that "our vote is for the work of the Republic's artists to be more Mexican, to the extent of being more universal and human."[46] Here, Azuela strategically redefines the notion of "universal[ity]" – which, of course, is often a term that is transparently European in its connotations – by equating it with the "Mexican"; however, unlike Breton's related gesture (i.e., Breton's equation of France with foreignness, noted earlier), Azuela's shifting of Mexico to the center and Europe to the margins is better read as critical *intervention* than (as it was in Breton's case) as a form of appropriation.

Amidst his precise redefinitions and recalculations of various cultural dogma, however, Azuela's version of artistic greatness remains very distinctly masculine. Significantly, Azuela's image of artistic failure is itself feminized: the worst an artist can do, in Azuela's terms, is to "play the role of courtesan." The masculine tonalities of Azuela's lecture emerge in part from the fact that Kahlo was one of only two women whose work was displayed at the 1937 exhibition; more broadly, however, they resonate within a particular national and historical context, one analyzed incisively in recent years by Jean Franco, in which this "messianic" (and explicitly masculine) view of the artist was prevalent. Franco notes that the aftermath of the Mexican Revolution was marked by a postrevolutionary "discourse that associated virility with social transformation in a way that marginalized women at the very moment when they were, supposedly, liberated."[47]

Two decades later, the reverberations of that "messianic" rhetoric can still be felt not only in Azuela's commentary, which constructs a politically exemplary art – transcendent, permanent, and heroic – in opposition to the "courtesan." In the specific context of Mexican cultural history, it is useful as well to consider the association of the politically ineffectual "courtesan" with the near-mythic figure of *La Malinche*, Cortés's Aztec guide, interpreter, and mistress, traditionally construed as a collaborator who capitulated to a brutal invasive force.[48] It would be a mistake, however, to consider Azuela's demonization of the "courtesan" solely as a cultural legacy of *La Malinche*; it is equally important to note the extent to which related metaphors of intimate servitude were linked, throughout a range of writings from the thirties left, with the problem of artistic complicity in repressive political regimes. For example, early in Breton's and Rivera's 1938 essay "Manifesto: Towards a Free Revolutionary Art" (which was coauthored with Trotsky, though he was not credited in the published text), we read that

> [t]he regime of Hitler, now that it has rid Germany of all those artists whose work expressed the slightest sympathy for liberty, however superficial, has reduced those who still consent to take up pen or brush to the status of domestic servants of the regime, whose task it is to glorify it on order, according to the worst possible aesthetic conventions.[49]

In 1939, Trotsky published a reply to Breton in which he reinforced this rhetoric, referring to the "sheep-like servility of the intelligentsia," who act as "purveyor[s] of bureaucratic heroism in prudently proportioned slices."[50] Kahlo's sole contribution to the 1937 show locates her firmly within the confines of her own patriarchal family – rather than outside it, where the servant is compelled to venture – in an image of a naked little girl who strikes a sassy pose, but who nevertheless stays resolutely in her place, holding in her hand a ribbon that binds three generations together (plate 1).

The following year, Breton famously described Kahlo's art as a "ribbon around a bomb,"[51] and in stark contrast to the group exhibit in Mexico City, Kahlo's one-woman show in New York was a distinctly feminine affair: it was enclosed within a promotional apparatus designed to situate Kahlo not only as a Mexican painter, but as a woman painter as well; "there is no art," Breton wrote in his catalog introduction, "more exclusively feminine."[52] Still, from the title of Breton's catalog essay, "Frida Kahlo de Rivera," to the sequencing of her paintings, to the kinds of publicity that her work went on to generate in North America and Europe, the brand of femininity that was foregrounded in the Levy Gallery show was one that cast the most flattering light possible on the male artists and intellectuals who surrounded her, especially those, like Breton, who were involved with the Surrealist project. Explaining what he means

1. Frida Kahlo, *My Grandparents, My Parents and I (Family Tree)*, 1936.

when he calls her work "feminine," Breton writes that "in order to be as seductive as possible, [Kahlo's art] is only too willing to play alternately at being absolutely pure and absolutely pernicious"[53]; in other words, it flirts with him. The irony here is a particularly harsh one: in the earlier show in Mexico, where Kahlo's work was marginalized, political and artistic failure were circumscribed by Azuela within the metaphor of the "courtesan," whose activities were defined by "flattery to the powerful"; to recontextualize Breton's and Rivera's 1938 phrase, she "glorif[ies the regime] on order." Under the direction of Breton and Levy, Kahlo's work was shifted to a position of centrality precisely by means of a parable of courtesanship in which the force of Kahlo's images was made to be contingent upon her biographical association with more famous and powerful men.

Breton's parable of courtesanship was also achieved by means of an image of Kahlo as one who binds generations together, although in Breton's account, it is artistic and intellectual – rather than familial – lineages that are joined in her work. Just after praising her as "a young woman endowed with all the gifts of seduction, one accustomed to the society of men of genius," Breton writes that

> Frida Kahlo de Rivera is delicately situated at that point of intersection between the political (philosophical) line and the artistic line, beyond which *we hope that they may unite in a single revolutionary consciousness while preserving intact the identities of the separate motivating forces that run through them.*[54]

In the group show in Mexico, Kahlo finds a proper place among the virile artistic "outlaw[s]" by working to bind the family together; in her one-woman show in the United States, she finds a place by binding together discrete, even competing intellectual tendencies embodied in the work of prominent men whom she knows intimately. In both, her primary role is as a mediator: one whose work establishes continuities, rather than marking discontinuities; on who connects, not one who intervenes.

Despite Breton's claims to the contrary, however, Kahlo's own career was punctuated by serious and quite explicit interventions into Surrealism's vision of its own cultural past. One of them, moreover, involved explicit reengagement of the figure of the woman-as-mediator: in this case, not the "courtesan," but her less privileged double, the prostitute. In order to illustrate this aspect of Kahlo's work, I will turn now to a little-known painting that Kahlo produced in 1938, the year of the Levy Gallery show: *Girl With Death Mask* (plate 2). In that painting, a little girl is dressed for a Day of the Dead celebration: she is wearing a pink dress trimmed with white lace and a skull mask on her face, and is holding a bouquet of flowers in her hand, while another mask sits at her feet. This painting contains one of Kahlo's most conventionally realistic children: along with *Dressed Up For Paradise*, which depicts the corpse of a small boy that has been elaborately arranged for a wake, *Girl With Death Mask* also shows a child who is ritually adorned for an occasion in which boundaries between life and death, between the human and the nonhuman, are crossed and troubled. Typically for Kahlo, the most realistic tableaux are ones in which definitions of "reality" are called most sharply into question.

Purely in terms of its subject matter, the painting is unremarkable; similar images can be found even in such humble (if politically troubling) contexts as tour guides to Mexico marketed to travelers from the United States around that same time. In Frances Toor's 1947 compendium, the *Treasury of Mexican Folkways*, for example, we find the following description, and later a photograph, of comparable scenes. Toor writes:

2. Frida Kahlo, *Girl With Death Mask*, 1938.

Even the paper masks, made in quantities and selling at ten centavos or two cents a piece, show imagination, fantasy, and great decorative talent. Of these, special ones are made for the Day of the Dead in the form of skeletons and skulls; for carnivals, to represent French and Spanish types; for other times, kings, birds, monkeys, as well as all sorts of fanciful faces, which delight youngsters and adults.[55]

With scant regard for their complex social function, Toor invokes these masks as instances of the "primitive" imagination at work.[56] What keeps *Girl With Death Mask* from serving merely as a plainly rendered visual account of an event that is repeated annually – and

3. Pablo Picasso, *Les Demoiselles d'Avignon*, 1907.

which can then, by means of its transparent evidentiary value, serve
as a fulfillment of or grounding for exoticist fantasy – is the strong
resemblance that it bears to one of Surrealism's best-known precursors, Picasso's 1907 canvas, *Les Demoiselles d'Avignon* (plate 3). This
painting, of course, shows a group of five nude prostitutes in an
Avignon brothel, partially draped in pink and white fabric, with
three of the figures wearing masks that recall similar African masks
that Picasso is likely to have seen on display at the Trocadéro in
Paris. At one level, Kahlo's response to Picasso can be read parodi-
cally: while Picasso's juxtaposition of pink body and African mask
means to be searingly disruptive, calling into question the bases of
Western epistemology by recombining the categories of self and
other, Kahlo's image appears plainly rendered and entirely contin-

uous with the painter's own historical reality. Thus, Kahlo demystifies Picasso's apparently radical gesture, showing how the disruption of cultural norms that he achieves through massive effort is, in terms of her own experience, a mere commonplace.

This reading matters, albeit primarily as a starting point; it coincides precisely with the oppositional readings of late-thirties Surrealism that I described earlier in the chapter. What it lacks, however, is a fuller consideration of the way in which *Girl With Death Mask* also works to problematize certain aspects of Kahlo's own, lived experience. While Picasso's present-day audiences are well aware of his fascination with African artifacts, which he collected and displayed in his studio and sought out at the Trocadéro, Kahlo's audiences have paid less specific attention to the fact that Kahlo, in her studio, surrounded herself with her own collection of pre-Columbian statuary. It would be a bit too simple to argue that, in depicting popular practices of masquerade in *Girl With Death Mask*, Kahlo was merely depicting her "own" historical reality; like Picasso, she too was a *student* of popular traditions, rather than a creator of them, and while her subjects were domestic and familiar – his were exotic and evocative of a violent colonial history – it is still important to acknowledge that Kahlo was separately situated, by means of class, from the artists who produced the masks that she depicts in her painting.[57]

In Kahlo's painting, however, there is a good deal of self-conscious consideration of the process and practice of cross-class appropriation. While the masks in Kahlo's painting are stylized and nonrepresentational, for example, the larger composition works in a realist mode; thus, Kahlo registers at the level of style a discrepancy between her own work and that of the anonymous artists who produced the masks. The painting's literalness, far from being plain or natural, is itself encoded as a departure from the abstraction of the masks created by popular artists. On the other hand, the stylization of Picasso's masks is continuous with the cubist fragmentation of the bodies of the models who wear them.[58] Moreover, and perhaps more graphic, there is Kahlo's adornment of the little girl in a frilly dress. Picasso's models – prostitutes posing in a brothel – are in many respects as marginal and anonymous as the mask-makers who produced the works on display in Picasso's studio and at the Trocadéro. Kahlo, on the other hand, explicitly evokes an economic situation that would enable this middle-class child to own her own small collection of popular art. Far from being a straightforwardly literal or confessional painting, *Girl With Death Mask* ponders with almost unreadable complexity the problems of modernist privilege and the construction of difference. Masking, moreover, is a crucial element in the history of Mexican popular art and costume, reflecting a complex range of traditions to which Kahlo alludes here; her picture makes a sharp, ironical point about art-historical narratives that insist upon interpreting popular art as purely naive, or, as Toor puts it, "primitive." *Girl With Death Mask*, however, also makes an ironical point about the activity of self-disclosure: painting back to Picasso, Kahlo does not present anything like raw self-revelation. Instead, she presents a little girl wearing a disguise.

Finally, however, we lose a great deal when we read Kahlo's painting *only* as a response to or revision of Picasso. It is just as likely that Kahlo, in *Girl With Death Mask*, was also revising one of her own, earlier self-portraits: *Between the Curtains* (plate 4), the painting that opened her Levy Gallery show, and that served as the foundation for the (still-evolving) legend of Kahlo as intellectual courtesan. Looking at *Girl With Death Mask* from the point of view of Kahlo's earlier self-portrait, *Between the Curtains*, we can see the fabric of her gorgeous Tehuana gown cut to a different pattern in order to fit a child's body, and a similar bouquet, simplified for the occasion of a celebration of the dead. We can also see how Kahlo, who was so often praised early in her career for her painterly "candor," nonetheless enacted in her paintings a continuous process of self-revision, offering her audience an unstable, discontinuous series of self-portraits that can only be called "confessional" in the most deeply problematical sense. *Between the Curtains* recalls Kahlo's connections to a series of famed male intellectuals – Trotsky, to whom the picture is dedicated; Rivera, at whose insistence she wore gowns like the one depicted in the painting; and Breton, who used the picture to introduce Kahlo to an international public. Kahlo's circulation among competing cultural formations dictated the conditions in which she enacted this variegated performance.

The curtains in the Trotsky portrait, like the masks in *Girl With Death Mask*, invest both poems with a theatrical quality. In making this claim, however, I come into direct conflict with Breton's own reading of Kahlo's work. Writing about her self-portrait for Trotsky, Breton observes that Kahlo "has painted herself dressed in a robe of wings gilded with butterflies, and it is exactly in this guise that she draws aside the mental curtain. We are privileged to be present, as in the most glorious days of German romanticism, at the entry of a

4. Frida Kahlo, *Self-Portrait (Dedicated to Leon Trotsky)*, 1937.

young woman endowed with all the gifts of seduction."[59] Although
Breton describes her costume in densely metaphorical detail, and
significantly refers to Kahlo's choice of a "guise," he nonetheless
goes on to read the portrait not as a calculated form of masquerade,
but as a blunter form of self-revelation. For Breton, "draw[ing] aside
the . . . curtain" is akin to lifting the veil: disclosing the putatively *real*
self, rather than calling that self into question. When Kahlo revises

her self-portrait, one year later, in *Girl With Death Mask*, she makes that "[dis]guise" more explicit, hardly ignorable.

Finally, returning to Picasso with Kahlo in mind, we can also see how Picasso's models in *Les Demoiselles d'Avignon* are likewise posing "between the curtains," in front of an open window that itself serves as a kind of stage. Picasso's own self-conscious reflection upon aestheticization of the "other" might be detectable in this gesture. Moreover, his choice of a brothel as a setting for his painting – a place where women play roles for money – further underscores the notion that his own painting contains within itself a deliberately constructed theatre of alterity. When Kahlo replaces Picasso's prostitutes with a little girl, she leaves the courtesan behind – not by replacing corruption with innocence (her little girl, decked out in a death mask, can hardly be called innocent; moreover, Kahlo would hardly have judged a prostitute in such moralizing terms) but by replacing the woman with a child: one too young to be caught within the adult cycles of female exchange.

4

Over the following decade, the context in which Breton met with Rivera, with Trotsky, and with Frida Kahlo was to change utterly. The Second World War began and ended; Rivera broke with Trotsky, and was briefly (and mistakenly) implicated in Trotsky's 1940 assassination; Breton's influence continued to wane, to the point where he ultimately merited only a brief and somewhat dismissive mention in Rivera's biography. Finally, until her death in 1954, Kahlo continued to distance herself, both publicly and privately, from her prior association with Surrealism. It must here be emphasized that I have examined only an extremely brief and idiosyncratic episode in Kahlo's professional biography. On the other hand, however, I would hope to suggest that for Bretonian Surrealism, the late 1930s constituted a crucial moment, a point of reckoning, a period when he – by means of his relations with second-wave affiliates like Kahlo – was brought face to face with the limits of the self-critical strategies that he had been carefully developing for nearly two decades.

By pointing out the brevity and quirkiness of Kahlo's public association with Surrealism, however, I do not mean to suggest that she ceased altogether to be critically, oppositionally engaged with its theories and practices. To briefly illustrate this, I will turn to Kahlo's 1944 self-portrait *The Broken Column* (plate 5), and one of its impor-

5. Frida Kahlo, *The Broken Column*, 1944.

tant antecedents, Giorgio de Chirico's 1924 canvas, *The Disquieting Muses* (plate 6). *The Disquieting Muses* is a text that was regularly enlisted in the services of Surrealism's version of its own history; de Chirico was positioned as a key predecessor by Breton and his cohort during the twenties and early thirties, and *The Disquieting Muses* played an important cameo role in the internationalization of the movement during the late thirties, when it was reproduced as the frontispiece for David Gascoyne's English translation of selected essays by Breton, published in 1936 by Faber and Faber under the title *What is Surrealism?*

In the painting, three fantastic stone figures, constructed of an

6. Giorgio de Chirico, *The Disquieting Muses*, 1924.

incongruous mix of architectural, anatomical, and mechanical forms, stand in a piazza. They are part column, part realistic representation of the human body, and part dressmaker's mannequin. Hardly the figures of conventional heterosexist fantasy, these "muses" are instead reminders of the constructedness of more traditional notions of the muse as an eroticized source of inspiration. Breton wrote of de Chirico that he "retains only such exterior aspects of reality as propose enigmas or permit the disengagement of omens and tend toward the creation of a purely divinatory art."[60] Indeed, de Chirico's painting, which constructs these "muses" out of images taken from his personal, idiosyncratic pictorial vocabulary, suggest that the muse is a container primarily of private meaning, an apparently arbitrary projection of the artist's own desires.

Kahlo's painting, however, interrogates de Chirico's by positioning the muse as a more than arbitrary figure. Portrayed in scholarly and popular media as a kind of muse throughout her career – as she has been again, in the context of her ongoing, posthumous celebrity – Kahlo was well aware that the fiction of the muse could not be disarmed merely be being de-eroticized, made private and arbitrary. She was accustomed not only to the company of men of genius, as Breton asserted, but also to their tendencies to cast real women in the role of diviners, of near-fantastic, exteriorized sources of inspiration.

Kahlo had, in the words of Nancy Deffebach Breslow, "spoofed" de Chirico before, in her 1938 painting *Four Inhabitants of Mexico*, one of the newer, more definitively local and politicized images that generated so little response during her 1938 New York show.[61] In the foreground of that painting, as Breslow points out, Kahlo replaced de Chirico's typically classicist figures with a series of identifiably Mexican ones, including a child resembling Kahlo herself. *The Broken Column*, however, is hardly such a celebratory image: one of Kahlo's most disturbing self-portraits, it shows a nude, weeping Kahlo, bound in a medical corset, with nails driven into her skin. Her body is split open from her neck to her hips, and in place of her spine she has painted a fragmented classical column. The cracked column, the white drapery, the anatomical torso, and the tiny shadows cast by the nails clearly recall the left-hand figure in de Chirico's painting. The corset recalls in more subtle ways the mannequins who, according to William S. Rubin, provided a visual source for the bulbous, distorted heads of de Chirico's muses.[62] Moreover, the deep, receding background of de Chirico's painting is echoed in Kahlo's; her cracked landscape mimics the cracks in her columnar spine, just as the smooth planes of de Chirico's piazza mimic the surfaces of his "muses," which bear only minor flaws.

Jean Franco has argued, persuasively, that Kahlo frequently disrupts conventionally masculinist fantasies about female interiority by portraying her own interior as the horribly wounded inside of her own body.[63] What is fascinating about *The Broken Column*, however, is that when Kahlo places the fantastically gruesome spectacle of her broken body on display, what the viewer finds inside is not some brute reality, but a painterly allusion of the most academic sort. Her apparently confessional gesture is at the same time a compressed intertextual engagement. Not merely reminding the viewer that fantasies of the muse are grounded in the historical oppression of women, in women's "concrete reality," Kahlo's image also suggests that women's self-representation is itself entangled with that history. Her candor has its limits. As such, *The Broken Column* points up the fact that even when de Chirico makes the strategically useful move of dispensing with conventionally eroticized configurations of the muse, he does little to address the problem of the histories of representation that have enabled that figure's persistence. Kahlo, on the other hand, reasserts both the historically subjugated female body, and that body's necessary imbrication within a range of misogynistic representational strategies.

Penetrated repeatedly in the painting, Kahlo's body nonetheless maintains an incongruous integrity: the nails on her skin cast shadows, and seem to float on its surface rather than to pierce it. Her tears appear to be suspended on the planes of her face. The shattered column maintains its shape, however tenuously. At precisely the points where the boundary between inside and outside has been crossed, the painting is unexpectedly decorous and discreet. Certainly squeamishness did not prevent Kahlo from pressing these images further. Like the open corset that binds her body tenuously in place, this painting is situated on the border separating inside from outside, and draws attention to that border's many functions: its frequent brutality, its occasional usefulness, and finally, its intermittent permeability.

In her influential mid-eighties formulation of a feminist "elsewhere" that is both inside and outside representation, Teresa de Lauretis uses language closely akin to Kahlo's pictorial vocabulary:

> That "elsewhere" is not some mythic distant past or some utopian future history: it is the elsewhere of discourse here and now, the blind spots, or the space-off, of its representations. I

think of it as spaces in the margins of hegemonic discourses, social spaces carved in the interstices of institutions and in the chinks and cracks of the power-knowledge apparati.[64]

Calling attention to "the blind spots, or the space-off" – a cinematic term that maps "the space not visible in the frame but inferable from what the frame makes visible"[65] – de Lauretis points towards structural weaknesses within the architecture of a range of "hegemonic discourses." In Kahlo's *The Broken Column*, those pressure points are themselves mapped onto a compressed consideration of the place of the insider-outsider, whose work deftly allegorizes the conditions of its own production as a process of multiple affiliation, registering both its own entrapment, and some tentative possibility of intervention.

Leonora Carrington's self-revisions

In 1939, twenty-two-year-old British painter and writer Leonora Carrington published a story entitled "La Débutante" in a collection of tales called *La Dame Ovale* (*The Oval Lady*); that volume also contained a series of illustrations provided by her lover, the much older and better-known painter Max Ernst. One year later, André Breton selected the story for inclusion in his monumental *Anthology of Black Humor*, a volume whose publication was then withheld by the Vichy government until the end of World War II. This brief period, framed by the two separate appearances of "The Debutante," of course, was one of extraordinary, grand-scale, international turbulence. This phase also comprises, at the present moment, the most closely scrutinized period of Carrington's own, ongoing career.[1] During those years, she began publishing and exhibiting her work under the tutelage of Ernst, a painter much admired by André Breton, just before World War II; when Ernst was arrested in France prior to the Occupation, Carrington made a difficult border crossing into Spain, and in the process had a nervous breakdown; after a brief period of institutionalization in Spain (recounted in her stunning early 1940s essay "Down Below"), Carrington emigrated to New York, where she was briefly involved with the Surrealist community-in-exile, publishing some of her work in the Manhattan-based Surrealist journal *VVV*. Soon after, she settled in Mexico, where she has lived part-time ever since.

"The Debutante" is the first-person tale of a reluctant debutante who visits the zoo on the morning of her coming-out party, and manages to persuade a friendly female hyena whom she meets there to attend the party in her place. Unable to devise a costume that will disguise her hairy snout, the hyena decides to kill and eat the narrator's maid, Mary, so that she might use Mary's face in order to mask her own. The hyena's plot elicits brief resistance from the narrator: "It's not practical," she tells the hyena, "She'll probably die if she hasn't got a face."[2] The hyena, however, proceeds with her grotesque plan. She eats Mary, leaving only Mary's face and feet, and ventures out in mask and full formal dress to the party, where her unlikely impersonation succeeds until her hyena stench finally gives her away. Found out at the end of the story, the narrator is left to contend against her mother, whom she pointedly describes as being "pale with rage."[3]

As an instance of Surrealist "black humour," Carrington's story presents a clear, sardonic challenge to the norms underwriting British aristocratic culture during the years leading up to World War II. Describing late-thirties debutante celebrations, for example, Christopher Ogden tersely explains how the typical "season" held "a more serious purpose than simple fun. Strip away the music, champagne, gowns and white ties," Ogden writes, "and the ritual was all about breeding and preserving or improving bloodlines."[4] Moreover, even the "simple fun" that Ogden describes had more profound resonances: as historian Angela Lambert has recently pointed out, the feverish activity of the prewar debutante season served, for those involved, to block from consciousness the disastrous implications of Hitler's steady rise. Lambert notes, for example, the (near-Surrealist) juxtaposition in late-thirties British newspapers of two kinds of notices: on the one hand, lavish descriptions of debutante balls, accompanied by long catalogs naming upper-class girls and describing their gowns, and on the other, scaled-down and increasingly despairing notices in the "personal" columns posted by Jews from Germany and Austria who were seeking domestic and service employment that would enable emigration to Britain.[5] The aristocratic preoccupation with "preserving or improving bloodlines" thus found its monstrous counterpart in the eugenicist technologies of National Socialism.[6]

Carrington's hybrid figure of the hyena–debutante – who manages, somehow, to pass for the narrator in the muted evening light – is assembled from the body of a domesticated animal and the blood of a domestic worker. In Carrington's reading, upper-class ritual, despite its overriding concern with the maintenance of "bloodlines," is quite literally pieced together from the sacrificial remnants of those from putatively lower cultural orders. She shows how the debutante's presentation, which is designed plainly to distinguish the upper from the lower ranks, in fact dramatizes the way in which the two are connected: the "high" defined by means of brutal negation of the "low." In the twilight grey of the party, human and animal, servant and aristocrat, high and low, light and dark – all mix, and become temporarily indistinct, until the violence latent in their relations is finally made plain by the intrusion into the dining room of a bad smell.[7]

Carrington was herself a reluctant debutante in London during one of the last "seasons" before World War II, a small biographical detail that rapidly assumed enormous public importance as her career got underway in the late 1930s. In autobiographical comments that she scatters throughout interviews given during the course of the 1980s, Carrington reconstructs her own mid-thirties "season" as a brief, idiosyncratic interlude – marking the end of a privileged but unruly adolescence, and the start of the best-known phase of her career: her years with Ernst, and her brief public association with Surrealism. In a final attempt to normalize her position in the world in which she had grown up, her parents placed her, as Carrington puts it, "on the marriage market."[8] In that, she failed nearly as extravagantly as did the heroine of her short story; rather than flirting with acceptable suitors during the Ascot races, Carrington recently told interviewer Paul De Angeles, she instead spent her time reading Aldous Huxley's just-published novel *Eyeless in Gaza*.[9]

Still, despite the blip-like quality of Carrington's coming-out season within the more extended and complex trajectory of her career, the image of Carrington as debutante has shown unlikely resilience, and has guided even her recent reception in ways that merit detailed examination. Major contemporary interpreters of Carrington's "The Debutante" have read the story as a wonderfully subversive performance, one in which the young heroine circumvents the patriarchal imperatives of the debutante ritual by setting in motion a wildly ingenious masquerade; by means of her plot with the hyena, the debutante dislodges her fixed place in the order of things, and destabilizes her identity.[10] I would argue, however, that the kinds of cultural critique embedded within Carrington's story are both somewhat less direct and somewhat more self-critical than this kind of reading might suggest. Carrington's short story, as I have tried to make plain in my own interpretive reconstruction, references the deep ambiguities located in her heroine's (and by extension, her own) position: on one hand, both serve as pawns in the patriarchal game of the "marriage market"; on the other, however, both are privileged beneficiaries of the rigidly stratified British class system who play a crucial part in its maintenance.

These sorts of ambiguities, I believe, are best sorted out by analyzing Carrington's own, acute self-consciousness about the workings of rituals – of which the debutante "season" provides a near-perfect example – in which women serve as mediators or objects of exchange between men. I argued in the previous chapter that André Breton, through his early promotional efforts during the late 1930s, helped to consolidate an image of Kahlo as a kind of intellectual courtesan, whose paintings were largely confessional. Despite the obvious reductiveness of these sorts of entrepreneurial fictions, however, I went on to show how they did in fact disclose something important about the role that Breton scripted for Kahlo in the ongoing institutional drama of Surrealism during the years leading up to World War II: concerned about the waning international significance of his own brand of Surrealist activity, he hoped through his promotion of Kahlo's work to consolidate his own connections to the Marxist intelligentsia in Mexico City – to use her work, in other words, as a mediator between Surrealism and another, emerging political avant-garde. The courtesan – as a figure who mediates between men – bears a clear relationship to the debutante, who in a spectacular public ritual, is "presented" to appropriate suitors in anticipation of later being "given away" by her father in marriage. Throughout her early writings, Carrington subjects these and related rituals to her own rigorously disruptive form of analysis.

In order to understand how these sorts of issues might have bearings upon readings of Carrington's work, it is first important to keep in mind how Surrealism in the late thirties was not by any means a monolithic movement, but was instead varied, internally conflictual, and precisely at that moment, reaching a point of dispersal. The competing Surrealist tendencies that Kenneth Burke described in 1940 – when he characterized the movement as simultaneously "cult[ish]" and "incongru[ous]" – were coming to crisis at precisely this time.[11] Carrington's own history is vividly illustrative: she was introduced to the movement in Britain in the late thirties by *Surrealism*, a book-length overview written by the conservative English critic Herbert Read, who (to the delight of some of Breton's detractors) had embraced the purportedly radical aesthetic during the thirties.[12] Carrington then became professionally entwined with the movement's French affiliates, by virtue of her connection to Max Ernst, a relationship that landed her temporarily in France, and that brought her into contact with many of the movement's key figures just prior to the war years. After her institutionalization in Spain, as I noted above, Carrington emigrated to New York and was associated there with a wide circle of European intellectuals-in-exile, as well as with David Hare's New York journal *VVV*, which had a line-up of advisory editors including Breton, Ernst, and Marcel Duchamp. Later, when Carrington came to rest in Mexico, she met Diego Rivera, Frida Kahlo, and Remedios Varo, who, of course, had their own take on the significance of the movement. In later years, she would tell Paul De Angeles that she was relieved, when in Mexico, to be finally disconnected from the orthodoxies of the Parisian circle.[13] These are just a few of the forms that the movement had assumed at this point in its history; aware of the possible attenuation of his own influence, Breton was necessarily concerned with the problems of formational continuity and dispersal, subjects to which he devoted much provocative analysis in his writings from the 1930s and early 1940s. Shuttling between different sites of Surrealist activity, Carrington helped to reinforce the increasingly tenuous connections between them.

In her late teens and early twenties, of course, Carrington would not have been likely to understand her own situation in the terms set down by contemporary feminist analysts writing about the "exchange of women" – theorists whose work I discussed at some length in the first chapter. Carrington did, however, have related terms at her disposal for understanding these issues, in the admittedly idiosyncratic form of Aldous Huxley's *Eyeless in Gaza*, the book that she claims to have read, somewhat fortuitously, during the course of her own debutante season. Huxley, as Jessica Mitford notes in her autobiography *Hons and Rebels*, enjoyed a brief vogue among artistically inclined British debutantes during the 1930s; he served, as Elizabeth Bowen put it in a 1936 review, as "the perpetual clever nephew who [could] be relied on to flutter the lunch-party."[14] As such, it is with surprising critical force that in *Eyeless in Gaza* Huxley takes up the issue of what it meant for a young woman to inhabit the role of "*sérieuse*" in interwar British culture.

At the center of *Eyeless in Gaza* is Helen Amberley, a rebellious teenage girl who attaches herself to Hugh Ledwidge, a tedious, middle-aged ethnologist, in an effort to transform herself into an intellectual. They get married. Helen follows Hugh through museums and consumes the reading lists that he dictates to her – dutifully, but with growing resentment, following his lead. Hugh, charmless and sexually clumsy, views Helen as a relief from his arid scholarly life, a guide away from intellectual abstraction and towards the pathways of genuine experience. Their desires clash, their misunderstandings fester, and they reach a point of crisis when Helen, reading a newspaper on a train, learns that Hugh has written a novel based on their relationship and entitled *The Invisible Lover*.

As described by book reviewer Catesby Rudge, Ledwidge's novel evokes a " 'Galahad-like spirituality.' " The reviewer goes on to claim that " 'This fantasy of the invisible but ever present,

> ever watchful, ever adoring lover and his child-beloved has an almost celestial innocence. If I wanted to describe the book in a single phrase, I should say that it was the story of Dante and Beatrice told by Hans Andersen . . .[15]

Enraged at finding her marriage thus falsified, Helen begins to laugh: "luckily," Huxley's narrator observes, "she was alone in the compartment. People would have taken her for a madwoman."[16] Helen bursts in upon a gathering of Hugh and his friends, where she proceeds to correct, in explicit, very public terms, his fantastical misreading of their relationship: " 'Hugh!,' she thought with a derisive pity. 'Enjoying his private and invisible fun, like Dante with his phantom, and then having to suffer the trampling intrusion of Signora Alighieri!' "[17]

Helen Amberley Ledwidge is portrayed in Hugh Ledwidge's novel, then recognized by the reviewer, as a type of Beatrice. Huxley plays with this configuration throughout the novel: Helen's husband, explicitly, treats her as the companion on a journey towards Paradise; her lover Anthony Beavis, on the other hand, imagines her repeatedly as a companion on a journey towards Hell. Despite her intellectual appetites, and despite her own violent, anarchic interruptions of the social order, Helen is rarely imagined, by the men around her, as anything other than compliant, a conduit to ecstatic, mysterious ranges of experience that await their delectation. But she also, and this is perhaps more important, provides a link between her husband Ledwidge and her lover Beavis, who is an old-school rival whom Ledwidge had both envied and feared; Helen's other type, in the logic of the novel, is Helen of Troy, a classical epitome of the exchanged woman. Huxley, perhaps unwittingly, offered up a parable about the position of women intellectuals in the midst of modernist discourses of cultural critique – fantasized as conduits of inaccessible experience, they served, in fact, as conduits between male-governed cultural formations.[18]

Carrington, in transit from her father's house to the "marriage market," was waylaid; she took up with Ernst, and when he was imprisoned before the Occupation, she became mentally ill, was institutionalized, and was compelled to marry another man in order to escape further institutionalization. Her account of that period, her autobiographical essay "Down Below," is titled as a guidebook. Complete with a map, it places Carrington in a position closely akin to that of Helen Amberley; she serves as a guide to the underworld – a part of the sanitorium that she refers to as "Down Below" – initiating her readers into a realm of secret knowledge. In that sense, her essay seems to serve a deeply conservative purpose, to perform the mediumistic function that her patrons and mentors continually assigned to her. It is in the contents of "Down Below," however, that that image is at least partly transfigured. In *Eyeless in Gaza*, Helen Amberley, after reading the review of her husband's novel, claims that she will " 'write a book called *The Inaudible Mistress*. A woman who says exactly what she thinks about her lovers while they're making love to her. But they can't hear her. Not a word' "[19] Carrington, as Helen Amberley imagined for herself, composed a work filled with both inaudible and audible protest.

As I will demonstrate by taking a closer look at the complicated textual history of Carrington's "Down Below," the place of women in Surrealism was at once clearly delineated and oddly unfixed: in other words, they were continually transported and trafficked for the purposes of providing some stability for a movement whose future, at that point, looked increasingly fragmentary and uncertain. All the while, however, their work was touted to the public as naive, untutored self-revelation. To recognize this is to recognize the institutional needs served by many of the women affiliated with Surrealism, and to see how those needs bore down upon their work and its subsequent reception. If, as I have been arguing, insider-outsider self-representation is continually shifting and transforming, we can also begin to pinpoint some of the reasons why: insider-outsiders continually needed to address different audiences, for different reasons, so that their self-disclosure constituted itself in a continuous process of revision. Finally, I will argue, as we recognize their apparent unwillingness to tell the mere plain truth about themselves, we can also come to grips with many of the blunter historical determinants of their shifting self-disclosure.

1

By virtue of its timing and broad visibility, the text that "consecrated [Carrington] as a Surrealist heroine"[20] was not "The Debutante," but was instead the autobiographical essay "Down Below," Carrington's searing account of the breakdown that she experienced during her efforts to cross the French border into Spain in 1940. "Down Below" began its circuitous publication history in the February 1944 issue of the American Surrealist-affiliated journal *VVV* – the fourth and final number of that journal's short run. At that time, the *Anthology of Black Humor* was still under wraps in France, where the original French version of "Down Below" ("En Bas") was also awaiting publication. "En Bas" appeared in France in 1945, one year later, as a volume (a pamphlet, really) in Henri Parisot's "L'Age d'or" series. The English and French originals then went through various reprints during the next four decades, and were finally put into definitive form by editor Marina Warner (in consultation with Carrington and Paul de Angeles) in a 1988 English-language collection of Carrington's writings entitled *The House of Fear: Notes from Down Below*.

Marina Warner and Susan Rubin Suleiman, who have done the most in recent years to revive critical interest in Carrington's work, have both observed how "Down Below" was appreciated by the Surrealists because it contained an insider's account of a condition – female insanity – greatly valued by them, but at the same time inaccessible directly to them. Warner writes that, in Breton's eyes, Carrington had "realised one of the most desirable ambitions of Surrealism, the voyage down into madness," and goes on to locate this "ambition" within the larger context of Surrealist practice between the two World Wars:

> [Carrington] was Nadja *retrouvée*, the heroine of Breton's text returned to "normal," an instrument of *l'amour fou* and its victim. She had truly experienced the dementia Breton and Paul Eluard had only been able to simulate in *L'Immaculée Conception* of 1930, though their impersonation of insanity later won Jacques Lacan's applause.[21]

Warner thus demonstrates how Carrington's earliest audiences found her in her work an authentic, experiential account, one that could be used in support of the "simulat[ions]" or "impersonation[s]" that Breton and Eluard had theretofore produced. As had happened in Breton's earlier promotion of Kahlo's work, he valued Carrington's as well for its truth-value.

This valorization of authenticity, of course, typifies the kind of critical attention accorded the modernist generation of women insider-outsiders, as I attempted to illustrate through various examples given in the previous chapter; like Huxley's fictional heroine Helen Amberley Ledwidge, those women were charged with the responsibility of disclosing alien vistas of experience to their audiences. Here, again, it is useful to consider the ironies, for interwar women working in the insider-outsider mode, of Walter Benjamin's 1936 remark that "experience has fallen in value": intellectual interest in their work was premised upon the condition of its intellectual devaluation, its presumed lack of self-consciousness.[22] Suleiman and other feminist readers have gone on more recently to point out the shortcomings of treating "Down Below" – as Breton did – as an absolutely raw, unfiltered, spontaneous account of Carrington's breakdown. Suleiman notes, as does Renée Riese Hubert in another sharp analysis, that "Down Below" is in fact intensely self-conscious, containing within itself many subtle, careful responses to and revisions of better-known Surrealist texts. Suleiman suggests that we read the text not in harmony with, but instead, in counterpoint to Breton's 1928 novel *Nadja*, and Hubert goes on to argue that Carrington's revisions of Surrealist masterworks contain a submerged narrative of "feminine liberation."[23]

Warner's, Suleiman's, and Hubert's commentaries supply important correctives to earlier interpretive mystifications of Carrington's painting and writing; to the extent that I will also be looking at how "Down Below" worked contrary to Bretonian expectations, my own reading will follow in pathways mapped out by theirs. What interests me primarily, however, is not Carrington's direct conflict with Surrealist mystifications of "Woman"; instead, it is her indirect engagement of a series of broader institutional imperatives that kept her – in ways that I described earlier – in constant motion, performing a complicated series of evasive maneuvers. Like Kahlo's painterly self-image – indeed, like insider-outsider work more generally – Carrington's autobiographical texts were themselves subjected to constant self-revision, a fact that stymies any effort to read their work either (as Breton did) as unvarnished self-display, or (in terms developed by more recent feminist critics), as a more complicated but still cleanly dialogical engagement with a privileged interlocutor. Like Kahlo, Carrington came to Surrealism with a set of motivations and concerns distinct from Breton's own, which are themselves reflected in her work; moreover, and again like Kahlo, she directed her critical responses not only towards Breton, but towards a "Surrealism" that was rapidly mutating, expanding and contracting in unpredictable and frequently ambiguous ways. As such, in my own reading, I will focus upon the ways in which Carrington's essay allegorizes the shifting position of women upon the equally unstable terrain of late-thirties Surrealism. I will turn first to the earliest published version of "Down Below" in order to consider how the essay is inflected by Carrington's concern with and attention to the problem of female exchange. I will argue that the figure of the debutante – the innocent female initiate, "given away" by her father, on the verge of her first encounter with wider ranges of experience – operates in somewhat conservative ways in the broader context of the journal *VVV*, where "Down Below" first appeared. I will then turn to the most recent version of the essay, published in 1988, in order to evaluate some of the important changes that the text has undergone since its initial publication.

"Down Below" in its original published form – in the February 1944 edition of *VVV* – is not by any measure an easy essay to read.[24] It opens with a doctor's diagnosis of "incurabl[e]" insanity, proceeds through a detailed account of brutal institutional therapies, and ends not happily, but inconclusively. During the period that she recounts, Carrington endures sexual assault, incarceration, seizure-inducing drugs, self-starvation, and near-inconceivable filth. Her own illustrations – a creepy portrait of her doctor, and cryptic guides and maps of the clinic where she was treated – look like weird pencil drawings left in the margins of a child's schoolbook. Thus, it comes as a bit of a shock when the essay ends with a formal photographic portrait of a lovely, tidy, and serene Leonora Carrington, accompanied by her mother, both of them dressed in pale evening gowns; the caption reads "Leonora Carrington the day of her presentation at court" (plate 7).[25]

The "author's photo," a common mechanism of contemporary spin control, often relies for its force upon the deliberate creation of interpretive dissonance. For example, Mary Gaitskill's first book of stories – the transgressively erotic *Bad Behavior* – has over the years gained some notoriety not only as a result of its content, but also because of its wildly incongruous back-cover portrait of a sweet-faced Gaitskill, dressed in a sailor shirt, looking a lot like a preadolescent tomboy. What Carrington's portrait establishes is an equally jarring contrast; it juxtaposes the essay's many verbal images of degradation and vulnerability with a photographic image of

7. Leonora Carrington and her mother during her presentation at court.

deliberately constructed purity and protectedness. Initially, the photograph evokes pity; looking at it, it is hard to keep from thinking that this teenage girl must have had no idea what lay in store for her. In certain other respects, and much less sentimentally, the portrait

8. Lee Miller, *Revenge on Culture*, from *Grim Glory*, 1940.

can also pass as an instance of cultural critique. Juxtaposed with "Down Below," the image of Carrington and her mother, poised and spotless on the eve of World War II, could serve much the same function as one of the most famous postwar photographs produced by Carrington's friend Lee Miller, the well-known model and photographer. Miller's *Revenge on Culture* (plate 8) uses the image of a broken stone statue of a woman lying in a pile of rubble as a reminder to complacent Europeans of the violent obliteration of many of their own most cherished cultural institutions; the debutante ritual in which Carrington participates, seen in light of the contents of her essay, thus assumes a quality of the absurd. Just as deliberate, however, and much more troubling, is the fact that the image also works, quite clearly, in order to titillate the reader. It casts a strangely erotic glow around the astonishingly unsexy essay that precedes it, helping to blunt the effects of "Down Below" by transforming it, in certain respects, into a kinky story about a debauched aristocrat.

What is transpiring in the photograph is the peculiar initiation rite of the British aristocracy that I have already discussed: a daughter is being "presented" at court – offered up to "the marriage market," in anticipation of later being "given away" by her father, to her husband, in marriage. Carrington is also, of course, being presented to an international reading public in her essay. (She had published stories and shown paintings before; none of them, however, had the kind of autobiographical vividness of "Down Below.") Her new readers would have been able to infer from the contents of Carrington's essay the outlines of a debauched debutante plot; at the start of "Down Below," for example, Carrington mentions her affair with Max Ernst, and goes on to describe her subsequent efforts to find other lovers after Ernst was incarcerated by the French. The artist's lover in the text and the virginal debutante in the photograph make a seductive combination. Accordingly, the irony generated by the portrait comes in large part at Carrington's own expense: rather than being "given away" to an upper-class suitor, Carrington lands in the arms of Surrealism itself. This oddball marriage – one that seems at first to undermine the pretensions, ignorances, and exclusions of the British aristocracy – is itself thoroughly problematical; through her affiliation with Surrealism, Carrington assumes a subordinate position (as a virginal initiate, poised on the threshold of maturity, awaiting defloration) that is structurally similar to the one she would have occupied in a much more conventional marriage.

Where these similarities become clear is in a broader examination of the journal in which the essay first appeared. The fourth and final number of *VVV* – in which "Down Below" was the final published piece – is an issue deeply concerned with the future of Surrealism: in it, the editors shift their focus towards a new generation of Surrealist-affiliated artists. Throughout its run, the journal, edited by David Hare with an advisory board made up of Breton, Ernst, and Marcel Duchamp, was distinctly expansive and forward-looking in its impulses. It foregrounded and encouraged interdisciplinary activity, seeking to create an international forum for discussion among psychoanalysts, anthropologists, social scientists, fiction writers, poets, and visual artists. Lévi-Strauss published an obituary for Malinowski in *VVV*; Aimé Césaire's poems appeared there; Pierre Mabille published essays on psychoanalysis; Carrington, Remedios Varo, Wifredo Lam, and many other painters had high-quality reproductions of their work put into print. At the end of their brief publishing run, moreover, Hare and his advisory editors seemed particularly concerned about Surrealism's future. Thus, in the journal's final number, a large share of the contributions come from the movement's second wave: poets and painters from the western hemisphere (Lam, Matta, Césaire), women artists (including Carrington and Jacqueline Lamba Breton), and at least one contributor notable primarily for his extreme youth (17-year-old poet Philip Lamantia, who published a reverential open letter to Breton). Read in this context, which was deliberately experimental, but also quite conservative in its concern for the movement's continuity, the contents of Carrington's essay begin to rhyme in unexpected ways with the image presented in her debutante portrait: to expropriate Christopher Ogden's sardonic description of the London debutante "season," the final issue of *VVV* was itself "all about breeding and preserving or improving bloodlines."[26]

In subtle ways, the editorial apparatus accompanying Carrington's essay works to obscure these blunt imperatives, making her contribution to the journal appear to be much more disruptive than it actually is. For example, Carrington's essay is accompanied by a curious italicized editor's note, *"as told to Jeanne Mégnen / translated from the French by Victor Llona,"* informing the reader that the essay was a translation of a transcript, twice removed from Carrington herself. (As I previously noted, the essay did not appear in the original French version until after the war ended.) What a reader of *VVV* might reasonably infer from the italicized editor's note that accompanies "Down Below" is that the essay, which throughout its length is addressed to a privileged but unnamed interlocutor, was composed in dialogue with Jeanne Mégnen, a woman whose husband, Pierre Mabille, was a psychoanalyst and essayist affiliated with the Surrealist circle. This scene is brimming with subversive interpretive possibility; the wife of one prominent Surrealist records the intimate confessions of the former mistress of another; Carrington credits her interlocutor, from the start of the essay, with great wisdom, addressing her as "you, whom I consider the most clear-sighted of all";[27] the photograph of Carrington with her mother appears just below the note mentioning Mégnen. The reader of "Down Below" seems to have entered into a private realm where women are together, apart from the men, telling their secrets to one another. In a journal whose red cover displays Matta's startling visual interpretation of a *vagina dentata*, one might infer that the editors have decided finally to allow the women to talk back, even to the extent of giving them the last word.

Such inferences, reasonable as they are, would nonetheless also be historically inaccurate. In recent years, Carrington has filled in the textual history of the essay, and we now know (as Carrington hints during the essay, and has more recently informed Marina Warner) that the "you" constantly addressed in "Down Below" is not Mégnen at all; it is Mégnen's husband Mabille, whose work Carrington alludes to at key points in her account, and who treated Carrington after she left Europe for the Americas in 1943. Mégnen, in time-honored fashion, acted as stenographer and witness, performing a mediating function closely akin to Carrington's mediation between different Surrealist coteries. The journal's glimmering indications of female solidarity and resistance are further undermined when the reader considers the fact that Carrington's mother, as shown in the photograph, is on the verge of relinquishing her daughter to the "marriage market." With this in mind, the function of the essay in the fourth number of *VVV* begins to seem perplexing and endlessly complicated. The journal creates an appearance of women on their own, running amok; the history that Carrington has recently enabled scholars to reconstruct, on the other hand, is a very different one.

The potential disruptiveness of Carrington's essay is also contained in other, somewhat more pointed ways. *VVV* 4 includes a companion article to Carrington's piece, one whose title, "Le Paradis," calls out to Carrington's "Down Below" across the table of contents. That article is written by Mabille, and contains a passionate call for his readers to abandon their habitual desires for order and stability – their "modération malicieuse."[28] These maliciously moderate desires are embodied individually in what Mabille calls a "complexe paradisiaque" and collectively in a "myth édénique"; both entail a rejection of worldly disorder, randomness, and transitoriness in favor of transcendence, of the continually deferred but purportedly endless pleasures of "Paradise."[29] Near the end of his essay, Mabille calls for his readers to relinquish these dulling, destructive habits of mind in favor of a Surrealist recognition of the marvelous embedded within quotidian experience. Mabille's essay, like Carrington's, carries with it striking illustrations: photographs of patients lined up on stretchers, in a sanatorium or spa, indistinguishable as mummies, and overseen by a line of attendants dressed in white – the imperious enforcers of the "paradise complex."[30] Mabille, himself a medical professional, clearly wishes to redefine the boundaries of what constitutes both treatment and health.

The antidote to all of this self-delusion, of course, can be found in Carrington's deeply disturbing "Down Below," whose title inverts Mabille's negative diagnosis of the "paradise complex," answering it with a detailed description of what Carrington has learned from her own hellish episode of insanity and her subsequent treatment by Mabille. Even her photographic illustrations are responsive to his: the attendants' plain cotton trousers and shifts find their opulent parody in her mother's and her own fluid, bias-cut gowns; her mother's ambition (i.e., a "proper" marriage for Leonora) is visually rhymed with these starchy attendants' efforts to lead their patients to "paradise." While Carrington herself is hospitalized, however, her own goal is to travel downwards, rather than towards "Paradise," in order to reach a part of the asylum that she calls "Down Below." She even provides a map to illustrate her institutional surroundings, one that traces out the geographical contours of her journey. Thus, Carrington's essay serves in many ways to reinforce Surrealism's vision of its own future; while Hare and his fellow advisory editors seem to relinquish control over the future of the movement – offering it up to the second wave – they in fact work quite hard to maintain their grasp on it. Like a more compliant version of Huxley's Helen Amberley Ledwidge, Carrington produces a tale that coincides precisely with the desires of the men who surround her.

From the start of the essay, however, there are indications of a more resistant voice at work, one whose tonalities are more closely reminiscent of Helen Amberley's fantasy of the "inaudible mistress." What is perhaps most surprising about "Down Below," given the circumstances surrounding its composition, is the extent to which Carrington's confession seems motivated and shaped by a profoundly critical awareness that the journey described therein is marked by her contact with a series of male authority figures who pass her – in some cases, quite literally – from hand to hand. Her illness follows closely upon the arrest of Max Ernst, whom she immediately attempts to replace with other lovers. In this, Carrington is following the advice of an English friend named Catherine, who arrived in France during the earliest stages of Carrington's breakdown: "Catherine, who had been for a long time under the care of psychoanalysts, persuaded me that my attitude betrayed an unconscious desire to get rid for the second time of my father in the person of Max, whom I had to eliminate if I wanted to live."[31] Although

89

Carrington ultimately rejects portions of Catherine's advice, calling them "fragmentar[y],"[32] she nonetheless proceeds by trying again and again to "eliminate" the father figures whom she repeatedly encounters on her journey, and who control her activities, enabling her escape from France, but also arranging her incarceration at a sanitorium in Spain.

Carrington is able to cross the French border, for example, only after gaining assistance from men connected to her father's business in England. After finally reaching Madrid, she fixates upon a shadowy Dutch businessman named Van Ghent, also connected in undetermined ways with her father's business, whom she is convinced is a Nazi agent involved in the mass hypnosis of the citizens of Spain. Following Van Ghent, she transfers her attentions to a "Mr. Gilliland," a British executive working for her father's chemical business in Madrid, and he passes her on to Dr. Pardo, who deposits her in the clinic where she remains until the conclusion of the early versions of the essay. After Carrington's madness is diagnosed and she comes under a doctor's care in Madrid, she has a brief affair with one of her physicians – "Alberto N." She claims that she "hastened to seduce him, for I said to myself: 'There's my brother who comes to liberate me from the *fathers.*' "[33] She finally concludes, however, that Alberto N. is himself attracted to her because "he was aware of the power of papa Carrington and his millions."[34] At stake in all of her movements is her will to escape her father's influence, out of which she weaves a densely speculative web that eventually, in her own imaginings, comes to include Franco and finally Hitler himself. Carrington, moreover, is acutely conscious of her own tendency to see everywhere the evidence of paternal manipulation and control; there is even an element of her famous "black humour" in the repetitive appearance and far-flung influence of her father's sinister envoys, who seem to be lurking around every corner.

The first of these rejected father substitutes who appears in "Down Below," of course, is Max Ernst, a painter much admired by Breton himself, and an advisory editor at *VVV*. Published in that journal, Carrington's descriptions of her activities and movements during her breakdown come to mirror her passage between and among different Surrealist coteries. Moreover, her journey turns out to be circular, leading her back to her point of departure: into the domain mapped out by Ernst and his cohort. Thus, Carrington's life as an artist, cured of her insanity, has direct continuities with the events that led up to her brief incarceration in Spain. Caught within, but highly aware of the processes that guide her, she ends up framing her own story in ways that implicitly indict those – Mabille, Ernst, and Breton – who are positioned in *VVV* as her saviors.

My reading is admittedly pessimistic: thus far, I have stressed the ways in which Carrington depicts her Surrealist cure as nothing more than a continuation of the illness from which she appears to have recovered; only the psychotic symptoms have disappeared, not their causes. The determinants of her most pronounced symptoms – her debilitating sense that all of her movements are controlled by her father – are by no means eliminated by her move to New York and her embrace by the Surrealist community-in-exile. Like the ill-fated protagonist of her short story "The Debutante," whose ingenious resistances only implicate her further within the very processes that she wishes to escape, Carrington in the 1944 version of "Down Below" remains caught.

2

Thus far, I have focused on the way in which the image of the debutante – a virginal initiate, standing on the threshold which marks her passage from an old master to a new one – operated during the early phases of Carrington's reception history. I have shown how that image worked to circumscribe her early writings, limiting their force by subordinating her concerns to those of Surrealism's first wave. I have also sought to illustrate, however, how Carrington's own rereadings of debutante rituals – her fascination with configurations of female "exchange" apparent in both "The Debutante" and in "Down Below" – can offer us a more fluid way of assessing her late-thirties work. Once we become aware of her as an intellectual *in transit*, moving from destination to destination and piecing together a method as she goes along, we can begin to see how her essay "Down Below," far from serving a straightforward autobiographical account, instead casts a gloweringly ironical eye on the exchange of women within Surrealism in the years during and just prior to the Second World War.

As I move towards my conclusions, however, I would like to turn back to the more purely autobiographical contents of the essay, in order to make a series of necessarily speculative remarks about the changes that "Down Below" has undergone since its 1944 publication. "Down Below" was finally published in an approved, finished form in Marina Warner's 1988 collection *The House of Fear: Notes From*

Down Below. That volume contains a long critical and biographical essay by Warner, a group of short works by Carrington, photographs of Carrington then and now, and selected reproductions of her paintings. At the end of the volume, in an editor's note, Warner explains the textual status of Carrington's reissued works:

> The texts in this volume were established by the author, in consultation with Marina Warner and Paul De Angeles, in 1987 ... Every attempt was made to remain true to the spirit and tone of the author's first-draft compositions of 1937–1943, while *minor revisions were made for the sake of clarity and accuracy.*[35]

Here, Warner assures the reader that the collected texts are "established," "true," "cl[ear]", and "accura[te]" – and indeed, the reader has no reason to suspect otherwise. The 1988 version of "Down Below," in fact, bears differences from its predecessor that, while small, are nonetheless radiantly significant; it includes a postscript supplying an end to the story (left inconclusive in the earlier versions), and contains textual alterations whose cumulative effects are quite striking.

The majority of the textual changes seem designed to make the essay read less like a translation (recall that Carrington dictated the text in French to Jeanne Mégnen, so that the English version of the essay printed in *VVV* was both a transcript and a translation): idioms are recast, awkward syntax is altered, and, most notably, the passive voice is repeatedly excised and replaced with the active. On the whole, the 1988 text is surer, more forceful, and more commandingly written than previous versions.

Twice, for example, Carrington deletes passages from the early versions in which she claimed to be incapable of describing her ordeal.[36] One might imagine that the tentativeness of the earlier versions contributed to the reader's sense of Carrington's well-known childlike charm;[37] here, that is no longer the case. The removal of the passive voice also has the effect of making Carrington seem less dependent than before upon the interlocutor whom she addresses. She has spoken in an interview with Suleiman of the phenomenon of "'opinion dependency'" – this, in reference to her youthful inexperience at the time of her affair with Max Ernst. To Suleiman, Carrington stated that

> "I think that a lot of women (people, but I say women because it is nearly always women on the dependent side of the bargain) were certainly cramped, dwarfed sometimes, by that dependency. I mean not only the physical dependency of being

supported, but also emotional dependency and opinion dependency."[38]

This "'opinion dependency'" is what Carrington works hardest to extricate, not only from the grammar of the essay but also, explicitly, from some of its important passages. In the first (and least significant of these), Carrington in 1944 argued briefly with Pascal, on the subject of conventional polarizations of reason and emotion;[39] in the 1988 version, she deletes any reference to Pascal. In another, more significant excision,[40] Carrington deletes a reference to Pierre Mabille's anthology, *Le miroir du Merveilleux*, which, according to her 1944 commentary, contains a passage from Alfred Jarry that has helped her to recover "the key to [her own] story." This omission explains an earlier one, where in the original version, Carrington had credited to her interlocutor her own use of the "mirror" metaphor; in the revised version, her phrase of deferral – "to resort to your own metaphor" – is deleted.[41] Thus Carrington, in the 1988 version, makes deliberate efforts to distance her narrative from recognizable "'opinion dependency.'"

While these sorts of changes might be the most pervasive, they are not the most startling. Perhaps the boldest alteration comes in her revision of a scene that transpires early in the essay, where Carrington – whose illness has by this time become acute – meets a group of soldiers in a bar in Madrid who force her to a strange apartment building, where they sexually assault her. In the 1944 *VVV* version (and its 1945 French equivalent), the soldiers attempt rape, but Carrington resists heroically, exhausting them, so that they finally give up their efforts and one of them returns her to her own hotel.[42] In the revised 1988 version, however, the soldiers rape Carrington "one after the other" before casting her out alone; disoriented and disheveled, she then wanders about in a public park until a policeman finds her and escorts her to her room.[43]

Even in the absence of the gang rape episode, "Down Below" is filled with instances of violation that carry with them strong sexual connotations. During her institutionalization, Carrington is repeatedly stripped and bound, prodded and penetrated, forced against her will to submit to invasive treatments of various kinds. For readers of the 1988 text who are unaware of the editorial changes, the episode of the gang-rape seems neither more nor less important than any of Carrington's other horrific accountings of her experiences. It is even possible to argue that, in certain respects, the outlawed rape (recall here that Carrington is rescued afterwards by a policeman) constitutes a less sustained and overwhelming violation than the institutionalized torture that she undergoes at the clinic: one is random, fleeting, and illegal; the other is systematic, extended over a long period of time, and authorized by both the medical establishment and by the government functionaries who admit her to the hospital in the first place. Finally, although it is impossible to say exactly why Carrington chose to make such a significant change in "Down Below," it is possible to assess the effects of her choice upon the essay itself.

Looking at these two versions of "Down Below" side by side, and considering further the complexity of the history of that essay's own origins, it is tempting to argue that Carrington, in her essay, is making a point about the indeterminacy of "experience"; in fact, she invites the reader to draw this conclusion. Throughout "Down Below," the boundary between fact and fiction, between history and hallucination, is continually explored. In a crucial and oft-cited passage which appears in all versions of the text, Carrington writes that "I am afraid I am going to drift into fiction, truthful but incomplete, for lack of some details which I cannot conjure up today and which might have enlightened us."[44] Renée Riese Hubert uses passages such as this as a basis for arguing that historical accuracy is not really the issue for readers of "Down Below": "we hardly need to know," Hubert writes pointedly, "the actual strength of the medication or whether she was really forced to lie naked in her excrement, for what really concerns us is how she views and interprets her ordeal."[45]

Hubert bases her claim, in large part, upon analyses of a single version of the essay, and in that context, her reading makes good sense;[46] "Down Below" is, as Hubert suggests, as centrally concerned with the process and manner of recollection as it is with the events recollected, which makes for a pointed *riposte* to Breton's claims about Carrington's raw, unvarnished sincerity. Reviewing variants of "Down Below," however, the reader is faced with a very different problem – that is, with significant new information that contradicts information given in the earlier accounts. Thus, one of the first questions that Carrington's revision of the sexual assault sequence conjures up is the question of which version comes closer to squaring with events as they actually occurred – not a trivial issue when the event that is described is a rape. The answer, however distanced from the text itself, is given by Marina Warner in her final editorial note: the 1988 version, according to Warner, was "reviewed and revised for factual accuracy by the author."[47]

What interests me most about this particular textual shift and the editorial apparatus that accompanies it is the fact that they take many of the most deeply ironical, sophisticated inflections of "Down Below" – its self-reflexiveness, its distrust of its own articulacy, its intertextual density – and work to reground them in the domain of "factual accuracy." Thus my own reading, which has thus far stressed the continuous destabilization of "Down Below," and carries with it a deep skepticism towards the authenticity of the self that is disclosed in that text, finally turns on a question of real events and their accurate depiction. I take this question seriously; morever, I think that it matters that we accept Warner's assurance of the "factual accuracy" of the 1988 text, along with the complex interpretive demands that that assurance makes upon the reader. It is to this apparent contradiction that I will turn as I move towards my conclusions.

Early in the essay, as Carrington flees France for Spain and her illness intensifies, she begins to experience frightening hallucinations: huge trucks hauling mutilated body parts, rows of coffins lining the roadside. She keeps quiet about this, in order to conceal her deteriorating condition from her friends. Later, however, Carrington discovers that she was not in fact hallucinating during the car trip; she and her friends had driven past a French military cemetery, and had actually witnessed those nightmarish scenes. Yet another example of Carrington's brand of "black humour," this sequence shows how the world around her had, in reality, taken on the quality of gruesome hallucination; the chief early symptom of her illness – a complete identification with the outside world, so that her personal anguish mirrored an anguished France – can thus be read as an extreme form of lucidity. These passages in Carrington's essay are reminiscent of Paul Fussell's well-known remarks about European border disputes that preceded the First World War, which themselves translate onto the geography of interwar Europe the skepticism towards "experience" outlined by Walter Benjamin in 1936: "Fragmenting and dividing anew and parcelling-out and shifting around and repositioning – these are the actions implicit in the redrafting of frontiers. All these actions betray a concern with current space instead of time or tradition. All imply an awareness of reality as disjointed, dissociated, fractured."[48] At the same time, however, Carrington later demonstrates how her identification with the world around her goes on to assume a hubristic and finally a delusional quality; her increasing inability to distinguish historical fact from private fiction is what finally marks her loss of control. Carrington's primary concern while ill is the possibility of intervening against Hitler's influence (she envisions herself, at times, as the political savior of Madrid); after her recovery, however, the index that she uses to chart her trajectory into madness is her loss of ability to recognize or to guage the significance of historical realities. Thus, while "Down Below" plays quite deliberately with the abstract peculiarities of perspectivism and madness, Carrington remains deeply concerned with the issue of how to perceive and articulate historical and political fact. One of Carrington's more evocative gestures before her incarceration is her shredding of "a vast quantity of newspapers," which she scatters in the streets, convinced that they are being used in order to hypnotize the Spanish public.[49] In a necessarily complicated way, Carrington wants to renegotiate the terms with which historical fact gets represented.

Why, then, would Carrington's most notable factual alteration take the form of her transformation of her earlier account of the rape? (In the later version, for example, no efforts are made to clarify the delusional readings of broader political events in Madrid; the reader is left to make those sorts of corrections and adjustments herself.) Moreover, why, if most of her minor revisions seem designed to depict a more forceful and assured narrator, would the one scene in "Down Below" in which Carrington triumphs over her victimizers be transformed utterly?

In order to suggest a few tentative solutions to these interpretive riddles, I will turn briefly to more recent feminist commentary on the issue of female "traffic." Throughout the eighties and into the early nineties, some of the most provocative new work on the old issue of the "traffic in women" has focusing on the problem of rape. Beginning with Patricia Joplin's 1984 essay "The Voice of the Shuttle is Ours," and moving up to more recent analyses of US popular culture by Susan Fraiman, feminist theorists have turned their attention towards the problematical agency of the exchanged woman, noting the way in which the mediating woman – crossing the threshold between men, thus cementing the bonds between them – is frequently denied any choice in the matter. Though Joplin's and Fraiman's analyses are very different, there are nonetheless important points of contact between them: while on one hand the woman's consent (or lack of consent) is rendered meaningless and inconsequential as she circulates among men, both Joplin and Fraiman point towards possibilities of resistant enunciations that take shape both inside and outside the cycle of exchange.[50]

In her 1939 depiction of the reluctant debutante, Carrington foregrounded the difficulty of refusing the cultural imperatives grounded in rituals of exchange; rather than saying "no," the young girl sends a masked substitute in her place, and in the process (by consenting to the murder of her maid, Mary) finds herself even more irretrievably enmeshed within the processes that she is attempting to resist. Among the Surrealists, Carrington found herself in similarly straitened circumstances, and also met with an even trickier philosophical problem: in a Surrealist (under)world where masculine and feminine desires are fully articulated – fully liberated from the paradisiacal constraints of habit and convention – there would be no reason for a woman to refuse in the first place. Female sexual consent is obviated, because rape would not exist.

Critics like Hubert, Suleiman, and Warner have (rightly) focused on Breton's 1928 novel *Nadja* as a point of departure for Carrington's "Down Below." In so doing, they have paid particular attention to Carrington's depiction of female madness, which differs so sharply from Breton's. Breton, of course, abandons his lover Nadja when she finally succumbs to insanity and is institutionalized; he adores the fantasy of *l'amour fou*, but cannot cope with its reality. Carrington, as they have argued in different contexts, presents in "Down Below" a powerful revision of Surrealist mystifications of female hysteria with her blunt account of her own illness and recovery.

In this context, however, it is also worth noting that in *Nadja*, Breton begins to withdraw from Nadja in advance of her institutionalization, and for different reasons – reasons that have to do specifically with problems of female sexual agency and consent. In an important sequence late in the novel, Breton somewhat ambivalently describes his disgust upon hearing from Nadja a brief story about her own sexual past: in her tale, Nadja describes her refusal of the advances of a man who approaches her in a restaurant. The man strikes her, and Nadja bleeds on him before she leaves. Susan Suleiman has argued that Breton's disgust might have been generated not – as he initially suggests – by the indignity of the scene, but instead by "the image" that Nadja presents to him "of a man spattered with female blood," which might have signified for Breton "the 'otherness' in femininity."[51] My own related sense is that one of the determinants of his revulsion is the bare fact of Nadja's sexual refusal, which Breton describes – in his own account of Nadja's account – as a cunning, calculated, even somewhat mean-spirited action.[52] He is as revolted by the possibility of Nadja's withholding of consent from the man as he is by the possibility, so vividly described by Suleiman, of contamination by " 'otherness.' "

The context of Carrington's refusal is of course different from that of Nadja's. Her attackers are soldiers, not ordinary men in a bar. They are official agents of repression, not quotidian, unofficial brutes. Her refusal, as such, makes for a happy conclusion to a Surrealist fairy tale, not (as Breton reads Nadja's story) for a humiliating and slightly sordid spectacle. In the early versions of "Down Below," Carrington emerges triumphant from her battle with the soldiers. She exhausts them with her superior strength and will, leaving intact her status as the heroine of a Surrealist fantasy of a world in which feminine sexuality refuses to be regulated and disciplined by the sinister agencies of popular morality, of the state, or of prideful individual caprice, and in which every sex act that is accomplished will, as such, also be desired. In the revised version of "Down Below," however, Carrington rends that fiction, as surely as she had shredded the Spanish newspapers during those final days before her institutionalization, demonstrating in graphic ways its distance from the world that she inhabits.

As Carrington's potent image of the shredded newspapers suggests, the terms of representation must constantly be shifted – *not* in order to disclaim the possibility of "factual accuracy" – but in order to achieve a more complicated version of what constitutes "fact." Thus, Carrington's self-revisions – like Frida Kahlo's mutating self-portraiture – work to unsettle the fixity of Surrealist hypotheses of feminine " 'otherness' ": in this sense, both women's works can be read as pointed interventions into more conventional Surrealist practice. As I have attempted in both cases to show, however, this denial of fixity is not by any means a utopian gesture, one that removes the female subject from the realm of historical necessity, creating for her a space of free self-inventiveness. Instead, it is a denial that is itself the product of a complicated set of historical exigencies that continually bore down on work by women insider-outsiders during the interwar years.

Hurston among the Boasians

Zora Neale Hurston's ethnographies played a major role in setting the agenda for the debates in which I now participate; her dazzling, boldly experimental ethnographic writings from the 1930s and early 1940s are often cited as an inspiration by contemporary scholars who are in the process of elaborating postmodern discussions of difference and oppositionality – scholars whose work, in turn, inspired my own, present analysis. The tendency among recent critics and theorists to treat Hurston as a contemporary rather than a historical presence has assumed a number of forms: bell hooks, as I noted in my first chapter, has shown that many of the self-reflexive techniques used by present-day experimental ethnographers were anticipated by Hurston more than five decades ago. Nathaniel Mackey, in his recent essay "Other: From Noun to Verb," turns to Hurston's 1934 essay "Characteristics of Negro Expression" in order to locate theoretical underpinnings for his description of the process of textual variation that he calls "othering."[1] In Barbara Johnson's 1985 essay "Thresholds of Difference," Johnson depicts Hurston as a kind of mentor: "I had a lot to learn," Johnson writes, "from Hurston's way of dealing with multiple agendas and heterogeneous implied readers."[2] And Trinh T. Minh-Ha, in her important 1986 lecture "Outside In Inside Out," cast major portions of her argument in the form of a collage of quotations in which she and other writers conversed with Hurston's 1943 essay "The 'Pet Negro' System."[3] In this respect, Hurston's case is by no means isolated: members of the interwar generation of insider-outsiders, including most of the women whose work I treat in this present volume, have repeatedly been configured as intellectual time travelers: their work is often seen as being much more clearly responsive to the concerns of the present day than it was to those of their own.[4]

I will eventually return to the question of what it means to displace Hurston's admittedly prescient interwar writings into the present. Here, however, I mean merely to point out how, in such an over-determined context, I approach Hurston's ethnographies with a peculiar kind of trepidation; I am fully aware that I run the risk of circularity, of merely affirming the obvious by pointing out just how precisely Hurston demonstrates the very strategies that her writings enabled me to seek out in the first place. What I hope to present in this chapter, instead, is a version of a Hurston who is somewhat less intimately familiar – who is instead firmly located within a distinct and distant moment. I will attempt first to trace out the circumstances that gave rise to precisely those aspects of her work that now seem so contemporary, and will go on to suggest ways of reading her ethnographic writings that account for both their strangeness and their familiarity, their oldness and their newness.

1

It is possible to map the northwest quadrant of Manhattan, *circa* 1925, as an intellectual battleground where two competing discourses – anthropological representation of African–American culture, and African–American literary self-representation – had it out, in muted but intensely serious ways, for a decade or so. Around 135th Street, with fluid boundaries moving to the north and south, were the artists, writers, patrons, performers, and public intellectuals who were participating in the late phases of what is now called the Harlem Renaissance. Around 116th, but also extending its influence well beyond its own well-tended borders, was Columbia University, home to Franz Boas's anthropology department. Between those two locations, which overlapped geographically but remained predictably distinct from one another, Hurston vacillated during her early years as a writer. In the course of this extraordinarily productive phase, Hurston produced an array of short fictional, nonfictional, and dramatic pieces for literary contests, magazines, and anthologies, a play coauthored with Langston Hughes, a scholarly monograph, two well-received novels, and two important book-length ethnographies.

Hurston, who was born in 1891 and spent important phases of her childhood in Eatonville, Florida, made her way up the east coast during her teens, working at various jobs, finishing high school, and then beginning college at Howard University. By the early 1920s, she had reached New York, where she emerged as a forceful if mercurial presence within the Harlem Renaissance. A favorite subject among Renaissance memoirists, historians, and novelists-à-clef, Hurston tended to be portrayed, up to the point of her mid-seventies revival, as a minor writer with a big and somewhat volatile personality; during that same time period, she left almost no traces at all in the equally voluminous archives of late-twenties Columbia.[5] Hurston was enrolled at Barnard in the mid-twenties, working towards completion of a B.A. in English,[6] when Gladys Reichard, one of her anthropology professors, spotted her talents and brought them to the attention of Franz Boas. For the next decade, Hurston would divide and mix her pursuits, both literary and anthropological. After enrolling officially in the graduate program in the mid-thirties, Hurston never completed her Ph.D. Despite this, she worked closely with a number of prominent Boasians, including Melville Herskovits, who cites her anthropometric research in his volume *The Anthropometry of the American Negro*,[7] and Ruth Benedict, with whom Hurston studied independently.[8]

Boas, by this time a very old man, pursued an agenda during the 1920s and 1930s that was widely varied, encompassing subjects from the most arcane to the most accessible. A sizable proportion of the research projects performed during those years by Boas and his colleagues were designed to counteract racism and xenophobia in both their homegrown and their international forms. Boas, moreover, had a talent for translating dense, tedious compendia of anthropological data into pithy public pronouncements; Arnold Krupat refers to this as Boas's "citizenly practice."[9] In the US, his research formed the basis for public arguments against the tightening of immigration restrictions, and in line with his international agenda, Boas spoke out against pernicious notions of national "purity" that circulated widely, under the banner of Aryanism, during the interwar years.[10] In February 1926, for example, Boas, working to counteract the mythology (as well as the pseudoscience) of the "Aryan," was quoted in *The World*: "Nationality is irrelevant," he stated there. "All nations are mongrel."[11]

As part of their broader antiracist agenda, Boas and many of his students devoted particular attention during the interwar years to research on Native American and African–American traditions throughout the western hemisphere. A large part of this effort was devoted to analysis of the effects of urban migration and industrialization upon rural traditions in the southeastern and western United States. Boas's student Margaret Mead referred to these projects, with characteristic gusto, as a "giant rescue operation," one designed to compile an archive of Native American and African–American oral traditions that were undergoing rapid transformation the early decades of this century.[12] According to the "rescue" mentality, those traditions were not simply experiencing inevitable historical change (as, in fact, they always had done, though admittedly not with this rapidity); to the contrary, they were disappearing completely, incorporating themselves into a broader national tradition that was itself inextricably mixed. These so-called "rescue operation[s]" – generally referred to as "salvage" efforts – provided the context for the research that Hurston compiled in her 1935 volume *Mules and Men*, a gathering of African–American folktales collected in her home state of Florida, and of information about hoodoo activity in and around New Orleans.

During the 1930s, Hurston's teacher Melville Herskovits was the resident expert on African–American subjects; himself a fascinating public figure, Herskovits spoke at NAACP banquets, published an article in Alain Locke's anthology *The New Negro*, and made detailed anthropometric studies in black neighborhoods in Washington, DC and New York. "Apparently," Renaissance historian David Levering Lewis notes somewhat sardonically, the white Herskovits had achieved the status of "an honorary 'New Negro.'"[13] In his *New Negro* essay, Herskovits made the now-famous observation that Harlem, rather than seeming culturally alien to a white observer, was "just like any other American community. The same pattern, only a different shade!"[14] Herskovits's brief comment on Harlem – which has since been quoted many times – works hard to contain many of the tensions within interwar Boasianism that made themselves felt not only in Hurston's writing, but also in writings by Ella Cara Deloria that I will go on to discuss in the following chapter. Both women found their work enmeshed within tensions inherent in the logic of "salvage" – a logic grounded in the thoroughly problematical assumption that some untainted form of cultural "otherness" could and should be retrieved, collected, and examined, and which tended to turn away from the complex particularities of post World War I (and, as Hazel Carby has noted, particularly of *urban*) black and Indian culture and history.[15]

Herskovits's famous encapsulation of a Harlem life is useful as an example of the central strategy by which the Boasians combatted white racism; they did this by ironizing whiteness, by making it seem strange to itself – provincial and a bit befuddled – rather than allowing it to remain an unexamined standard against which everything else could then be measured.[16] This ironizing impulse is at work throughout Herskovits's essay, which begins with him noting how his own ignorance about urban black life was challenged during his first visit to Harlem, leaving him "bewildered at [Harlem's] complexity."[17] He continues with a lively, detailed description of what he saw when, for the first time, he witnessed the spectacle of "the great teeming center of Negro life in Harlem":

> And so I went, and what I found was churches and schools, club houses and lodge meeting-places, the library and the newspaper offices and the YMCA and busy One Hundred and Thirty-fifth Street and the hospitals and the social service agencies. I met persons who were lawyers and doctors and editors and writers, who were chauffeurs and peddlers and longshoremen and real estate brokers and capitalists, teachers and nurses and students and waiters and cooks.[18]

Herskovits's twice-repeated claim that Harlem is "the same pattern, only a different shade" means to call into question assumptions about white cultural singularity by presenting Harlem as one among many, differently tinted versions of a single "American" pattern; implicit in Herskovits's remark is the notion that Morningside Heights is merely another version, no more and no less.

Cultural historian Richard Handler – borrowing a phrase from prominent Boas student Edward Sapir – has referred to this process, which runs throughout published writings by Boas-influenced anthropologists, as "'destructive analysis of the familiar.'"[19] It is a comparative method that engenders reflection not only upon an "[un]familiar" culture, but also (and more critically) upon the observer's own. As I noted in chapter 1, Clifford Geertz, writing in detailed ways about this form of self-critique in Ruth Benedict's writings, refers to the process as "self-nativising," which he defines as "the juxtaposition of the all-too-familiar and the wildly exotic in such a way that they change places."[20] The relationship between Boasian "self-nativising" and the forms of Surrealist self-critique that I discussed in the previous chapters should be clear; these sorts of parallels formed the basis for James Clifford's influential early eighties hypothesis of an "ethnographic Surrealism."[21]

In the context of my own analysis of insider-outsider activity,

Geertz's phrase – "self-nativising" – is enormously suggestive, seeming at first to serve as an apt description of what it might have meant to work, as Hurston did, within a discipline where she would her*self*, under more usual circumstances, have occupied the position of the *native*. In Geertz's usage, however, the "self" to whom he refers is a white, North American self; moreover, the "natives" put to work in the services of the ironization of the white "self" themselves tend to be presented as fixed, static points of comparison, rarely allowed to display complexities, contradictions, or self-ironies of their own.[22] Thus, Herskovits's description of Harlem – "the same pattern, only a different shade!" – while prefaced by an acknowledgment of the "complexity" of black Manhattan, nonetheless freezes it, like a negative for a photograph of white Manhattan. Rather transparently, Boasian "self-nativising" is intended as a strategy to be used by white speakers, one that serves primarily in order to enable white audiences to reflect critically upon their own ignorance.[23]

In light of Geertz's remarks about Boasian "self-nativising," moreover, David Levering Lewis's apparently casual designation of Herskovits as an "honorary 'New Negro'" begins to assume a more pointed significance. Boasian "self-nativising" works by striking an alienated pose, by adopting the voice of someone who looks at euroethnic, North American culture from an external position – in short, *by adopting the voice of one who is not white*, by performing a complicated kind of cross-cultural ventriloquism.[24] Even Herskovits's more detailed description of Harlem, quoted at some length above, partakes of this ventriloquistic strategy: the image of a black man (or occasionally of a black woman) from the provinces setting foot in 1920s Harlem for the first time, and marveling at the broad array of black experience on show in one place all at once, has been a set piece throughout this century in African–American fiction. The difference is subtle but distinct. In work by black writers, this image is commonly used in order to defamiliarize blackness; in Herskovits's, on the other hand, it defamiliarizes whiteness by making Harlem look familiar to a white viewer. It would not be possible for Hurston (or for Deloria) to simply step into the "self-nativising" position assumed by Herskovits; Boasian processes of "self-nativising" – like Surrealist hypotheses of "Woman," to which they bear a complicated resemblance – recall once again Teresa de Lauretis's terse and extraordinarily useful claim that the theoretical position of *"woman"* is "vacant, and what is more, cannot be claimed by *women*" (emphasis added).[25] In Hurston's (or, for that matter, Deloria's) case, a further complexity comes by way of the fact that as a woman, Hurston was also unable to speak fully as a representative of African–American "folk" culture; in Hurston's work, as Mary Helen Washington has argued more recently, "the female presence was inherently a critique of the male-dominated folk culture and *therefore could not be its heroic representative*" (emphasis added).[26] I will go on to demonstrate how this form of ventriloquistic self-critique works in much more explicit ways in experimental versions of Boasian ethnography; in order to get to that point, however, I will need first to deal more explicitly with Hurston's own intellectual relationship to the Boasians.

2

One of the most notorious documents to emerge from that early period in Hurston's reception history is the preface that Franz Boas provided for *Mules and Men*, Hurston's 1935 account of her field research into rural African–American storytelling and conjure traditions. Boas opens his brief essay by claiming that "ever since the time of Uncle Remus, Negro folklore has exerted a strong attraction upon the imagination of the American public."[27] Despite this longstanding "attraction," Boas continues, "the intimate setting in the social life of the Negro has been given very inadequately." Boas goes on to argue that the "merit" of Hurston's work lies in the fact that, as a black woman (or, as he pointedly puts it, as "one of them"), Hurston was able to "penetrate through [her informants'] affected demeanor," in order to disclose, by means of her "revealing style," her informants' "true inner life."[28] Critics have since gone on to make clear the ways in which Boas's comments are patronizing, voyeuristic, exclusionary, and (in light of the complicated ironies that suffuse Hurston's prose) just plain wrong; as an effort to situate Hurston's work, the preface is full of its own, woeful inadequacies.[29]

Read as a indicator of methodological debates that were then developing within Boasian anthropology, however, Boas's preface is, in fact, quite revealing. It could be read, in part, as a critical reflection upon the relationship between Boasian methodology and Joel Chandler Harris's controversial representations of African–American idiomatic speech: although Boas's antiracist politics were, of course, distinctly different from Harris's plantation nostalgia, both of them made strategic use of cross-cultural ventriloquism. Moreover, and more generally, Boas's implicit comparison of Hurston to Joel Chandler Harris points to broader disciplinary concerns, shared among many of Boas's colleagues and students, about the limits of the detached analytical style that they had habitually adopted in their writing. Increasingly, as Richard Handler, Arnold Krupat, and Kamala Visweswaran have pointed out in important recent commentaries on the "literary" Boasians, Boas and his students were turning their attention towards literary models in order to formulate fresh stylistic strategies.[30] Pointing out how *Mules and Men* improved upon Harris's "Uncle Remus" stories, Boas was not merely damning Hurston with faint praise; he was also making an important disciplinary leap, pointing to the increasing plausibility of weighing the relative merits of fictional and ethnographic description – at that time, an undeniably daring move. Moreover, Boas's stress upon the "true inner life" (a phrase that he twice uses in the preface) reflects not only an essentializing tendency to assume the presence of a unified other perspective; it also reflects a broader, emerging awareness of the manner in which the ethnographic encounter is motivated and abutted in unpredictable ways by the consciousnesses – the "inner li[ves]" – of both observer and informant, who bring to their relationship a series of different expectations and attitudes.

I make these points not in order to defend Boas against his recent critics in the field of Hurston studies, with whom I am in basic agreement; instead, what I wish here to emphasize are those aspects of Boas's preface that bring him into close, unacknowledged contact with his neighbors just to the north in Harlem. "Unacknowledged" is the operative term here; what is particularly striking about Boas's mention of Harris's "Uncle Remus" stories is the way in which it erases a long history of debate among African–American intellectuals over the question of how to transpose oral traditions into written form; in the figure of Joel Chandler Harris, Boas blots out a series of highly contentious arguments about the representation of vernacular speech that reached their most complex, concentrated form during the Harlem Renaissance.[31] Moreover, the justifiable concerns that Boas expresses about the tensions generated during encounters between middle-class academic observers and their rural, working-class informants – tensions that are, according to his reductive reading, resolved by Hurston's blackness – might have themselves been illuminated by some of the novels of the Harlem Renaissance in which this issue is treated in subtle, profoundly complicated ways. The middle-class, biracial narrator in James Weldon Johnson's

The Autobiography of an Ex-Coloured Man (1912/27), for example, plays quite deliberately with the problem of social-scientific perspective: he travels up and down the east coast, passing alternately as white and black; he takes notes and makes classifications; he learns new languages, skills, and decorums with near-miraculous ease, observing everything and everybody from a slightly chilly but still-imperceptible distance. Johnson's unnamed narrator achieves a kind of "participant-observation" ideal, able to insinuate himself into any given situation without undue notice. Johnson's treatment of the issue of cross-racial passing, looked at from this (admittedly limited) perspective, turns "passing" into a rich, politically complicated metaphor for anthropological fieldwork.[32]

What I mean to point out here, in a preliminary fashion, is the way in which Harlem continually gets erased from the annals of Columbia, despite the fact that Renaissance-based discourses and debates might well have clarified many of the blurrier areas of Boas's own analyses. What the reader finds, in its stead, is a series of references to the authenticity of Hurston's research, which are bolstered by praise for her insider's perspective, and enclosed within the private domain of what Boas calls her "loveable personality."[33] In Kahlo's and Carrington's cases, I demonstrated how the rhetoric of authenticity was deployed in order to mask their function as envoys between cultural formations; by limiting our focus, for example, to the private debate between Kahlo and Breton, we miss the larger conflict that was carried out over the body of Kahlo's work between the Paris-based Surrealists and the Mexico City intelligentsia. Hurston – circulating between "Harlem" and "Columbia" – was embroiled in a similar dynamic.

Historian Walter Jackson, who has has produced one of the most informative studies thus far of relations between the Renaissance and the Boasians, illustrates this dynamic at work in his article's single reference to Hurston. The larger purpose of Jackson's analysis is to clarify the ways in which Herskovits was influenced by his contact with Renaissance intellectuals. In the course of Jackson's detailed exposition, however, Hurston makes a brief but unforgettable appearance. Describing Herskovits's correspondence with German ethnologist Erich von Hornbostel, Jackson writes:

> Herskovits made it clear that his views were not the result of abstract speculation. He had had the opportunity to observe the motor behavior and gestures of his research assistant, Zora Neale Hurston, who was then an anthropology graduate

student at Columbia. Although she was "more White than Negro in her ancestry," her "manner of speech, her expressions, – in short, her motor behavior" – were "what would be termed typically Negro." Herskovits had noted Hurston's motor behavior while she was singing spirituals, and he suggested that these movements had been "carried over as a behavior pattern handed down thru [sic] imitation and example from the original African slaves who were brought here."[34]

Jackson, who is primarily interested in Herskovits's interactions with the Renaissance men, allows this anecdote to pass without commentary; admittedly, this rather painful episode – where Hurston's "'motor behavior'" is fixed by means of Herskovits's analytical gaze – speaks quite loudly for itself. Rather than reading Hurston's work, Herskovits reads Hurston's body; in fact, the Harlem-based research with which Hurston assisted Herskovits was anthropometric, involving the quite literal measurement and reading of bodies.

In an oft-cited 1989 discussion of the ways in which work by black women intellectuals is put to use in writing by white feminist and African–American male critics, Valerie Smith notes a tendency among them to continually "[re]ground" their discourse in the image of the black woman's body; Smith notes that "although ... the impulse to rehistoricize produces insightful readings and illuminating theories, and is politically progressive and long overdue, nevertheless the link between black women's experiences and 'the material' seems conceptually problematic."[35]

In Jackson's anecdote, we have a striking interwar example of a related tendency – Herskovits "[re]ground[s]" his own analysis by interpreting Hurston's performance as an unmediated example of African–American authenticity. Readers of Jackson's essay have no way of reconstructing the circumstances in which Hurston came to be singing spirituals for Herskovits; for all we know, she might have been quoting for him from her own early 1930s theatrical experiments, in which she attempted to use African–American musical traditions as the basis for New York stage shows. Herskovits might have interpreted Hurston's musical performance in any number of "abstract" ways – as a complicated exchange between two colleagues of unequal rank, for example – but instead, in this instance, he turned to her precisely in order to turn away from "abstract speculation."

Returning Hurston's work to the realm of "abstract speculation," however, we encounter an altogether different set of interpretive problems; almost without exception, major recent interpretations of Hurston's *Mules and Men* (and of *Tell My Horse*, as well) have rested upon a particular set of assumptions about Hurston as a subtle, skillful manipulator of literary language, who found herself both stylistically and philosophically at odds with the more empiricist dictates of Boasianism. Robert Hemenway presents a pointed, clear, and highly influential version of this argument in his 1977 biography of Hurston: there, he writes that she "learned that scientific objectivity is not enough for a black writer in America, and ... went on to expose the excessive rationality behind the materialism of American life, the inadequacy of sterile reason to deal with the phenomena of living."[36] In Hurston's work, according to Hemenway's reading, African–American oral traditions were recodified by means of the delicate instrument of literary storytelling; among the more conventional Boasians, on the other hand, those traditions were dissected with the blunt tool of empirical science. Thus, as critic after critic has observed, both *Mules and Men* and *Tell My Horse* work against the grain of the kind of scientific analysis that Boas generally demanded of his students, shifting the focus to the ethnographer's own manipulation of her subjects, and performing the complicated task of calling into question the very possibility of ethnographic objectivity. It is for these reasons that bell hooks credits Hurston for the part she played in "saving Black folk culture."

There are, of course, good reasons for distinguishing Hurston from the Boasians in this way, as can in fact be seen from a brief comparison of two texts from within Hurston's *own œuvre*. The first, her 1931 monograph "Hoodoo in America," appeared in the *Journal of American Folk-Lore*, and was written in a highly conventional, detached scholarly style. It begins, for example, with a sober title page and a cursory historical overview. Hurston writes:

> Shreds of hoodoo beliefs and practices are found wherever any number of Negroes are found in America, but conjure has had its highest development along the Gulf coast, particularly in the city of New Orleans and in the surrounding country. It was these regions that were settled by the Haytian emigrees at the time of the overthrow of French rule in Hayti by L'Overture. Thousands of mulattoes and blacks, along with their white ex-masters were driven out, and the nearest French refuge was the province of Louisiana.[37]

On the other hand, the "Hoodoo" section of Hurston's 1935 collection *Mules and Men*, which is based upon the same research, opens with a spectacular drawing (by noted illustrator Miguel Covarrubias) of a nude Hurston undergoing an initiation ritual, followed by a verbal portrait of Hurston the ethnographer: "Winter passed and caterpillars began to cross the road again. I had spent a year in gathering and culling over folk-tales. I loved it, but I had to bear in mind that there was a limit to the money to be spent on the project, and as yet, I had done nothing about hoodoo."[38] The larger historical frame drops away, and what the reader finds, in its place, is a complex description of the motivations and anxieties of the ethnographer herself: love, and money, and most of all, a sense of unfinished business.

By poising Boasian empiricism against Hurstonian literary experimentation, however, one is forced to overlook not only the variety of Hurston's own ethnographic output, but also the ways in which Hurston's "literary" innovations placed her firmly within the emerging Boasian agenda; it also enables one to ignore the crucial but frequently suppressed connections between the Boasians and Renaissance. More recently, some scholars have begun to complicate this polarity in important ways; in an early 1990s essay, for example, Deborah Gordon noted the ways in which Hurston's liminal position *between* disciplines enabled her to experiment – most notably in the 1938 volume *Tell My Horse* – with generic intermixture and blur.[39] And Hazel Carby, in a 1990 commentary on Hurston's ethnographies, pressed these issues further by pointing towards the understated philosophical tendencies shared among certain Renaissance- and Columbia-based intellectuals.[40] Bearing in mind these more recent analyses, it is useful to recall that rather than being a narrow enterprise with unbreachable stylistic decorums, Boasian anthropology was itself a dynamic and often conflictual arena made up of variously experimental thinkers, for whom the boundary between fiction and ethnography – a boundary which, as Arnold Krupat and others have noted, tended most often to be strictly policed[41] – was nonetheless periodically transgressed. A widely noted instance of this form of transgression was a 1922 volume, *American Indian Life*, edited by Elsie Clews Parsons; that collection contains a series of efforts to recast ethnographic findings in the form of fictional biographies or autobiographies of imagined informants, including a well-meaning (if rather plodding) effort by Boas himself entitled "An Eskimo Winter." I noted earlier how Boasian "self-nativizing" works according to an implicitly ventriloquistic logic, by approximating the tonalities of one who is not white; I argued, further, that in Herskovits's essay "The Negro's Americanism," one can find a subtle example of this logic at work. In some of the contributions in *American Indian Life*, this ventriloquistic impulse – dramatized in a series of first-person fictional autobiographies of Native American informants – becomes much more explicit. These issues come to crisis in Edward Sapir's fascinating review of *American Indian Life*, which appeared in 1922 in the periodical *The Dial*.[42]

Even Sapir's title, "A Symposium of the Exotic," points to epistemological difficulties: the "exotic" mentioned in his title, rather than referring to something distant or outside, is meant instead to refer to a series of western-hemispheric traditions whose adherents were actually quite close at hand, and moving ever closer as a result of rapid cultural change during the interwar years. In his review, Sapir holds fast to a desire for mimetic fidelity, but concludes, in an interesting paradox, that fiction has the potential to be more faithfully mimetic than a strictly scientific transcription of findings, in that fiction enables the writer to represent the idiosyncracies of "consciousness," rather than merely an environment or an inventory of customs. "Those tracks of the individual consciousness," Sapir writes, "are the only true concern of literary art."[43]

A tension permeates the essay, however, over precisely this issue of consciousness: Sapir seems indecisive in his distinction between the consciousnesses of observer and informant. He argues, for instance, that Conrad's *Lord Jim* and *Heart of Darkness*, while failing to attain "perfection,"[44] are nonetheless the best examples in the language of attempts to represent the "exotic." Sapir ignores, however, the discrepancy between Conrad's minute exploration of his narrator's consciousness and his portrayal of the "exotic" terrain as an incomprehensible void. Immediately after his endorsement of Conrad, Sapir moves in another direction, and approaches the suggestion that ethnographic texts be written by the informant herself or himself: "It would almost seem that the bare recital of the details of any mode of life that human beings have actually lived has a hidden power that transcends the skill or the awkwardness of the teller."[45] Here Sapir strains against an insight-that would in many respects have made the job of the anthropologist obsolete. However, his elaborate qualification – "*it would almost seem*" – discloses his ambivalence, and with his next sentence, Sapir reveals that the "teller" to whom he refers is in fact the anthropologist, writing a fiction based upon his own experience in the field. "A great deal might be done," Sapir concludes,

> to capture the spirit of the primitive by adhering, so far as possible, to its letter – in other words, by transcribing, either literally or in simple paraphrase, personal experiences and

other texts that have been written down or dictated by natives.
In any event, the accent of authentic documents always reveals
a significant, if intangible, something about native mentality
that is over and above their content.[46]

Now this is an extraordinary passage: it suggests that the anthropologist should act merely as a facilitator, as a receptacle through which
barely mediated examples of other voices could be made audible
outside of their own context. Sapir's metaphors, however, suggest a
somewhat stronger effort at control: he mentions his desire to
"capture" the spirit of the "primitive," and suggests that the value of
"native" documents is not in their own content, but in that "something" that is "over and above their content" – that is, apparently, in
the superior subtlety of ethnographic interpretation. Sapir anxiously
picks at the problem that looms over the entire project: the problem
of its own possible superfluity. While many of the stories in *American
Indian Life* work by ventriloquising the voices of real or imagined
"others," Sapir briefly entertains – but then backs away from – the
notion that anthropologists should stop *writing*, and learn instead to
read the texts of Native American self-representation.[47] Finally,
however, Sapir assumes a position much closer to that of a writer like
T. S. Eliot – who dealt somewhat imperiously with "exotic" cultural
materials in his *The Waste Land*, which also appeared in that issue of
The Dial – than to those of contemporaneous Native American
intellectuals working on related issues.

The Harlem Renaissance, coexisting uneasily in northwestern
Manhattan with the Boasian project, thus exerted a peculiar form of
pressure. Working in a discipline that placed great stress upon
representing the "native point of view," the Boasians sensed the
presence of a "bewildering complexity" that had already made itself
felt in commentaries, poems, novels, and debates generated by
several generations of African–American intellectuals, but that did
not lend itself to the kinds of clear formulations and neat "pattern[s]"
that they had tended to privilege in their own scientific writings.
During the interwar period, however, as they began to turn tentatively towards other-than-scientific models in their efforts to approx-
imate more closely the "accent of authentic documents," the
Boasians looked to the south, rather than turning their attention just
to the north. Historian George Stocking, commenting in 1976 on the
literary aspirations of many of the Boasians, remarks that for some of
Boas's students, "The Greenwich Village of the New York *avant-garde*
and the Southwest of D. H. Lawrence and Mabel Dodge Luhan were

both important Boasian milieux; Boasians wrote poetry for little magazines and articles for the liberal weeklies."[48] More recently, Stocking has trenchantly analyzed the exoticist impulses that fueled the activities taking place within those various "Boasian milieux": in their search for literary models, the Boasians looked again and again to the traditions of white writing.[49]

It is an interesting but rarely mentioned fact that Hurston's publishers saw to it that her novels as well as her ethnographies were advertised to anthropological professionals; perhaps her anthropological readership saw *Jonah's Gourd Vine* – as Herskovits saw Hurston's musical performance – as a plain, unvarnished depiction of the univocal reality of African–American culture. It seems to me just as likely, however, that they saw it, and other novels produced by black writers during the early decades of this century, as an indicator of the representational possibilities that operated just beyond the boundaries of their own closed circle of self-irony and "self-nativising," and thus, just beyond their grasp. In their tendency to read Hurston as a black cultural exemplar (as if such a position were possible), rather than as a black woman intellectual with a specific set of commitments of her own, the Boasians referenced their anxiety about the narrowness of those boundaries.

3

By suggesting the limitations of an analysis that poises the "scientific" Boasians against the "literary" Hurston, I mean to show how during the 1920s and 1930s, Columbia-based anthropologists were in the process of performing a series of writing experiments that overlapped in important ways with those already underway in Harlem. Put more bluntly, Harlem had already produced what Columbia was just beginning to envision: a subtle and contentious tradition (by then several decades old) of experimental efforts by urban intellectuals to transpose oral traditions into written form. As such, Hurston negotiated between and among a series of artistic and scientific disciplinary protocols that up to that point had kept Columbia distinct from Harlem in the public mind.

Where these kinds of negotiations are most clearly visible are in Hurston's constant uses of textual self-revision. Even more clearly than Kahlo or Carrington, Hurston was a prodigious producer of textual variants – so much so that this has recently emerged as one of the most charged topics in Hurston studies. While much discussion of

Hurston's self-revision has centered on the differences between the thorny, politically provocative manuscript of her 1942 autobiography *Dust Tracks on a Road* and its muted, conciliatory published version,[50] this is an issue that also bears in direct ways upon readings of Hurston's ethnographic texts. By the time Hurston's *Mules and Men* was published by Lippincott in 1935, for example, substantial portions of the volume had already appeared in print elsewhere, in different versions – notably in "Hoodoo in America," Hurston's scholarly monograph published by Ruth Benedict in the *Journal of American Folk-Lore* in the early 1930s. Current debates about revisions contained in Hurston's 1942 autobiography tend to circulate around questions of relative truth-value: which version of *Dust Tracks* comes closer to representing Hurston's own sentiments, political or otherwise? One might pose a similar question about Hurston's ethnographic publications: that is, which version of her research presents the most faithful representation of the contents of the folkloric archives?

The search for the "truth" of Hurston's texts is without question a problematical undertaking, as critic after critic has acknowledged, but it would be too easy, I think, to dismiss such a search as (at best) theoretically naive or (at worst) utterly misguided. I do not consider such queries to be wholly inconsequential: their seriousness is underscored by the fact that a substantial amount of scholarly work has followed in the pathways marked out by Hurston's groundbreaking folkloric research.[51] I will, however, be approaching these issues from a slightly different perspective. My own sense is that a good way of getting at the complexity of Hurston's ethnographic process is not by privileging a single, authoritative text – *Mules and Men*, for example – but by examining in detail her revisions themselves. In this context, Nathaniel Mackey's "Other: From Noun to Verb," is again extraordinarily useful; his emphasis upon "'versioning'" enables a method of reading insider-outsider texts that shows how they

> react against and reflect critically upon the different sort of othering to which their practitioners, denied agency in a society by which they're designated other, have been subjected. The black speaker, writer, or musician whose practice privileges variations subjects the fixed equations which underwrite that denial (including the idea of fixity itself) to an alternative.[52]

"Othering," in the terms developed by Mackey, operates simultaneously in two directions: it "reacts" against a series of external constraints, i.e., the "de[nial of] agency" that "fix[es]" the so-called "other," reducing her complexity and rendering her static; however, it also "reflect[s] critically" upon the way in which categories of "Otherness" are created, opening outward to the possibility of "alternative[s]."[53]

What Mackey envisions here is a politically and philosophically complicated alternative to the harsh but necessary choices that Hurston's readers have made, again and again, throughout her reception history. By virtue of her association with the Boasians, as I have noted, Hurston was isolated as an African–American cultural exemplar or spokesperson; this troubling form of isolation was something that she shared with other women insider-outsiders of her own generation, including (in ways that I have already noted) Kahlo and Carrington. As a result of this, critics have had to tangle, again and again, with Hurston's own attitudes towards these claims of exemplarity: did Hurston resist the dictates of Boasianism, or was she fully implicated within them? Did Hurston, as bell hooks has argued, transcend her early faith in the tenets of the Boasian "rescue operation," and go on to invent a complex and self-critical method for "saving black folk culture"; or was she, as Hazel Carby has argued to the contrary, a more or less nostalgic and uncritical proponent of the Boasian logic of cultural "salvage"?[54] Put more bluntly, did Hurston collaborate, or did she resist? The answer, I think, is both – or perhaps, over the extended course of her career, more than both – and Mackey's attentiveness to processes of " 'versioning' " allows for a method of analysis that is both conscious of Hurston's textual metamorphoses *and* of the historical determinants and political implications of those metamorphoses.

The arduous revision process that led to the publication of *Mules and Men*, for example, was guided by a cacophony of voices – including those of Hurston's friends, editors, colleagues, teachers, as well as of her famously manipulative patron, Charlotte Osgood Mason. At the same time as it registers the force of a variety of pressures that abutted her work, however, Hurston's self-revision also offers insight into the way in which variation and improvisation helped her to devise strategies for freeing herself from the competing demands and agendas with which she met as she negotiated between Harlem and Columbia. On one hand, then, self-revision reflects the sharply determined limits within which Hurston operated – it is a form of self-censorship and a sign of either voluntary acquiescence or victimization; on the other, however, and less pessimistically, it represents a constant inventiveness. In order to illustrate Hurston's self-revisionary process at work, I will turn to a particularly vivid example: a small tale that Hurston rewrote repeatedly during the course of her career, and that bears in important ways upon Hurston's attitudes towards her own research.

The tale that concerns me involves a small-town rivalry between a male hoodoo practitioner and his female competitor, whom he terrifies into silence and acquiescence. The plot appears in Hurston's writing in at least five full-fledged variations, written in a range of modes including fiction, scholarly and popular folklore, and autobiographical anecdote. It surfaced first as a brief tale interpolated within a longer 1925 story entitled "Black Death," which Hurston submitted to a literary contest at *Opportunity*, and which remained unpublished until 1995.[55] In "Black Death," Hurston sets the scene for her story by describing the conflict between "Old Man Morgan," an exceptionally powerful hoodoo doctor, and "Old Lady Grooms," a conjure woman who "laid claims to equal power."[56] Old Man Morgan, weary of her boasting, decides to "put an end to it and prove his powers."[57] He exerts his influence over Old Lady Grooms, so that she is drawn, irresistibly and against her will, to "Lake Blue Sink, the bottomless,"[58] where she slips and drowns. A white coroner then arrives at the scene, and explains how her death was the result of an epileptic seizure. In the context of "Black Death," Hurston uses the story primarily in order to draw a contrast between the black townspeople's knowledge of the cause of Old Lady Grooms's death, and the white coroner's inaccurate and myopically rational diagnosis. A broad joke directed towards white ignorance, the brief story works in many respects to include Hurston's primarily black readership at *Opportunity* within the circle of the knowledgeable.

Six years later, in its earliest published version, the tale appeared in Hurston's 1931 *Journal of American Folk-Lore* monograph "Hoodoo in America." By that time, however, the emphasis of the anecdote had shifted. Hurston's ridicule of white rationality was sharply muted – perhaps due to the fact that an important segment of her early thirties audience was composed of white readers with a social-scientific bent – and Hurston focussed instead upon the plight of the woman hoodoo doctor. "Aunt Judy Cox," as she is called in her "Hoodoo in America" incarnation, suffers much more vividly at the hands of her male rival, but survives her ordeal and manages to make her story known. The salient element of Judy Cox's ordeal, in the revised version of the tale, is her temporary loss of the power of speech. After Aunt Judy has fallen into the lake and called for help, her rival "Old Man Massey" commands her to be silent:

> "Hush!" he commanded. "Be quiet, or I'll make an end of you right now."
> She hushed. She was too scared to move her tongue. Then he asked her: "Where is all that power you make out you got? I brought you to the lake and made you stay here till I got ready for you. I throwed you in, and you can't come out till I say so. When you acknowledge to yourself that I am your top-superior, then you can come out of the water. I got to go about my business, but I'm going to leave a watchman, and the first time you holler he'll tear you to pieces. The minute you change your mind – I'll send help to you."[59]

Massey then transforms himself into an alligator, and keeps watch over Aunt Judy until she is finally rescued. Although she survives her ordeal in this version of the story, she nonetheless gives up conjuring for keeps.

In both of these early versions of the tale, Hurston shifts her emphases in ways designed to make the tale more palatable to her anticipated audiences; here, Barbara Johnson's mid-eighties commentary on Hurston's shifting "structures of address" is directly pertinent.[60] In this particular context, moreover, Hurston's manipulation of her subject matter seems to indicate a troubling willingness to satisfy the desires of her readership – to do what she must in order to please. As Johnson argues, however, Hurston's gestures towards her audience are themselves regularly fraught with ambivalence, and radiant with multiple significances. While Hurston's story "Black Death," for example, is structured around a polarization of white ignorance and black knowledge, the meanings of "blackness" shift throughout the story, from the title onwards. The opening sentence of the story sets up this division:

> The Negroes in Eatonville know a number of things that the hustling, bustling white man never dreams of. He is a materialist with little ears for overtones.[61]

From the start, however, there are tensions within this apparently clear polarization of "Negroes" and the "white man." The "Negroes" to whom she refers, for example, are specifically located "in Eatonville," while her prospective readership at *Opportunity* would have been largely urban and middle-class. In the paragraphs that follow, moreover, Hurston's pronouns become more complex: she refers to her black characters in Eatonville as "they," indicating a difference from herself, and finally as "everybody," a pronoun that erases her black, urban readership as well as the story's lone white character. The broad polarization of black and white that structures her story gives way to a more complicated (and much more understated) consideration of African–American cultural heterogeneity – one that works to challenge, rather than to flatter, her readership.

Likewise, while the story in its "Hoodoo in America" incarnation seems to have been revised in such a way as to flatter her (mostly white) audience by muting her critique of white ignorance and provinciality, it is important to recall that by publishing the tale in *any* form in the context of a social-scientific journal, Hurston was at the same time issuing an important challenge to the decorums that guided Boasian field research. As Hurston described those decorums in her autobiography, Boas had a "genius for pure objectivity. He ha[d] no pet wishes to prove. His instructions [were] to go out and find what is there."[62] While the story of the showdown by the lake might well have originated in a tale that Hurston recalled from her own childhood, she had already incorporated it into her literary repertoire some years before she performed the field research published in "Hoodoo in America." By no means was she merely "find[ing] what [was] there"; she was actively manipulating the archives. Robert Hemenway has explained, to my mind satisfactorily, Hurston's use of "signature" stories in her published folkloric research; he argues that Hurston, for many years a lay folklorist, was "a product of a tradition in which narratives were community property rather than any individual's private possession, [and] simply transferred a part of her repertoire to the typed page."[63] As a breach of Boasian decorum, however, Hurston's gesture remains significant, shedding critical light upon the way in which *all* field-work – no matter how "objectiv[ely]" performed – involves the selection and manipulation of information, and carries within it an implicit claim, on the part of the researcher, to ownership of the materials that he or she has gathered. In this light, it is significant that in both of these early versions, Hurston subtly disavows authorship or "ownership" of the tale; as such, in both "Black Death" and "Hoodoo in America," Hurston presents the story as a collocation of popular rumors that circulate among the residents of Eatonville.

In her 1942 autobiography *Dust Tracks on a Road*, Hurston presents yet another, very different, version of this same plot; in this retelling, as she is describing the evolution of her own career as a fiction writer, Hurston claims that this was a story that she made up during her girlhood, at a point when she was growing less interested in abstract, fantastical children's games, and more interested in the complexities of stories with full-blown human characters. The protagonists in this version are "Mr. Pendir," an elderly bachelor who lives alone in Eatonville, and "Mrs. Bronson," another neighbor from her childhood. Hurston begins by providing the basic outlines of the plot: Mrs. Bronson, fishing alone one day, falls into the lake and is unable to pull herself out: "She said," according to Hurston, "that she screamed a few times for help, but something rushed across Blue Sink like a body-fied wind and commanded her to hush-up. If she so much as made another sound, she would never get out of that lake alive."[64] A sympathetic white doctor arrives soon after her rescue, and explains that Mrs. Bronson has had a stroke: he offers persuasive physical evidence for his diagnosis – "one whole side of her body was paralyzed" – and notes, as to her other injuries, that "her terror and fear had done the rest."[65]

Hurston, a little girl hearing the doctor's explanation, believes otherwise:

> Right away, I could see the mighty tail of Mr. Pendir slapping Old Lady Bronson into the lake. Then he had stalked away across the lake like the Devil walking up and down in the earth. But when she had screamed, I pictured him recrossing to her, treading the red-gold of his moon-carpet, with his mighty minions swimming along beside him, his feet walking the surface like a pavement. The soles of his feet never even being damp, he drew up his hosts around her and commanded her to hush.
>
> The old woman was said to dabble in hoodoo, and some said that Pendir did too. I had heard often enough that it was the pride of one hoodoo doctor to "throw it back on the one that done it." What could be more natural then than for my 'gator-man to get peeved because the old lady had tried to throw something he did back on him? Naturally, he slapped her in to the lake. No matter what the doctor said, I knew the real truth of the matter.[66]

In the *Dust Tracks* version, significant aspects of the earlier versions are recombined in order to create an entirely different effect. The white doctor asserts himself and offers his rational explanation, but – in contrast to the earlier version – his presence is apparently benign, and his diagnosis is implicitly supported by Hurston-the-writer, even as it is repudiated by Hurston's former self, the imaginative child whom she is in the process of describing. The hoodoo-based rivalry between Mr. Pendir and Mrs. Bronson is depicted as the invention of a little girl, not as a communally based rumor that grows out of a repertoire of shared stories and traditional practices. Moreover, the *Dust Tracks* version, unlike the 1931 "Hoodoo in America" text, makes highly conventional claims about authorship: in it, Hurston seems much less critical than before of the idea of individual – as opposed to communal – creative process. The 1942 version of *Dust Tracks on a Road*, of course, has been seen by many critics as one of the low points of Hurston's career: a conciliatory volume in which Hurston buckles under, again and again, to demands made by her white editors.[67] And this brief parable of the "birth of the author" would in fact seem to reflect these kinds of capitulations, presenting the reader with a conservative meditation on the private genesis of creative genius.

Looked at in the broader context of *Dust Tracks*, however, many of the story's meanings are much less clearly graspable. In a fascinating confluence of prior texts, Hurston opens her autobiography by narrating the story of her *own* birth – the quite literal "birth of the author" – by telling how when Hurston was born, the local midwife, fortuitously called "Aunt Judy," arrived too late to assist Hurston's mother. Instead, according to the *Dust Tracks* account, Hurston was midwifed by a helpful white man who happened along after her mother quite suddenly went into labor. "Aunt Judy" finally arrives in a huff, after the baby is born, and complains of the man's incompetence, noting that the baby's "belly-band had not been put on tight enough."[68]

Some pages later, Hurston goes on to tell how as a girl, she dreamed – like Hurston's best-known fictional heroine, Janie Crawford – of journeying towards the horizon, of "riding off to look at the belly-band of the world."[69] The midwife "Aunt Judy" – who possesses detailed knowledge of the workings of the "belly-band" – thus assumes vast, if understated, importance in the early pages of *Dust Tracks*; her function, however, has already been usurped by the white man, and she is left merely to mutter in frustration. Although some of Hurston's recent critics have noted, with good reason, that this male "midwife" seems designed to garner the approval of a white readership, it seems to me arguable that his is not entirely a benign presence. Instead – like the white doctor who comes along later in the autobiography to diagnose Mrs. Bronson's illness – he is a white mirror image of "Old Man Massey," "Mr. Pendir," and a range of patriarchal figures who form rivalries with and finally subdue the women who dare to challenge their authority.

The problem of creative usurpation – marked by gender and by race – surfaces again and again in Hurston's work, but nowhere more clearly than in this particular "conjure story," which was, to my knowledge, Hurston's most frequently (perhaps even obsessively) repeated tale. What makes this most compelling is the fact that many critics who have written about Hurston during the last decade – notably Marjorie Pryse and Houston A. Baker, Jr. – have argued that in the workings of conjure, Hurston found a suitable metaphor for the work of the African–American woman artist.[70] I would suggest, however, that if one wishes to view conjuring as Hurston's trope for black female creativity, then it becomes necessary to account for the clear ambivalences that can be found throughout her writings on the subject.

Throughout Hurston's work, as can be seen in the above-noted tales, the practice of conjuring is fractured, fraught with rivalry and conflict, and contains within it a continual threat to the power and effectiveness of women's work. Many readers assume that Hurston finds her own, true vocation by virtue of the fact that during her research trip to New Orleans, she is apart from the Boasian milieu and among "the people" (as she sometimes calls her informants), ensconsed in the protective secrecy of the New Orleans hoodoo underworld. Nonetheless, when Hurston's claims to those sorts of authority are strongest – when, for example, she describes her own participation in successful conjure rituals – she repeatedly denies her reader the easier satisfactions of a pure, unfiltered insider's view. She describes instead a world as variegated, stratified, differentiated as that of the more readily observable dominant culture. In fact, Hurston encounters subtle exclusions during her various New Orleans hoodoo apprenticeships that turn those encounters into weird mirrorings of her experiences both at Columbia and within the largely male-governed Harlem Renaissance: in both places, Hurston must subsume her own expression within the various stories, rituals, and explanatory vocabularies of others; in both places, moreover, the master narratives that she is taught fail to square with her reading of her own experience.

Hurston frames her "Hoodoo" narrative in *Mules and Men*, for example, with stories of her apprenticeships with two female conjurers – making possible the claim that she is celebrating the superior power of the female "two-headed doctor." It is significant, however, that both of those apprenticeships with women end inconclusively. Eulalia's narrative, which opens the "Hoodoo" section, ends before her rituals have even begun;[71] Kitty Brown's "death to the enemy" dance, near the close of "Hoodoo," is thwarted when the contrite "John Doe" returns to his abandoned love, Rachael Roe.[72] From Hurston's earliest writings on the subject, conjure is the site of rivalry between the sexes, and is used, more often than not, to reinforce extremely conventional erotic plots, plots that differ vastly from those of Hurston's own novels. Hoodoo restores order, rather than calling it into question; it intervenes where love or marriage fail, providing either vengeance or somewhat shaky assurance of a "happily ever after" ending.

During Hurston's hoodoo apprenticeships, the majority of her clients are women attempting to win (or to win *back*) a husband or lover; Hurston, however, in her accounts of those apprenticeships, embodies the contrary of this tightly circumscribed domestic ideal. She travels from teacher to teacher, refusing their requests for her to stay once her training is complete, showing no particular loyalty to any. In one of "Hoodoo'"s great comic interludes, Hurston even goes so far as to assist one of her teacher's wives in her (ultimately unsuccessful) effort to leave her husband and set up shop on her own.[73] While "Frizzly Rooster," as he is called, is preoccupied with fixing other people's marriages, as well as with his own affairs, his wife attempts to appropriate his power in order to free herself from him. Hurston, unlike the various wives and lovers whom she assists, remains restlessly unsituated, constantly in motion. As long as her grant money holds out, she can go as far as she must in order to "know the end of the talk."[74] Moreover, although Hurston supplies only sketchy information about her life apart from the series of apprenticeships, she receives repeated orders from her instructors to abstain from various activities – from eating certain foods to disclosing pieces of information to having sexual relations. Telling the reader what she cannot do, however, Hurston gives tantalizing hints of what she *might* do; her self-disclosure, however, is negative, delivered in the form of the master's "Thou shalt not."

Finally, in a somewhat distant sense, I do in fact agree with Pryse and Baker that in Hurston's work, "conjure" serves as a metaphor for Hurston's own writing practice – not, however, as a source of "'ancient power,'" as Pryse argues, or as a storehouse of "ric[h] cultural wisdom," as Baker does.[75] Instead, it is a sharply contested site, one that provides Hurston with ways of renegotiating her anomalous position within and among a series of cultural formations: in Harlem, at Columbia, in Eatonville, and in New Orleans. More crucial, perhaps, is the way in which it enables her continually to consider and reconsider the problematical status of the female "medium" – a status so often ascribed to the insider-outsider intellectuals during the interwar years.

4

In the course of Hurston's '"versionings"' of the tale of the showdown by the lake, one strange rewriting – notably different from the others – appeared in the late 1930s in the context of a WPA-sponsored Florida guidebook. There, Hurston wrote that

> There is a legend that has grown up about the huge alligator which inhabits Lake Belle at Eatonville. He is said to be an ex-slave who escaped from a Georgia plantation during the Indian wars in Florida. On his escape he made his way down into Florida and joined the fighting forces of the Indians under Osceola and Billy-Bowlegs. When they were defeated and scattered, this Negro made great African medicine on his own on the shores of what is now known as Lake Belle and at the finish he transformed himself into the American counterpart of his clan god, the crocodile, and slid into the waters to wait a friendly time. He had said time and time again to his comrades that he would never die by the hand of the white man nor be re-enslaved.[76]

In this version, Hurston's earlier depictions of male-female rivalry disappear, and the tale is set in the context of the much broader histories of African–American and Native American resistance to slavery and conquest. I began this chapter by noting the way in which African–American and Native American oral traditions were contained in similarly troubling ways within the Boasian logic of "salvage"; Hurston herself draws this cross-cultural parallel, in understated ways, at key moments in her own research. In the above story, Hurston moves beyond anecdotal comparison, taking the significant leap of imaging *communities* of resistance to the "hand of the white man," made up of people who join together as "comrades" across cultural lines.

For Hurston, however, this vision of coalition remained the material of folkloric possibility, of shared revisionary imagining; her own position was far too isolated to allow for the actual formation of these kinds of coalitional bonds. When contemporary critics and theorists working on the analysis of insider-outsider activity treat Hurston as a peer and a metaphorical contemporary – a strategy that

I noted in my introduction, apparent in work by hooks, Johnson, Mackey, and Trinh – my sense is that this gesture represents an important effort to remove Hurston from isolation, to displace her from a position of false exemplarity and engage with her in substantive debate, and perhaps most of all, to take seriously the complexities of the theoretical and methodological interventions that she developed more than a half-century ago. In the chapter that follows, however, I will look at how debates among insider-outsiders were already beginning to take shape during the 1940s, by turning to Ella Cara Deloria, and her careful intertextual reengagement of Hurston's work.

5

Dreaming history: Hurston, Deloria, and insider–outsider dialogue

Hurston and Deloria, performing what is sometimes referred to as "anthropology at home,"[1] were engaged during the 1930s and 1940s in related ethnographic experiments, both in the field and in their writings. Hurston, as I noted in the previous chapter, performed important portions of her research in Eatonville, Florida, where she spent parts of her childhood and adolescence. Deloria, a Yankton "Sioux" anthropologist born in South Dakota in 1889, was educated at mission schools and at Oberlin and Columbia, and then returned to South Dakota to live, intermittently, and to do fieldwork.[2] Hurston's and Deloria's careers have thus far been read by scholars as running parallel to one another, not touching. In this chapter, I will argue (in what is necessarily a speculative way) that at certain key points, their intellectual paths did in fact cross; I will illustrate this by showing how Deloria's historical novel, *Waterlily*, responds in precise ways to several of Hurston's important published texts from that same time period.

Waterlily, which Deloria finished in the late 1940s, but which remained unpublished until 1988, is frequently and appropriately praised for its "ethnographic density" and for the "balanced picture of Sioux life" contained within its pages – a "picture" that, as Alanna Kathleen Brown has noted, "would have been innovative and threatening to WASP assumptions about racial superiority."[3] Julian Rice, who in recent years has contributed most to Deloria studies, has gone so far as to read the novel as a "guide" to Deloria's nonfiction study of Dakota oral traditions, *Dakota Texts*.[4] According to these readings, the novel cuts two ways: it is faithfully responsive to the nineteenth-century Dakota context that Deloria depicts, and critically responsive to the "WASP [mis]assumptions" that had theretofore dominated the field.

In an important review that followed the 1988 publication of *Waterlily*, however, Arnold Krupat made some useful observations about the limits posed by readings that focus too tightly upon Deloria's historiographical nuance and accurate cultural description. Making a significant (and, in Deloria studies, a rare) comparison to Zora Neale Hurston, Krupat notes that the term "ethnographic novel" – which he somewhat reluctantly uses in order to describe *Waterlily* – presupposes a kind of linguistic transparency and directness. He argues, for example, that the term is clearly not suited to a contemporaneous text like Hurston's *Their Eyes Were Watching God*, much less to more recent novels by Erdrich, Momaday, Silko, or Welch; "their linguistic and formal ingenuity," he writes, "are simply too great for that."[5]

Krupat seems willing, nonetheless, to place *Waterlily* within the category of the "ethnographic novel," stressing its historical learnedness and accuracy over its "linguistic and formal ingenuity." Following Krupat's own suggestions about the limitations of such readings, however, I will argue that a third dynamic was also at work in Deloria's novel: that is, Deloria's intertextual responsiveness to Hurston's own concurrent efforts to depict, in literary form, the workings of African–American oral traditions. Writing in 1987 about contemporary "revisionist" histories of Indian–white relations, Deloria's nephew Vine Deloria, Jr. makes a series of pertinent observations; he writes: "Whether we can clean out the emotional swamp of white America and recount Indian–white relations more objectively or whether we must continue to struggle with old beliefs and shibboleths when we could be doing more important work remains to be seen."[6] In this metaphorically compressed passage, what Vine Deloria suggests is the possibility that the massive intellectual burden imposed by the need to dismantle age-old misinterpretations might be getting in the way of creating newer ones. Here, he sums up an issue that is central to the analysis of *Waterlily* that I will undertake. Ella Deloria, constantly read as a writer who responded critically to white misconceptions, might at the same time have had other work on her mind. At stake in Deloria's engagement with Hurston, I will suggest, was the possibility of forming a community of readers who shared many of Deloria's own philosophical and methodological dilemmas – as Hurston, her contemporary and fellow insider-outsider, certainly did

– and with whom Deloria could further explore one of her own novel's central concerns: the relation between female eloquence and feminine sexuality, and the disruptive role that both play in processes of cultural description.

1

Describing the changes brought about by the increasing professionalization of academic anthropology during the interwar years, historian George Stocking notes that the "ethnography of academic anthropologists tended to follow a 'one ethnographer/one tribe' pattern." As such, Stocking continues, "the methodological values of the new ethnography encouraged a 'my people' syndrome – the effects of which were reinforced by a strong sense of institutional territoriality among emerging academic centers."[7] The possessive personal pronoun in the phrase " '*my* people' " denotes an attitude of private ownership on the part of the (presumably white) anthropologist towards his or her (presumably nonwhite) subjects, an attitude that encompasses not only discrete investigative findings, but also entire matrices of cultural information. Thus, a critical rereading of anthropological research as a form of appropriation or even of theft – which is embedded in complex ways in much recent writing on what James Clifford calls "ethnographic authority" – is also implicit in Stocking's remarks.[8]

Stocking's summary, accurate as it is as a critique of broader institutional imperatives that were at work during the twenties, applies in only limited ways to the insider-outsider research that I am here considering. Of course, both Ella Deloria and Zora Neale Hurston performed much of their interwar research in places that they considered to be their homes; in both of their cases, rather than signaling a claim to private ownership, the phrase " 'my people' " denotes a more public and somewhat more complicated form of connectedness than that implied in Stocking's comments about "institutional territoriality." In these two women's cases, the pronominal modifier " 'my' " would carry within it a sense not only of active possession, but also of being possessed *by*: one's people being the people *to whom* one belongs. And perhaps above all, while the "syndrome" that Stocking describes is most often marked by the assumption that the " 'people' " in question are homogeneous and totalizable – and thus, that they can, at least in a metaphorical sense, be possessed – both Hurston and Deloria describe " '[their] people' " as split, divided, almost endlessly diverse, and always elusive of the investigator's grasp.

Hurston's 1942 autobiography, for example, includes a chapter entitled "My People! My People!," which opens with the following sentences:

> "My people! My people!" From the earliest rocking of my cradle days, I have heard this cry go up from Negro lips. It is forced outward by pity, scorn and hopeless resignation. It is called forth by the observation of one class of Negro on the doings of another branch of the brother in black.[9]

Hazel Carby has written that this passage, and others like it in Hurston's writing, "signif[y] the division that the writer as intellectual has to recognize and bridge in the process of representing the people"[10] – a division, Carby argues, which is constituted by differences of class, which in turn are differently enforced in rural and in urban settings. In Hurston's usage, the phrase " 'my people' " is deeply ironical, an expression of difference, rather than of identity. With it, she points up African–American heterogeneity, rather than enforcing a fantasy of "black culture" as a neat parcel of cultural property that can be gathered up and owned by a researcher.

Ella Deloria, in her 1944 popular ethnography *Speaking of Indians*, makes a related point, albeit in a much different way. Deloria writes, in the course of one of her many critical interpolations on the crucial historical issue of naming and nation, that

> a few words on the background of the Dakotas are needed here. They are the second largest tribe and live principally in South Dakota. They divide naturally into three parts: those farthest east are the Santees; then come the Yanktons; and still farther west, beyond the Missouri, are the Tetons. They are all Dakotas, but they group on the basis of dialects. I am a Yankton and not a Teton; ... among them, I am presenting a Teton picture primarily.[11]

Deloria, here as elsewhere in *Speaking of Indians*, points towards the diversity that is present among the vast conglomerate of "Indians" who appear in the title of her book; she does so even as she is in the process of naming herself in relationship to the subjects of her research. Moreover, she notes that in this part of her discussion, she will focus upon a group to which she does not, herself, belong. Rather than invoking " [her] people,' " she invokes a people who are pointedly *not* hers. Finally, as can be seen in her variation of first- and third-person pronouns in the passage above, Deloria repeatedly foregrounds the partiality of the view that she is presenting, rather than situating herself as the all-knowing expert.

Ella Deloria had scholarly qualifications that Franz Boas described, in a 1937 letter of recommendation, as "unique," in that they were grounded in part in her personal history, and in part in her lifelong research into Dakota linguistics, history, and culture.[12] Deloria assisted Boas on numerous projects during the twenties and thirties, coauthoring one article with him, and providing ethnological data that underwrote many others.[13] Boas considered her work indispensable to aspects of his own, once writing to Benedict during one of his department's frequent funding crises, asking for money because he could "not afford to lose [Deloria's] services just now."[14] Even now, authorities in the field remain profoundly respectful of and indebted to Deloria's research; citing her linguistic and archival work, Julian Rice recently made the bold claim that "for the literary study of American Indian oral tradition, no tribe has been more enriched by the work of a single individual than the Lakota have been by Ella Deloria."[15]

During the mid 1940s, Deloria was immersed in the preparation of two lengthy, much-anticipated manuscripts that were set to cap her twenty-year research career. One was an enormous, authoritative study of the everyday lives of the Dakota, now commonly referred to as "Camp Circle Society." The second was a historical novel set among the nineteenth-century Dakota, entitled *Waterlily*. In large part due to the shifting priorities of the postwar publishing industry, however, neither of these books would see print during Deloria's own lifetime. (*Waterlily*, as I noted, was eventually published in 1988; "Camp Circle Society" is not yet available in print.) While working on these two manuscripts, Deloria received valued responses from a wide and distinguished circle of readers, including relatives, editors, and professional colleagues. Despite their consistent praise and engaged responses, however, Deloria was plagued by uncertainties as she wrote, and rewrote; by far the most complex and unrelenting criticisms of those two books-in-progress were scripted by Deloria herself.

Elaine Jahner precedes me in noting the critical and theoretical importance of Deloria's letters to her colleagues. In her introduction to the James Walker collection *Lakota Myth*, Jahner charts the emergence of a series of analytical paradigms for the study of Lakota oral traditions through the course of Deloria's voluminous correspondence with Franz Boas.[16] Thus, above and beyond the biographical interest that they undoubtedly hold, Deloria's letters constitute a crucial component of the textual output by a writer whose major works went unpublished during her own lifetime, and whose research provided the scholarly undergirding for work by many of her better-known peers. In Deloria's correspondence with Ruth Benedict, a related but slightly more self-reflexive form of commentary also takes shape. In a February 1947 letter to Benedict, for example, Deloria wrote of her "Camp Circle Society" manuscript:

> I simply can not write it as a real investigator, hitting the high spots and drawing conclusions. There is too much I know. I made a hundred false starts, and can't tell you how many times I've torn up my Ms. and begun again. I think the most you can say for it is that it is a composite of Dakota information, and that I am the glorified (?) native mouthpiece. My section on courtship and marriage is the worst; so terribly wordy and mixed up. I tell one thing – and fearing it will be misunderstood, I tell something else on the other side, and so it goes.[17]

Eavesdroppers into this epistolary exchange between Deloria and Benedict might be tempted to take this merely as a private moment of diffidence and frustration: indeed, it sounds a lot like a bad case of writer's block. What Deloria is describing here, however, strikes me as being both more controlled and more politically complicated than that. Her letter might be read, otherwise, as a meditation upon the practice of self-revision, which, I have argued, is a practice central to insider-outsider writing. She expresses pointed skepticism towards clear, clean scholarly generalities, which, she implies, tend to be grounded either in the deliberate exclusion of contrary information, or in simple ignorance. Deloria's claim that she is unable to play the part of a "real investigator" should not by any means be interpreted as self-deprecation; it is important to note how she describes her dilemma in terms of her own excess of knowledge, rather than in terms of some scholarly lack. As Janet L. Finn has written with regard to Deloria's correspondence with Franz Boas, such passages "illustrat[e] the complex web of responsibilities in which [Deloria's] scholarship was enmeshed."[18]

Further, and more to the point, Deloria in this passage implicitly criticizes the unexamined presumption of mastery that informed so many ethnographic studies from that same period. In her own words, quite simply, "there is too much [she] know[s]." In these remarks, I think, Deloria anticipates in important ways more recent commentators on insider-outsider activity, including Trinh T. Minh-Ha, who noted in a 1986 lecture entitled "Outside In Inside Out" that

> The moment the insider steps out from the inside, she is no
> longer a mere insider (and vice versa) ... unlike the outsider,
> she also resorts to non-explicative, non-totalizing strategies that
> suspend meaning and resist closure. (This is often viewed by
> the outsiders as strategies of partial concealment and disclosure
> aimed at preserving secrets that should only be imparted to
> initiates.)[19]

What Deloria presents to Benedict as an inability to achieve completion might thus be read, through Trinh's commentary, as a "suspen[-
sion of] meaning and resist[ance to] closure."

With this, Deloria expresses one of the central epistemological
cruxes of insider-outsider method: expected to reveal secrets and fill
in gaps, and often, as a result, either criticized for personal bias,
praised with unwitting condescension for raw, unvarnished authenticity, or alienated from a home audience by the scholarly demand
for distance and broad simplification, the insider-outsider is more
likely to be aware of just how much she knows that cannot, for a
variety of reasons, be properly expressed in summary or argumentative form. In this, Deloria's work from the 1940s also anticipates
recent historiographical commentary by Vine Deloria, Jr., who wrote
in 1987 that

> [p]resumably the attractiveness of the subject matter and the
> lack of clarity make it [i.e., the history of Indian-white relations]
> a field that appears to have many hidden and exotic secrets
> which need to be unfolded. The great mass of material in the
> field, much of which has not been brought into the arena of
> popular consumption, suggests that *all of us could labor the
> remainder of our natural lives without acquiring a more precise
> knowledge of our subject* [emphasis added].[20]

Ella Deloria reveals the inadequacies of the two roles that she is
expected to play – the "real investigator" and the "glorified (?) native
mouthpiece" – knowing all too well that Dakota life is too complex
to be summed up in any clear, plain-spoken way. There will always
be, as she puts it, an "other side" to the story.

In another letter on similar subjects written two months later,
Deloria goes on to clarify these concerns, focusing in this instance
upon the crucial issue of audience:

> I was a little cramped too, in wondering how some of those nice
> old men of the APS [the American Philosophical Society, which
> had provided some support for Deloria's field research] might
> take my stuff. O yes, and the missionaries! They keep asking
> about my ms. and "can hardly wait!" I wish I could pick my
> readers![21]

The desire that Deloria expresses here – to choose her own audience – was a way of coping with the competing agendas of her various, split potential audiences. In one letter, Deloria even goes so far as to suggest to Benedict strategies for keeping readers at bay, discouraging them by making her material public to only a very limited, technical readership, publishing the text in serial form (rather than as a whole) in several issues of a small scholarly journal.[22] In this letter, Deloria tangles with a problem that Carla Kaplan addressed in an important 1995 reading of Hurston's *Their Eyes Were Watching God*: the problem of finding a "fit listener."[23] There, reengaging the oft-debated question of the politics of voice in Hurston's novel, Kaplan suggests that "feminist and African–American fiction ... often seeks to dramatize its *lack* of listeners, the impossibility of finding competent – let alone ideal – interlocutors."[24]

While in this context Kaplan limits her commentary to the specific sphere of "feminist and African–American fiction," I hope to suggest that her comments apply by extension to Deloria's work, which, as I will go on to argue, was intimately engaged with Hurston's own. For the moment, however, what is of particular concern to a reading of Deloria, as Deloria herself notes in this and other more intimate letters, is her effort to avoid offending the sensibilities, trampling upon the discretions, blotting out the complexities, or otherwise failing to meet the expectations of readers in the home community that she so valued.[25] Here, Deloria reflects, at least in part, upon a charged "ethical" dilemma that has recently been expounded publicly in commentary by Paula Gunn Allen, who has noted that she chose to "specializ[e] in teaching *contemporary* literature to avoid as many ethical violations as I could, believing that I might teach it and evade or avoid queries about arcane matters" (emphasis added).[26]

What Allen describes as a more general concern with "ethical violation" seems, in many respects, to run counter to Trinh's aforementioned critical commentary on purported "strategies of partial concealment and disclosure." Working through this tension, Deloria's particular concerns are illustrative. In Deloria's case, expository elisions seem to have been situated in specific ways around the topic of female sexuality. In the first letter quoted above, to give one example, Deloria describes how her research on courtship and marriage caused her particular difficulties once she reached the point of writing it up. And in Deloria's correspondence with Benedict, to give another, we find one letter in which Benedict asks Deloria to query her informants about a series of exceedingly intimate sexual matters (concerning, for example, the violation of sexual prohibitions, or the practice of abortion); Deloria's response to Benedict is belated, rushed, and also notably and quite uncharacteristically opaque.[27]

Thus, while Trinh suggests that it is important not to overemphasize "strategies of partial concealment and disclosure" in writing by insider-outsider intellectuals, it is critical to point out that in Deloria's case, this very real need for "partial concealment" had precise historical and cultural determinants that bore down in important ways upon her writing process. Explaining certain elisions in her research in a pointed letter to Benedict, Deloria noted that her own status as a sexually inexperienced, unmarried woman made her acutely vulnerable to criticism from a home audience who might go on to speculate about the sources of her knowledge about women's erotic lives, presuming those sources to be personal and autobiographical, rather than derived from interviews in the field; here, in a weird instance of mirroring, we find Deloria expecting to be cast in the role of "native informant" by both home and by institutional audiences. Deloria dramatizes this tension – this problematical relation between ignorance and knowledge – in the early pages of her novel *Waterlily*, where the character Blue Bird gives birth, in solitude, to her first child:

> An eternity passed – and then, the child was a girl. Of that she was vaguely aware as she picked it up from the soft grass on which it lay and fumbled for her knife in its case hanging on her belt. Cleanly and quickly she cut the cord, as old wives said it should be cut. She herself had never beheld such a thing. Unmarried young women did not witness births.[28]

In this passage, Deloria manages both to describe and to fail to describe an event about which she would, herself, have had no intimate knowledge; the birth takes place in an inarticulate space marked by dashes, and is followed immediately by brief comment on the sorts of knowledge available to and withheld from "unmarried young women" like Deloria herself.

The point that I am making here is understated but critical: Deloria's apparent diffidence, spoken with such paradoxical eloquence in the letters to Benedict, might find adequate theoretical explanation either in Trinh's "resist[ance to] closure" or in Allen's concern with "ethical violation"; my sense, however, is that in Deloria's case, the explanation lies somewhere between, in the rather more concretely determined realm of the various allowances, expectations and prohibitions of a reading audience that for Deloria was *always* construed as split, multiple, and heterogeneous. I stress this point in part because of the aforementioned assumption of much Deloria criticism – one supported, I should note, by many of Deloria's own remarks about her work – that the task that she set herself was, in Kamala Visweswaran's words, to "persuade a potentially hostile white audience of the value and worth of Indian lifeways."[29] Further, I believe that Deloria's nuanced textual treatment of "insider information," to which she has no sanctioned access – especially information purportedly available only to sexually active women – dramatizes in important ways the Hurstonian paradox of "familiar strangeness": the way in which the apparently full and intimate understanding of the "insider" observer is marked, is indeed defined, by an awareness of the *limits* of her own knowledge. Finally, however, what is most crucially important about Deloria's theorizations of her own writing practice in her correspondence with Benedict is her disclosure of her own negotiation of a series of conflicting imperatives and prohibitions that bore down upon her work, creating within it an array of tensions that are palpable, despite the oft-noted expository elegance of her published and her unpublished texts.

These kinds of considerations about her fragmented audience and its various requirements inform many of the strategies that Deloria developed as she was writing *Waterlily*. In that novel, as in the "Camp Circle Society" manuscript, one important expectation that Deloria faced was, as I noted above, that she would revise or correct the manifold white-authored misreadings of "Sioux" culture that had emerged in the nineteenth century and continued to appear well into the twentieth. To be fair, this kind of "revisionary" activity did matter very much to Deloria, who witnessed and (in her writings) bore witness to many of the harsher political consequences of cross-cultural misreading. As her biographer Janette K. Murray has noted, important passages in Deloria's published research contain pointed, specific rewritings of historical episodes – for example, one notorious incident in which a white man was killed by two Dakota men, former prison inmates whose release the white man had negotiated – that had been previously subjected to racist or sensationalist treatment.[30]

To suggest this, however, is also to suggest that Deloria's works were *solely* engaged in dialogue with the hegemonic tradition of cultural description, and that the audience that she envisioned for her books was itself primarily white. As I argued above, Deloria's many concerns about the response of a home audience would seem, in part, to belie this assumption. Moreover, I would like to suggest also that in her efforts to imagine an ideal text with which to engage in dialogue, as well, perhaps, as what Kaplan calls an "ideal reader," Deloria chose her insider-outsider peer and contemporary, a woman who was herself an innovator in the representation of marginalized feminine sexualities: that, of course, is Zora Neale Hurston.

When Hurston makes the rare cameo appearance in Deloria scholarship – as she does, for example, in Krupat's important review to which I have already referred – her image tends to be situated at the margins of the historical frame. Krupat notes, for example, that Deloria's late-twenties research collaboration with Boas in New York coincided exactly with the beginning of Hurston's graduate work at Columbia, but he does not pursue the issue at any length.[31] Kamala Visweswaran notes coincidences between the two women's professional histories with similar tentativeness, and goes on to mount a brief but suggestive contrast between Hurston's *Tell My Horse* (1938) and Deloria's *Speaking of Indians*.[32] There are sound reasons for Hurston's marginal status within Deloria studies: beyond the temporal coincidence that Krupat and Visweswaran note, Deloria's historical connection to Hurston is in fact quite difficult, if not impossible, to document. Hurston eventually enrolled in the Ph.D. program at Columbia, while Deloria remained unofficially affiliated, working independently with Boas and Benedict; thus we cannot assume that the two women would have met in the common setting of the classroom. Added to this was the fact that for both women (as for all fieldwork trainees), Columbia was only a temporary dwelling place. Their time in Manhattan was punctuated by frequent voyages out into the field. As a final impediment to historians seeking out connections between the two women, there are, at least to my knowledge, no letters, footnotes, or other conventional documentary signs of intellectual relationship between Hurston and Deloria.

At the same time, however, I think it is fair to say that it would be highly *unlikely* if Deloria were *not* acquainted with Hurston's work: here, I double-negate in an effort to be judicious, rather than evasive. Deloria's published scholarship, for example, discloses an extensive knowledge of contemporaneous Boasian work, while her private correspondence contains numerous, passing references to this book or that article that informed her formal and methodological decision-making processes. Moreover, both Hurston's first novel, *Jonah's Gourd Vine* (1934) and her later ethnographic text,

Mules and Men (1935), were known to Deloria's own academic circle, advertised by Hurston's publishers among members of the American Folklore Society, and widely reviewed. The best evidence for Hurston's importance to Deloria, however, comes not from the archives, but from Deloria's own published writings, which at certain key points are clearly and profoundly responsive to Hurston's. Many cultural historians have noted, in separate discussions of each of these two women, that a central task for both Hurston and Deloria was the transposition of oral traditions into a written register. For Hurston, this took the form of her complicated and oft-analyzed experiments with the representation of rural, African–American idiomatic speech. One of Deloria's central scholarly legacies, moreover, was her development of methods for transcribing Lakota oral narratives.[33]

Thus, it is unsurprising that a notable point of contact between their writings comes in the form of a pair of stories concerning the tension between oral and written language: in their published research, both women include important anecdotes about the kinds of cross-generational miscommunication that might result from this tension, anecdotes that echo each other in muted but clear ways. Hurston's comes in her 1936 volume *Mules and Men*, in the famous tale, told in the voice of informant Robert Williams, about a young woman who goes to college, returns to Eatonville, Florida, and then attempts to transcribe a letter, dictated by her father, and addressed to her uncle. As the woman records a story that her father tells about his exceptionally obedient mule, she finds herself unable to properly transcribe the clucking sound that her father uses for coaxing the mule to work. The father asks his daughter, " 'Is you got dat?' " She replies:

> "Naw suh, Ah ain't got it yet."
> "How come you ain't got it?"
> "Cause Ah can't spell (clucking sound)."
> "You mean to tell me you been off to school seben years and can't spell (clucking sound)? Why Ah could spell dat myself and Ah ain't been to school a day in mah life. Well jes' say (clucking sound) he'll know what yo' mean and go on wid de letter."[34]

By the end of the story, the woman – unable properly to transcribe her father's idiomatic speech – ends up serving as the book-smart butt of a joke that will be shared between the two brothers.

Most critics, I believe accurately, have taken this tale to be one of

Hurston's self-reflexive signatures: a consideration of the problem of ethnographic representation, and of her own role as observer.[35] I would add to these earlier commentaries that the daughter's role as stenographer also contributes to Hurston's career-long, highly self-conscious consideration of her scripted role as a female medium, a vehicle through which information could be exchanged between men. In her own popular ethnography *Speaking of Indians*, published in 1944, Deloria presents a strikingly similar story about cross-generational tensions between speech and writing, which I will quote here at some length:

> When the first enthusiasm passed, adult interest in learning to write slowly waned in inverse proportion to the growing ability of their young to do so. "My little boy can write now; I needn't exert myself longer," a parent might say. It had never been any too simple. There was no tradition for it, and most of the people had tried it too late in life. They began to throw their pencils aside and depend on the school children.
>
> But the children were in most cases better versed in writing English and found it easier than trying to write Dakota. Some of the letters resulting from the youngsters' attempts to put their elders' ideas on paper have been marvels of interpretation. Some dignified old grandfather, proud and confident, would dictate formal words to a distant relative whom he wished especially to honor. There he would sit with eyes shut, the better to compose fine sentences, while his overrated grandchild struggled to translate and transcribe the involved speeches into English. "And now, dear relative, it is enough; I will now cease to address you for this time," might come out as "Well, so long, friend, I have to ring off now." No child would mean to be flippant with his grandfather's letter. He would be doing his level best, imitating something he had heard. Of course the old man would assume it was perfect. Fortunately at the other end another school child was sure to read the recipient's letter to him, and he couldn't help turning it into good Dakota idiom, for that was all that was possible to do. It wasn't funny to him either. And so the old timers imagined they had addressed each other with their habitual dignity, and never guessed the metamorphoses their serious sentiments had undergone en route. Such were some of the milder casualites in the struggle with acculturation.[36]

Letter writing, as commentators (including Deloria) routinely note, provides one of the clearest and most immediate practical advantages to those in the process of acquiring literacy, in that it allows for rapid long-distance communication.[37] Thus, in both Hurston's and Deloria's work, anecdotes about cross-generational letter writing are nearly inevitable, so much so that it might be possible to write off the similarities between these two stories as mere coincidence.

What a juxtaposition of the two texts does reveal, however, is highly significant. Hurston's is presented as a tale, Deloria's as a factual anecdote. Beyond that, the clearest difference is in the framing of the two anecdotes: Hurston tells hers in the voice of her informant, dwelling upon the particularity of his idiomatic speech. Deloria's, on the other hand, is told in the same expository idiom that she uses throughout the book, serving as part of her brief history of literacy instruction and educational policy early in this century. While the complexity of Hurston's shifting idiomatic registers in *Mules and Men* is unignorable, and has been repeatedly noted and analyzed by critics, in *Speaking of Indians* the shifts of register are much less clearly marked. The men and boys in Deloria's anecdote are speaking to one another in Dakota, while the boys' transcription and Deloria's re-telling are in English.

Like Hurston, however, Deloria does make delicate changes in order to register the different tonalities of grandfathers' words and grandsons' transcriptions. This is particularly apparent in her repro-duction of the boys' idiomatic English: "I have to ring off now" is a phrase that mirrors the larger anecdote by metaphorically substi-tuting one communicative technology (the telephone) for another (the letter written in English), which is itself a substitute for oral communication (between grandfather and grandson) in Dakota. Curiously, while the boys do not attempt an on-the-spot translation of a formal Dakota farewell into English written prose, Deloria herself attempts to do so: "And now, dear relative [etc.]." As Williams's tale commented on histories of migration and reverse migration, of literacy, the emergence of class divisions, and the role of the ethnographer herself, Deloria's anecdote evokes the violences (in her terms, the "milder casualites") wrought by government enforcement of educational policies on Dakota reservations, and implicitly equates those with her own role as a cross-cultural translator.

Deloria's anecdote also serves other, equally self-analytical purposes, functioning in subtle ways as a critical reflection upon Deloria's own engagement with Hurston's work. What is particularly striking in Deloria's brief anecdote is her description of the grand-sons, who produce "marvels of interpretation" and "metamorphoses ... en route" while appearing to serve as simple transcribers of their grandfathers' words; the grandfathers, meanwhile, are apparently unaware of what is happening before their very eyes. In Williams's tale, published several years earlier, the daughter is alone in her effort, and is dealt a sharp rebuke by the story and its teller. Hurston, as numerous readers have seen, uses the tale, in part, in order to show how gender divisions are at work in the community where Hurston performs her research; the daughter's literacy is immediately put to use in the services of her father, who then deems her efforts inadequate. Deloria's scribes are boys, and Deloria is careful to explain that there is no conflict – no "flippan[cy]" – at work in their efforts to transcribe their grandfathers' speech; they are doing their "level best" to perform a difficult task. In Hurston's tale, on the other hand, the tensions between father and daughter are foregrounded. Deloria revises Hurston by removing the obvious gender stratifications from her anecdote. At the same time, however, her implicit equation of herself (as ethnographic scribe) with the young boys in her anecdote introduces an entirely new set of gendered issues into the analysis. These are the issues to which I will turn in my discussion of *Waterlily*.

2

Deloria's *Waterlily*, composed during the mid-forties, is a multi-generational saga of nineteenth-century Dakota life, focusing on the experiences of two women characters, Blue Bird and her daughter Waterlily, and set during a time (Krupat places it in the 1840s) when contact with whites was minimal. Her novel opens with the afore-mentioned scene in which Blue Bird gives birth, alone and in silence, to her daughter. Blue Bird, who goes into labor during an arduous, extended march from an old camp circle site to a new one, finally dismounts her horse and walks alone into the woods alongside the column of marchers:

> ... grandmother once said: "No woman cries out like a baby; people ridicule that. To carry a child is an awesome thing. If one is old enough to bear a child, one is old enough to endure in silence."
> Blue Bird clung to those words with desperate tenacity and allowed not a moan to escape her, though she was alone. An eternity passed – and then, the child was a girl.[38]

For Blue Bird, giving birth in silence is an imperative handed down from grandmother to granddaughter, grounded at once in a complex, shared sense of the "awesome[ness]" of maternal power and, in less easily sentimentalizable terms, of the mother's broader kinship obligations; it is an overdetermined gesture, both voluntary and enforced, and is narrated in such a way that these conflicting determinants are equally apparent.

Zora Neale Hurston's 1939 retelling of the Moses story, *Moses, Man of the Mountain,* also opens with a discussion of silence and childbirth, albeit one that unfolds in a radically different setting. A Hebrew woman, enslaved with her people in Egypt, is anxiously preparing to give birth in secret, in the wake of the pharoah's order for the death of all male Hebrew children. The narrator sets the scene:

> "Have mercy! Lord have mercy on my poor soul!" Women gave birth and whispered cries like this in caves and out-of-the-way places that humans didn't usually use for birthplaces. Moses hadn't come yet, and these were the years when Israel first made tears. Pharoah had entered the bedrooms of Israel. The birthing beds of Hebrews were matters of state. The Hebrew womb had fallen under the heel of Pharoah. A ruler great in his newness and new in his greatness had arisen in Egypt and he had said, "This is law. Hebrew boys shall not be born. All offenders against this law shall suffer death by drowning."[39]

In Hurston's book, silent labor is also an imperative, but one unambiguously the product of political oppression; thus, it makes sense that the silence is occasionally broken, as the women whisper or cry out for mercy. In both Deloria's and Hurston's books, the women's silence testifies to their powers. While in Hurston's text, keeping mostly silent is a response to tyrannical restraint imposed from without, in Deloria's, it is an act whose logic Blue Bird has partly internalized. While I will return in due time to this striking textual echo, it will suffice for now to point out the clear contrast between them: while Hurston's book opens with the sound of an isolated verbal protest, an unnamed woman's whisper, Deloria's opens with an image of a communal march whose strict decorum is carefully observed.

These parallel scenes evoke in shorthand the kinds of questions that I will pose regarding the intellectual relations between Deloria and Hurston. In general, how is cultural description affected when it is marked by the specificities of women's histories? What does it mean to be a woman and to assume the role of culture-bearer? More precisely, what kind of political charge is carried by female eloquence? Early in his 1988 "Afterword" to *Waterlily,* Raymond DeMallie takes up some of these issues in relation to Deloria's novel, noting that "the book's focus on the experiences of the heroine Waterlily and her mother and grandmother make it a major contribution to understanding women in traditional Sioux culture. Yet," he continues, "Ella Deloria surely did not intend the book to be construed as a feminist statement."[40] DeMallie may well be correct in his assessment of Deloria's own, particular intent; it is unlikely indeed that she would have described her manuscript as "feminist" in any specific sense. At the same time, however, it is worth considering the ways in which Deloria's novel does in fact transmit subtle feminist resonances, not only, as Visweswaran has argued, by "emphasizing again and again the range of women's roles among the Dakota,"[41] but also and more pointedly by means of its intertextual reengagement of Hurston's writings.

One of the primary concerns shared by Deloria and Hurston – their concern, shown in the passages above, with the dynamic relation between female eloquence and female silence – is precisely the one that has guided much recent feminist criticism of Hurston's fiction. In her 1990 introduction to the HarperPerennial edition of *Their Eyes Were Watching God*, for example, Mary Helen Washington points out how Hurston's female characters are often set at odds with the rural, working-class communities in which Hurston performed her research, and which served as the setting for much of her best-known fiction. Washington writes, in a passage that I quoted in my earlier discussion of Hurston, that "when Hurston chose a female hero for [*Their Eyes*] she faced an interesting dilemma: the female presence was inherently a critique of the male-dominated folk culture and could therefore not be its heroic representative."[42] For the most part, in recent years critics have defined Hurston's "feminism" in terms of her complicated depiction of female eloquence as a weapon used against the constraints embedded within "male-dominated folk culture."[43] In that same essay, however, Washington also describes a 1979 public debate that gave rise to a major discussion of the political significance of Janie Crawford's voice. According to Washington, Robert Stepto argued that while "the frame story in which Janie speaks to Pheoby creates . . . the illusion that Janie has found her voice ... Hurston's insistence on telling Janie's story in the third person undercuts her power as a speaker."[44] Noting that Alice Walker spoke from the audience in order to emphasize the importance of both Janie's speech *and* of Janie's periodic silences, Washington goes on to describe Walker's remarks as "the earliest feminist reading of voice in *Their Eyes*, a reading that was later supported by many other Hurston scholars" – scholars including Washington herself.[45]

Although *Waterlily* did not see print until 1988, I would like to suggest that Deloria's 1948 manuscript, which languished for forty years in the archives, itself may have contained one of the "earliest feminist reading[s] of voice in *Their Eyes*." While Deloria's approach is positioned less distinctly than Hurston's as antipatriarchal critique, I believe that *Waterlily* directly engages Hurston's novel in an effort to examine, as more recent critics have, the ways in which both female voice *and* female silence have a variety of uses and significances; thus, in the opening pages of her novel, Deloria raises important questions about the value of voice in Hurston's writing by initially proposing silence as a complicated form of expressivity. In the dialogue that she sets up with Hurston, Deloria also anticipates a number of broader, contemporary reconsiderations of the shifting resonances of speech and silence that have recently emerged across a number of fields. "Postindian" novelist and theorist Gerald Vizenor, for example, has recently argued that "performance and human silence are strategies of survivance."[46] Anthropologist Lila Abu--Lughod, also taking seriously the tactical value of reticence, has written about the complicated purposes served by women's modesty in Bedouin culture.[47] Moreover, King-Kok Cheung has written critically of the unexamined overvaluation of eloquence in much western feminism. Reading texts by Asian–American women writers in her book *Articulate Silences*, Cheung reexamines "the social norms concerning speech and silence in North America, especially the premium placed on assertiveness in educational institutions and in society at large ... Such a logocentric tendency obscures the fact that silence, too, can speak in many tongues, varying from culture to culture."[48]

Finally, and most recently, Carla Kaplan has explained in complex and nuanced terms how, in Hurston's *Their Eyes*, "Janie's various refusals of public voice, self revelation, and fighting back do constitute an important form of political protest."[49] Where these interrelated observations leave us, I believe, is in a position to reconsider DeMallie's assessment of Deloria's "feminism"; the complexity of that term, which is itself left unexplored in DeMallie's commentary, can be partly unraveled in a comparison of Deloria's and Hurston's varying but intertwined treatments of the issue of female voice.

I agree with Washington's claim that Janie Crawford is continually at odds with the "male-dominated folk culture" that she inhabits. From the earliest pages of *Waterlily*, on the other hand, Deloria's female characters are defined by and enmeshed within a delicate web of community relationships that provides comfort and mutual security. Janie's resistance is mapped out over the course of her own, individual journey. For Deloria, however, the idea of a lone romantic quester would have been anathema. Rereading Hurston, Deloria looks for a way of exploring the nuances of female voice without doing direct violence to the communal networks through which that voice transmits itself. By arguing with Hurston, however, I believe that Deloria was at the same time attempting to map out new structures of community in an intertextual conversation with another insider-outsider intellectual who, by virtue of her situation at Columbia, shared many of Deloria's own concerns.

The clearest way of measuring the points of contact between Hurston and Deloria is to first consider how both women adapted their ethnographic research to fictional form; in this, their tactics were similar. Both attempted to transform analytical issues that were central to interwar Boasian research into their fictional counterparts: thus, the women's empirical observations about patterns of kinship and migration were transformed into their fictive equivalents – narratives of courtship and journeying. Performing this transformation, Hurston and Deloria concocted plots that shared a number of points in common: they both told stories of migratory women protagonists, whose lives are shaped in decisive ways by their departures from the stability of home (embodied in the figure of the grandmother) and their marriages to a series of men. My admittedly cursory plot summary points to a series of smaller and perhaps more significant echoes: the pivotal, early scene of a young woman's communion with nature; the forbidden courtship with a disreputable man; the tense departure from a grief-stricken grandmother; the public humiliation of a wife by one husband, and the tragic death and burial of another husband; the lengthy and strategically crucial recitation of a communal history; the grand-scale, death-dealing catastrophe; and many others. Woven through these sorts of obvious similarities are more subtle considerations of the relationship between eloquence and silence.

While I do not have the space to examine each of these crossing points in detail, what I would like to do is to closely analyze a few of them in order to advance my claims about Deloria's interrogation of the individualism that many critics have located at the heart of *Their Eyes Were Watching God*. In *Their Eyes Were Watching God*, as I have pointed out, Janie's progress is often indexed by her moments of public eloquence, and capped by her recitation of her own story to her friend Pheoby in the novel's frame.[50] In this, Janie is fulfilling a revised form of her grandmother's wish, expressed early in the novel, to find a "pulpit" from which she might preach a "great sermon." Janie's grandmother tells her, in an important speech, that

> Ah wanted to preach a great sermon about colored women sittin' on high, but they wasn't no pulpit for me. Freedom found me wid a baby daughter in mah arms, so Ah said Ah'd take a broom and a cook-pot and throw up a highway through de wilderness for her. She would expound what Ah felt.[51]

The "highway through de wilderness," of course, finds a form in Janie's journey through a series of marriages, each marked by departure and movement, each impelling her towards the embodiment of the desire that she imagined, as a girl, in her vision under the pear tree of a communion between bee and blossom; early in the novel, Hurston's narrator tells the reader that

> [Janie] had been spending every minute that she could steal from her chores under that tree for the last three days. That was to say, ever since the first tiny bloom had opened. It had called her to come and gaze on a mystery. From barren brown stems to glistening leaf-buds; from the leaf-buds to snowy virginity of bloom. It stirred her tremendously.[52]

For Janie, the individual quest, the use of eloquence, and the fulfillment of erotic desire are linked in complicated but inextricable ways.

In Deloria's *Waterlily*, desire and articulacy also matter a great deal, but rather than being imagined as individual achievements, each becomes part of a larger network of communal relations. Early in *Waterlily*, just after Waterlily's birth, her mother Blue Bird has a vision that echoes Janie's vision of the pear tree in near-uncanny ways:

> All around the waterlilies in full bloom seemed to pull her eyes to them irresistably, until she turned to gaze on them with exaggerated astonishment. How beautiful they were! How they made you open your eyes wider and wider the longer you looked – as if daring you to penetrate their outer shape and comprehend their spirit. She glanced from one to another, and suddenly it was impossible to distinguish them from her baby's face. A new sensation welled up within her, almost choking her, and she was articulate for the first time. "My daughter! My daughter!" she cried, "How beautiful you are! As beautiful as the waterlilies. You too are a waterlily, *my* waterlily."[53]

In Hurston's rendering, the communion with the pear tree results in what most readers, following Henry Louis Gates, Jr., now interpret

144

as an orgasm. It is a near-Whitmanian moment, one that involves the temporary putting aside of habit and duty (stealing away from one's "chores") and seeking, in solitude, after desire. In Deloria's rendering, on the other hand, the "new sensation" that wells up within Blue Bird is relational – growing out of connectedness to an other, the child – and her new eloquence results in a cascade of wordplay: simile ("as beautiful as the waterlilies", metaphor ("you too are a waterlily"), and personification ("*my* waterlily") – that enacts itself in the naming of her daughter, drawing her into a broader and mostly supportive kinship network.

In *Their Eyes Were Watching God*, the sensations accompanying Janie's communion with the pear tree "emerged and quested about [Janie's] consciousness,"[54] setting in motion Janie's own quest, her departure from her grandmother's home with her first husband, Logan Killicks. On the other hand, immediately after Blue Bird gives birth to Waterlily, she "quietly" rejoins the march, a very different kind of journey:

> By now the sun hung low. Blue Bird walked quietly alongside the line as if looking for her people, until a woman who was a social cousin noticed what had happened and took charge of her. After sending her family on, she turned her packhorse out of the line and settled the mother and child on the travois seat behind and began leading the horse at an even slower walk so that its delicate burden should not be jolted by hidden bumps and stubble.[55]

Like Hurston's novel, Deloria's is shaped by the travels of her heroines – first Blue Bird, then her daughter Waterlily. All of those travels, however, are contained within larger patterns of movement: on the march from one camp circle site to another, or between camp circles, where the women (or occasionally, the men) travel after their marriages, to join their in-laws.

Within these contrasts – which typify the clearest distinctions between Hurston's and Deloria's novels – is, of course, a distinct difference in the way in which Hurston and Deloria depict female eroticism. It is no accident that Janie's solitary orgasm under the pear tree, an outlaw moment described by Kaplan as "one of the sexiest passages in American literature,"[56] corresponds in Deloria's novel to a scene in which a newborn child is named by a mother whose respect for cultural decorum is obvious at every turn: Hurston's narrative tends to posit transgression as triumph, while Deloria's tends to measure its heroines' successes in terms of their obedience.

For in Hurston's novel, as successive generations of critics have noted, female desire is most often subversive, at odds with the needs of the community. From the earliest pages of the novel, when Janie's grandmother panics after she sees Janie "letting Johnny Taylor kiss her over the gatepost,"[57] to Janie's unsatisfactory marriages to respectable men, to her final, passionate, and volatile marriage to Tea Cake, a man who gambles, flirts, never stays put, and is much younger than Janie is, Hurston shows how female desire poses a continuous threat to communal stability, to the values embedded within what Washington called the "male-dominated folk culture." In Deloria's novel, on the other hand, there is a more understated effort to depict ways in which female desire and communal obligations constantly negotiate with and against one another. This effort is brought to crisis when Waterlily is "bought" by her first husband, Sacred Horse, whom she has not yet formally met. She is ambivalent and afraid: her family could well use the horses that have been offered in exchange for her, but she hesitates, initially, to consent to marry a stranger.

In a conversation between Waterlily and Blue Bird, Deloria goes on to dramatize the ways in which law and desire, which seem at first to be wholly at odds with each other, are partially reconciled; voluntary and coerced actions are again intertwined in highly self-conscious ways:

> Waterlily had to go all the way now. " 'Mother, tell me straight. Do you think I should agree to this marriage so that the horses can be used in the redistribution rites?' " There, it was out. She held her breath for the answer. Surely her mother must say, "Certainly not, my child. We don't do things that way in this *tiyoṡpaye* [camp circle]. You do not have to marry unless you wish to!"[58]

Waterlily imagines that her mother will tell her to follow her private wishes; instead, however, her mother answers her with a careful speech about kinship imperatives. When Waterlily acquiesces, after much ambivalent consideration, the narrator rewards her with what turns out to be a good marriage; moreover, after her first husband's tragic death, Waterlily gains the further reward of marriage to a man that she had earlier chosen for herself, in a moment of wild self-assertion. Deloria does not attempt to smooth over the difficulties for her women characters of subjecting themselves to broader communal obligations; what she demonstrates, however, again and again, is the way in which those obligations contain within themselves enough elasticity, enough improvisatory space, that private desire and broader cultural imperative can in the end, if only with difficulty, be made to mesh with each other.

There is ample textual support for the contention that Deloria responds to Hurston by interrogating Hurston's romantic individualism and replacing it with more communitarian values. To stop here, however, would be to risk simplifying the efforts of both women, and perhaps more important, to risk collapsing their efforts into a hackneyed and ultimately misleading polarity: a strong, assertive black woman poised against a stoic, silent Indian, with a bit of bad-girl/good-girl dualism thrown in for good measure.[59] "Feminism" as debated and disclosed by both Hurston and Deloria is necessarily more complicated and multidimensional, restlessly working itself out somewhere in between. Here, it is important to reconsider Walker's and Washington's remarks, noted earlier, about the strategic importance of Janie's periodic silences, which serve important critical purposes throughout *Their Eyes Were Watching God*. Kaplan, in the most complete and persuasive analysis to date of Janie's self-silencing, has argued that Janie's silences most usefully read in the context of Hurston's own skepticism towards

> narrative's social and psychological status ... [Hurston, in contrast to a broad, influential range of Renaissance-based commentators] does not represent narrative as constitutive of social or personal identity. And for her, its salutary psychosocial outcome is always contingent and circumscribed, never guaranteed.[60]

In the argumentative tradition leading from Stepto to Walker to Washington to Kaplan – a tradition that is, I would suggest, anticipated in important ways by Deloria – dominant readings of Janie's eloquence have been countered by readings of her refusal of eloquence. Deloria's privileging of silence, so apparent in the passages that I have discussed, brings this highly counterintuitive interpretation of Hurston's work to the surface, by dramatizing in *Waterlily* the ways in which social decorums ranging from gentle cajoling to harsh prohibition circumscribe her heroines' speech.

Further, Deloria was well aware that her own verbal portraits of nineteenth-century Dakota community ran the risk of static idealization, and mentioned several times to Benedict her desire to engage more recent concerns about cultural conflict and change.[61] Thus, it is also important to consider the subtle ways in which Deloria includes within her novel some conventionally Hurstonian moments,

moments when cultural imperatives generated by the community are themselves called into question. *Waterlily*, for example, is populated by a series of minor female characters who, unlike Waterlily herself, fail to conform to their various kinship imperatives – adulterers, sexually experienced young women who pretend to be virgins, and the like – but who are in the main granted the same narrative sympathy and generosity as is routinely accorded to the novel's more obedient characters. While Hurston places Janie Crawford, the female erotic outlaw, at the center of *Their Eyes*, in *Waterlily*, such characters remain on the margins. Conversely, in Hurston's novel, a marginal character like Pheoby, who is respectable and conforming but remains Janie's "kissin'-friend,"[62] has much in common with Deloria's protagonist.

I want further to examine this last point by considering closely how the implicit "critique" (Washington) that Janie posits of Eaton-ville culture might find echoes in Deloria's text. In my introductory set of parallels between Hurston's *Moses, Man of the Mountain* and Deloria's *Waterlily*, I deliberately elided an important question: by replacing the pharoah's tyrannical regime with the admittedly gentler coerciveness of Blue Bird's grandmother, was Deloria, in any sense, calling into question the rule of feminine silence in which her heroine acquiesces? Moreover, in her revision of Hurston's ethno-graphic anecdote about the effects of literacy across generations, was Deloria, by associating herself with young boys – rather than, as Hurston did, with a young girl – commenting in subtle ways upon the ways in which her place as a cross-generational scribe, who is deeply concerned with community loyalties of various kinds, compels her to understate her specifically feminist concerns? In order to suggest some answers to these questions, I will consider two passages from *Waterlily*: one in which Waterlily's relationship with her mother-in-law is described, and another in which Deloria develops her crucial characterization of Dream Woman, Waterlily's aunt.

Thus far, I have devoted much attention to the way in which, in Deloria's rendering, various kinship obligations work together, with the help of pointed interventions by a kindly narrator, in order to give support and coherence to the plots inhabited by women characters who are willing to conform to them. At times, however, Deloria is careful to depict how improvisation and minor transgres-sion are necessary, beneficial, and most of all inevitable in the stories of her women characters. When, for example, Waterlily leaves her own camp circle for that of her first husband, Sacred Horse, she is homesick, bewildered by the various formalities and avoidances that are required of her in her role as an adult, as a wife.

In the midst of this, her husband's mother, Taluta, recognizes Waterlily's homesickness, and deliberately shirks the avoidance taboos that usually circumscribe the relations between mother-in-law and daughter-in-law. Her transgression takes the form of a series of prohibited conversations:

> This surprised [Waterlily], for she had never before met a woman so independent of the avoidance taboo. And indeed some friends of the mother-in-law openly criticized her for it. "But it is too much liberty that you take, the way you talk so freely with your son's wife." To which she replied, "What of it? I can't let that rule stop me. She is only a child, after all, and far from her own people because we carried her off. She must be homesick at times. If I can cheer her up, what is so bad in that?"[63]

In fact, throughout the novel, there are many small transgressions much like this one, entering the narrative at pivotal points and, in the main, treated as ordinary events: apparently a sharply rule-governed culture, it contains mechanisms within it that allow for improvisation and gradual change.

Where this issue reaches its most pointed articulation is in Deloria's characterization of Waterlily's aunt, Dream Woman. An artist, Dream Woman is well known for the delicacy and above all for the originality of her designs. Originality and innovative self-expression might seem to run contrary to the rule-governed consistency that forms the basis for Deloria's description of nineteenth-century Dakota life: they are more clearly the characteristics of Hurston's heroine Janie Crawford. When Waterlily is a child, for example, Dream Woman makes toys for her:

> Dream Woman did things like that, quietly making her relatives happy and saying little. That was why she was named Dream Woman, because, like one who dreamed or saw visions of beauty and then remembered them, she worked such designs as nobody else imagined or originated. Women said she had supernatural help or she could not be so skilled in art. Be that as it may, Dream Woman was not one to divulge any secrets though she was often teased to say where she got her designs.[64]

Dream Woman's creativity, however, is associated not only with innovation; it is also linked to communitarian values and to silence.[65] It would be a mistake to read Deloria's depiction of Dakota culture as one that is static and unyielding, enforcing silence so as to better suppress any kind of innovation and change, especially among the women characters. Deloria paints a picture of a way of life that is at once rule-governed and immensely elastic; female innovation, which is presented in Hurston's book as an implicit challenge or threat, is used in Deloria's novel to show how cultural change – including (even primarily) change instigated by women – is a constant, near-imperceptible fact of life.

At this point, however, it becomes possible to look back to Hurston, via Deloria's rereading, from a slightly different perspective. Although the figure of the female dreamer has many important precedents within Dakota culture, it is also useful to consider the fact that in *Their Eyes Were Watching God*, Hurston's own depiction of the female dreamer is absolutely central, providing the book with its opening, which includes what are perhaps Hurston's most famous lines: "Now, women forget all those things they don't want to remember, and remember everything they don't want to forget. The dream is the truth. Then they act and do things accordingly."[66] Reconsidering these lines in light of Deloria's commentary on Dream Woman – who steadily, stealthily introduces cultural innovation and change – we might take Hurston's famous lines as a commentary on Hurston's own role in the manipulation of the African–American cultural archives, a commentary that shows how Hurston and Deloria have more in common than is at first apparent. Early in *Moses, Man of the Mountain*, Hurston shows how Miriam – Jochabed's daughter and the older sister of the newborn boy – is told to watch over the newborn son after he is cast out in the water in a small basket. Miriam becomes distracted and loses sight of the infant, and when she returns home, despondent, she invents the story of the child's rescue by the pharoah's daughter. The widespread rumor of a Hebrew baby growing up in the pharoah's household leads, eventually, to a revolution led by Moses, who may or may not be Jochabed's son. Hurston showed how a small tale invented by a little girl leads, finally, to massive social upheaval – showed, in other words, a girl whose invention or "dream" assumes the form of a complicated kind of truth – and in this, she might well have been reflecting in decidedly optimistic ways upon her own role, as an insider-outsider ethnographer, in the manipulation of the African–American cultural archives. Likewise, Deloria's Dream Woman reflects Deloria's own concerns, as a writer of historical fiction, about what it means to reinvent a temporally distant cultural milieu. The

"dream" – defined by both women as the process of female reinven-
tion of the terms through which a communal history is understood –
can itself perform important cultural work.

Where all of these concerns come together and reflect more
largely – if more guardedly – upon Hurston's and Deloria's projects
is in both women's more explicit considerations of the question of
what it means to carry and transmit a communal history. In *Their
Eyes Were Watching God*, the communal history is recited early in the
novel by Janie's grandmother, who spins a tale that is, at least
initially, fiercely resented by Janie. In *Waterlily*, community history
comes by way of the multivalent performance of Woyaka, an oral
historian who spends a season in the camp circle of Blue Bird and
Waterlily. Janie's grandmother, Nanny, tells the story of the end of
the Civil War, beginning with a painful, private account of the
departure of the slaveholder who had fathered her child (Janie's
mother, Leafy), her further abuse by his wife, and her ultimate
escape with the newborn baby. Nanny's story then opens outward,
into a description of the arrival of the Union army and her
emancipation, followed by a commentary on the lasting oppression
of African–American women. Janie, made miserable and guilty by
her grandmother's recitation, sets aside her own desires and allows
herself to become caught within Nanny's tale: she marries Logan
Killicks, whom her grandmother had chosen for her: "out of
Nanny's talk and her own conjectures she made a sort of comfort
for herself."[67] Not surprisingly, given Janie's desire to make her
own way, her marriage to Killicks does not last. Janie, however,
eventually assumes the role of historian, much like the role assumed
by her grandmother earlier in the novel; she tells her own story to
her friend Pheoby, in a way that negotiates a pathway between her
grandmother's intense sense of historical determinism and her own
romantic individualism.

In Deloria's engagement of the question of how to find the means
with which to express a communal history, the metaphorics of
captivity are also present, albeit in a much different form: Deloria
reflects, self-consciously, upon the dangerous process by which a
single historian can take captive the history of an entire people.
Woyaka begins his recitation with a bit of metacommentary, describing how he assumed his role after a strict course of training by
his grandfather:

> "The day I was born [my grandfather] looked on me and
> vowed to make of me the best teller of stories that ever lived

among the Tetons. And to that end he never gave up training
me. I was, you might say, my grandfather's prisoner, for I did
not have the liberty enjoyed by other boys; I did not go about at
random; I did not run with my own kind or engage in idle
play."[68]

The historian's task itself constitutes a kind of captivity, making him
in certain respects "a strange man,"[69] forever distanced from forms
of wordplay engaged in by others: "he did not enter freely in the
bantering and good-natured joking that went on about him."[70] Here,
Woyaka echoes Janie's resentment of her grandmother's constant
backward glance. Woyaka, however, goes on to suggest that he,
himself, has become a kind of warder; when his grandfather offered
up prayers for his grandson, he prayed that, in Woyaka's words, "I
be enabled forever to hold captive everything I heard."[71]

Through the characters of Nanny and Woyaka, both Hurston and
Deloria reflect self-consciously upon the burden that they ambivalently assumed, among the Boasians, by taking on the role of
communal historians. This role carried with it a charged (indeed, an
impossible) responsibility that constituted a form of captivity for the
tale-teller – as it did for Woyaka and for the young Janie Crawford.
Moreover, in both Hurston's and Deloria's work, there is a more
troubling and understated consideration of the possibility that, by
enclosing a communal history within their own words, they were
taking captive an inventory of events, traditions, and practices that in
fact belonged to no one person.

3

I began with a discussion of cultural ownership and cultural theft,
and I will turn to these issues briefly as I move towards my own
conclusion: not coincidentally, these subjects have been prominent
throughout much of the literature of Indian–black literary relations in
the Americas. I have discussed elsewhere the prominence of the
figure of the stolen text in western-hemispheric traditions – beginning with Caliban's plot against Prospero and his books, and moving
through more recent works by such writers as José Martí, Roberto
Fernández Retamar, Jamaica Kincaid, Charles Johnson, Louise
Erdrich, and Michael Dorris. In postmodern reconsiderations of the
history of European conquest in the western hemisphere, African–
American, Native American, Latino/a, as well as Anglo writers have
responded to each other across apparently discrete literary traditions

by deploying this figure again and again. What began as an effort to revise the significance of Shakespeare's *The Tempest* eventually developed into a charged intertextual conversation *among* contemporary western-hemispheric writers.[72]

I have suggested in the preceding pages that Deloria's novel, frequently and appropriately praised for its sharp revision of hegemonic representations of "Sioux" cultural traditions, and for fidelity to its traditional Dakota sources, nonetheless found one of its primary inspirations in a major work from the African–American tradition. To compound the speculation in which my chapter is already grounded, I would like to conclude by suggesting that Deloria's work might also have inspired at least one contemporary African–American historical novelist, a writer who has also, like Deloria, been praised for her historiographical nuance: that is Toni Morrison, whose 1987 novel *Beloved* reaches its climax in a scene that might well have found its own source in Deloria's 1944 book *Speaking of Indians*.

The scene to which I refer comes late in *Beloved*, and involves the novel's heroine, Sethe, a woman who escapes from slavery after being sexually assaulted by a group of white men, and then kills one of her children in an effort to prevent the child's capture and return to slavery. Years later, Sethe mistakes another white man, Edward Bodwin – an abolitionist, as it turns out, and Sethe's landlord and occasional benefactor – for the schoolteacher who had orchestrated and then coldly observed her assault. Late in the novel, Bodwin arrives at her home in a cart; recalling her earlier assault, Sethe attacks Bodwin with an ice pick, finally directing years of suppressed anger against a man who for her embodies the source of all of her rage.

In her 1944 nonfiction book *Speaking of Indians*, Deloria includes an account – given in the voice of an informant – of two Dakota men beaten and imprisoned after being arrested while attempting to bury their uncle. Enraged, they vow to kill the first white man that they see upon their release from prison. After they are released, they carry out their plan, killing a white man who rides by them in a cart, and who turns out, by coincidence, to be the man who had intervened on their behalf and negotiated their release from prison:

> "Riding home that evening, happy no doubt over having befriended the injured, he came down a lonely hill, crossed the stream, and started slowly up the next hill. The two men who had been released that afternoon waited in ambush. Yes, it was

a white man all right, driving in a little black buggy. They fired
at him from behind, killing him instantly. Imagine how they felt
when they learned that they had killed their own benefactor!"[73]

In Morrison's novel, Edward Bodwin is also driving a cart, unaware
of his surroundings because he is lost in prideful recollections of a
time, years before, when he had intervened on Sethe's behalf after
she was imprisoned for killing her child. When Bodwin rounds the
curve and Sethe spies him, then attacks him and is restrained by
friends, all that he can do is look at her, as the schoolteacher had
watched years before. Both Deloria and Morrison, in their careful
emphasis upon the psychology of both parties in the assault, clarify
in subtle ways the complicity of the "benefactor" in the oppressive
system that he merely seems, by virtue of his actions, to resist.
Moreover, in their examination of the motivations of the assailants,
Deloria and Morrison show how their apparently chaotic, unfocused
rage has its basis in specific injustices in which the "benefactor" is
subtly implicated.

bell hooks has made tentative suggestions about the cross-currents
between the history depicted in Morrison's *Beloved* and the history of
Indian–white relations:

> In the United States it is rare for anyone to publicly acknowl-
> edge that African Americans and Native Americans are the
> survivors of holocaust, of genocidal warfare waged against red
> and black people by white imperialist racism. Often it is only in
> the realm of fiction that this reality can be acknowledged, that
> the unspeakable can be named. Toni Morrison's novel *Beloved*
> seeks to acknowledge trauma of slavery holocaust, the pain that
> lingers, wounds, and perverts the psyche of its victims, leaving
> its mark on the body forever.[74]

It is possible to argue that Morrison – in her apparent allusion to
Deloria's *Speaking of Indians* – was attempting in *Beloved* to find a
specific form for expressing the historical connection that hooks
makes in this essay. hooks argues that "only in the realm of fiction"
can this breadth of suffering be acknowledged, but I will presume to
add to hooks's observation that only in that realm of fiction can this
kind of cross-historical improvisation be performed: one that draws
connections and forges intimacies by (in a more benign but still
active and somewhat risky sense) "stealing" a text from another
tradition, and recasting it as fiction. In a final connection to both
Hurston and Deloria, Morrison herself has implicitly equated the
creation of historical fiction with the act of dreaming; Morrison's

meditation on the 1955 lynching of Emmett Till took the form of a 1986 play entitled *Dreaming Emmett*.

During the thirties and forties, when Hurston and Deloria were at work, dreaming was most often interpreted, via psychoanalytic theory, as a process through which individual, idiosyncratic desires gain expression. Through the intertextual dialogue between Hurston and Deloria, however, we can also begin to interpret "dreaming" – redefined by both women as the renegotiation of the terms through which communal histories are understood – as a form of coalitional cultural work. Thus, while it matters a great deal that Deloria's new readers acknowledge her "revisionist" impulse and her fidelity to Dakota traditions, I would argue that it is also important to consider the subterranean connections that she established, by means of her muted dialogue with Hurston, with African–American cultural traditions.

6

"Lyrical interrogation":
H.D.'s training–analysis

1

The tension between psychoanalysis and feminism has been an enormously productive one for feminist theorists during the last two decades, generating a body of commentary that appears inexhaustible. The history of the relation of women intellectuals to the evolving discipline of psychoanalysis, however, has only just begun to be written.[1] In part, this is indicative of the fact that until the mid-eighties, debates about the role played by women in the initial phases of the evolution of psychoanalysis were in large part focused upon the extent to which Freud's earliest women analysands, rather than his later women disciples, contributed to the development of the discipline.[2] In part, however, the privileging of theoretical speculation over historical research within recent discussions of women and psychoanalysis points to the fact that this particular history is still very much in the process of unfolding.

Classical psychoanalysis, like interwar anthropology, was in part dependent for its formulations upon the testimony of an untutored other (the female hysteric, the anthropologist's informant).[3] I have discussed, with regard to Hurston's ethnographies, how Boasian theory subtly precluded the possibility of a writing informant, even as, in practice, the Boasians solicited Hurston's contributions for the purpose of establishing cross-formational dialogue between "Columbia" and "Harlem."[4] In Freud's psychoanalysis, the notion of a writing analysand was equally disruptive, the status of the female student-analysand equally problematical. As I argued in the case of interwar Boasianism, I will suggest as well that for psychoanalysis, the insider-outsider served as a figure through which the institution

– in this case, psychoanalysis as practiced by Freud and his students during the years just prior to Freud's death – could explore and extend its own extradisciplinary applications.[5]

In *Tribute to Freud* (1974), her two-part account of her 1933/34 training–analysis with Freud, H.D. situates herself on the borderline between the opposed positions of the "analysand" and the "analyst," in a mixed affiliative situation structurally similar to those occupied by Kahlo, Carrington, Hurston, and Deloria in the cases I have already examined. For Freud, women analysts performed functions that gave rise to tensions and ambiguities that should by now – in light of these preceding discussions – be strangely familiar. In important respects (as Freud himself confirmed, at times in unexpectedly straightforward ways) women analysts were valued as sources of practical commentary against which their male colleagues might ironize their own positions; the women's work, as such, often served as a ground upon which increasingly nuanced theorizations could be produced by Freud himself and by his male disciples.

In his early thirties lecture "Femininity," for example, Freud discussed contributions made by women colleagues to his own inquiries into the development of feminine sexuality in precisely these terms; he claimed that

> [i]n recent times we have begun to learn a little about this, thanks to the circumstance that several of our excellent women colleagues in analysis have begun to work at the question. The discussion of this has gained special attractiveness from the distinction between the sexes. For the ladies, whenever some comparison seemed to turn out unfavourable to their sex, were able to utter a suspicion that we, the male analysts, had been unable to overcome certain deeply rooted prejudices against what was feminine, and that this was being paid for in the partiality of our researches. We, on the other hand, standing on the ground of bisexuality, had no difficulty in avoiding impoliteness. We had only to say: "This doesn't apply to *you*. You're the exception; on this point you're more masculine than feminine."[6]

Here, Freud positions the woman analyst as a container of experiential knowledge about differences between the sexes and the "prejudices" that might ensue from them; the sexed distinctions between men and women that the woman analyst insists upon drawing, however, are useful primarily as empirical foils to Freud's own more subtly gendered distinctions between "masculin[ity]" and "femi- nin[ity]." The division that Freud draws here – between the systematic theoretical intellection engaged in by "male analysts," and the sassy empiricist back talk of his "excellent women colleagues" – has been cited again and again by recent feminist theorists as evidence for the thoroughly problematical situation of women analysts in the early years of psychoanalysis. "So," Luce Irigaray wrote in 1974, in a memorably irreverent paraphrase of Freud's above-cited remark, *"their practice* has brought us some information that elucidates *our theory"* (emphasis in original).[7]

What Freud's remarks should also recall, more broadly, are the parallel circumstances within which insider-outsider intellectuals made their way into late-thirties Surrealism and Boasian anthropology. I have discussed throughout the preceding chapters the manner in which insider-outsiders articulated themselves into metropolitan intellectual life by generating a compensatory form of "experien[tial]" discourse during a time in which – as Walter Benjamin noted in 1936 – "experience ha[d] fallen in value";[8] however densely ironized their self-inscriptions might have been, they were regularly taken as raw fodder for more advanced interpretive activity, satisfying what I have termed a "desire for mimesis." Between Boas's preface to Hurston's *Mules and Men,* Breton's catalog essay for Kahlo's gallery show, and Freud's "Femininity" lecture, we can discern continuities in this palpably reductive tendency to "authenticate"[9] the work of the insider-outsider – to associate it, in Irigaray's terms, with plain, unnuanced *"practice,"* rather than with scrupulously self-resistant *"theory."* In order to demonstrate how these shifting valuations of the "practic[al]" and the "theor[etical]" work to blur a series of sharper institutional concerns – which were enacted, as in these aforementioned cases, in a process of interdisciplinary crossover and conflict – I must first sketch out very briefly the context of H.D.'s own encounter with psychoanalysis.

H.D.'s training-analysis with Freud transpired during 1933 and 1934 in Vienna, a setting richly evocative both of the many stresses that threatened the continuity of Freud's discipline, and of his final efforts to create a stronghold against a world (his world and others') that was rapidly disintegrating.[10] Freud was seventy-seven, H.D. forty-seven. Freud's Vienna, which he described in the mid-thirties as the most "valuable" home to psychoanalysis,[11] was more than ever for him a place of weirdly paradoxical domestic exile. Although Freud refers in his writings to Austrian antisemitism at least as early as 1900, *Moses and Monotheism* (published after his 1938 move to London) necessarily paints a much bleaker picture than his earlier works. In *Moses and Monotheism*, the threat is at once more generalized and much closer to home: the volume contains comments about the impossibility in his present time and place of publishing writings on religious subjects, and the book's discontinuous and repetitive essays are interspersed with autobiographical details about his flight from Vienna to London. Inside Freud's office, however, he had created a world apart, filling the space with his famous collection of Greek, Roman, Chinese, and Egyptian antiquities. Lynn Gamwell, curator of a late-eighties exhibit of Freud's antiquities, noted that his choice of collectables was itself idiosyncratic, out of sync with his surroundings: "he was in Vienna," Gamwell observes. "He could have collected Biedermeier or Baroque, which were in vogue. He didn't do that."[12] His office provided elaborate shelter from, and contrast to, the world outside of it. Bracing himself against the political onslaught that would force him to flee the country in five years' time, he was holed up in a tiny empire of his own with his wife and youngest daughter, his physician, a protective coterie of late-era disciples and patrons, and a small number of hand-picked analysands.

H.D., who approached Freud out of a desire to free herself from "repetitive thoughts and experiences – [her] own and those of many of [her] contemporaries"[13] – describes an equally incongruous setting: her shopping trips, visits to coffeehouses, and nostalgic forays through the city where her mother and father had honeymooned are punctuated by a disturbing inventory of images of Vienna just before the war: showers of confetti printed with Nazi slogans, swastikas chalked on sidewalks, rifles piled on street corners. She was, moreover, unable to write, complaining of "a growing feeling of stagnation, of lethargy" that was exacerbated by her acquaintance with a new group of younger poets who were both more politically committed than she was, and somewhat less fearful in their anticipation of another world war.[14]

Freud was attempting not only to safeguard but also to extend the applications of his own life's work, a process that led him to a series of interdisciplinary efforts (which included *Moses and Monotheism*) during his final years. Since his early teens, as if by reflex, Freud had greeted crises of disciplinary continuity by attempting to enlarge the scope of psychoanalysis. During the years of Jung's defection, for example, he produced some of his earliest anthropological speculations, notably *Totem and Taboo* (1913). It is significant that H.D. met Freud when he was old and in extremely fragile health, and was encountering what was undoubtedly his greatest challenge of continuity; "frail as he was," Susan Stanford Friedman has written, he was nonetheless, at the end of his life, quite "deeply concerned about the future of psychoanalysis."[15] Freud's interdisciplinary experiments, at this point, were growing increasingly bold and turbulent, imaginative and unguarded. *Moses and Monotheism* – a near-Surrealist mixed bag of psychoanalysis, cultural history, Egyptology, and anthropology, with a bit of literary criticism thrown in – caused him particular worry; Freud wrote in 1936 to Max Eitingon of his fears that "experts would find it easy to discredit [him] as an outsider"[16] – a concern that seems, nonetheless, to have exerted scant inhibiting force upon the text as it was finally published. (Writing to Lou Andreas-Salomé, he would describe his speculations on Moses as comprising "a kind of historical novel."[17]) Moreover, despite Freud's very real if most often muted self-doubts, some of his disciples were following his lead, venturing into literary criticism, education, and other fields. Like Hurston and Deloria, who became affiliated with Columbia's anthropology department at a moment when literary experimentation was on the rise, H.D. met Freud during a time when his institutional energies were in many respects centrifugal. Attempting to regenerate her own, temporarily declining powers, H.D. was prepared to traverse the boundary between psychoanalysis and a range of distinct but nonetheless related disciplines.

The relation of H.D.'s work to Freud's has been the subject of copious commentary on the tense connectedness of feminism to psychoanalysis;[18] within this broader field of inquiry, the more specific problem of disciplinarity has given rise to a series of discrete arguments about the position of women within the psychoanalytic institution. Susan Stanford Friedman, whose extensive research and commentary has set the tone of H.D. studies for over a decade, has described H.D.'s relation to Freud in terms of an "improvisation[al]"[19] dynamic of "collaboration and intimacy" that discloses itself within H.D.'s distinctly literary memoir of her own analysis. Friedman makes her argument in response to François Roustang's mid-seventies claims that Freud's male disciples were impelled into a series of rivalries which enforced their doctrinal conservatism, and which Freud went on to dramatize in his psychoanalytic myth of the "primal horde."[20] Against Roustang's reading of Freud's disciplinary rigor – a reading largely unconcerned with work produced by Freud's women followers – Friedman argues that "Freud's patronizing attitude" towards his women students had the "paradoxica[l]" effect of "allow[ing] them more room to maneuver,"[21] creating space for a multiplicity of resistances that emerged within H.D.'s own work.

At the other end of this particular argumentative continuum, Klaus Theweleit's early nineties commentary on psychoanalytic object-choice provides an alternative to Friedman's reading, one that is much less sparing in the claims that it makes about the position of women within the psychoanalytic institution. Drawing in part upon a range of cases in which early women student-analysands were caught within triangulated relationships between male analysts – notably Sabina Spielrein's and Joan Riviere's – Theweleit describes the "medial" position so often inhabited by women intellectuals affiliated with psychoanalysis during its early phases.[22] Like Friedman, Theweleit argues that Freud's treatment of his women student-analysands had "more to do with literature and play than [with] conventional medicine"[23] – thus, the "improvisat[ory]" dynamic that Friedman describes. Unlike Friedman, however, Theweleit argues that Freud "manage[d] to turn the treatment into a training method and patients into informants and helpers in the expansion of psychoanalysis,"[24] putting their marginalized labors to work for Freud's own purposes. Within the institutional context that Theweleit traces out, his brief commentary on H.D., while richly nuanced and largely nonjudgmental, is also extraordinarily severe; he positions H.D. as a "special daughter," who demonstrates in her *Tribute* how Freud "gives at least *some* women a little help" (emphasis in original), regardless of the manner in which *other* women might have "suffered" as a result of Freud's analytic and institutional machinations.[25]

As I have argued throughout this present study, however, my own sense is that by framing debates about female affiliation within polarized notions of resistance and complicity – a polarity that implicitly underwrites the stances of both Friedman and Theweleit – we are steadily making our way towards a critical impasse. In the case of women and psychoanalysis, as Sarah Kofman suggested more than ten years ago, such debates tend inevitably to criminalize the woman intellectual: either she turns herself into an outlaw by refusing to cooperate with the masters, or she betrays her sex by complying with them.[26] My own understanding, as such, makes its way between the contrasting positions mapped out by Friedman and Theweleit. On one hand, Theweleit's reading of interwar psychoanalysis – which he calls a "daughter state under male sovereignty"[27] – maps out a "medial" position for women that coheres in broad terms with my own claims about the mediating activities performed by interwar women insider-outsiders working across a range of disciplines. At the same time, however, as I have demonstrated throughout the preceding chapters, I am at least as concerned with the ways in which these women manipulated their circumstances as I am with the ways in which they were manipulated by them; these are questions that Theweleit largely leaves open in his 1990 volume *Object-Choice*. Friedman, who by contrast to Theweleit develops far more detailed strategies for reading H.D.'s specifically feminist interrogation of psychoanalysis, emphasizes H.D.'s resistances in such a way as to give only brief (albeit highly suggestive) hints of the strategic usefulness of H.D.'s work to Freud's own.[28] What I would suggest as an alternative to both Theweleit's and Friedman's commentaries, therefore, is a reading that conjoins the severity of Theweleit's account with the feminist emphasis of Friedman's – a reading, in other words, that comprehends cross-disciplinary expansion and drift as a defining activity of mid-thirties psychoanalysis as practiced by Freud, and as enacted in increasingly self-critical ways over the course of H.D.'s own postanalysis career. As such, in the pages that follow, I will read H.D.'s version of psychoanalysis neither as a radical violation of psychoanalytic protocols, nor as an innocuous form of creative experimentation, nor as an instance of complicitousness on H.D.'s part; her work has previously been read in each of these ways. Instead, I will read her memoir *Tribute to Freud* and her long poem *Helen in Egypt* as realizations of and (more pointedly, if also more implicitly) as commentaries upon some of the expansive tendencies of late-thirties psychoanalysis, tendencies within which H.D.'s work was itself enmeshed.

2

In Louisa May Alcott's *Little Women* (1868), Jo March, living away from home in New York, begins writing in a journal that she addresses to her mother and her sister Beth. In her opening entry, Jo recalls her "dreadfully improper" behavior from earlier that day, when she had "peeped" through the curtains of a glass door in order to find out who was singing "Kennst du das Land" – Mignon's lyric from Goethe's *Wilhelm Meister's Apprenticeship* – in the boarding-house parlor. What Jo saw was Professor Bhaer, the middle-aged

German scholar who would eventually become her companion, her mentor, and her husband, and whom she goes on to describe in her journal in copious and occasionally unflattering physical detail.[29] In "Writing on the Wall" (1945/46), the first section of her two-part volume *Tribute to Freud* (1974), H.D. punctuates her reminiscences of her training-analysis with Freud, her own "Professor," with the same lyric – "Kennst du das Land, wo die Zitronen blühn?" – which she recalls from her own childhood, and which she locates not in this charged scene from Alcott's novel, but in its source in Goethe.[30]

I will return later in this chapter to the specific significances of Goethe's lyric within H.D.'s memoir. For now, however, I mean merely to specify a complicated textual crossing point, wherein a twentieth-century American woman writer and her nineteenth-century fictional counterpart confront the memory of their older and purportedly wiser "Professors": Jo March carefully observes Bhaer, unbeknownst to him, as he hums in the parlor, and then shares her observations, rather indiscreetly, with her mother and sister; H.D., on the other hand, submits enthusiastically to therapeutic observation by Freud. In *Little Women*, however, Jo indirectly turns her own written reminiscences of her life with her sisters over to Professor Bhaer, for his scrutiny and approval, thereby reversing the specular dynamics enacted in the earlier passage. H.D., in a contrasting gesture, proceeded after Freud's death to publish one of the most provocative, intimate, and empirically vivid accounts of the therapeutic setting and process ever produced by one of Freud's own analysands – an account that initially appeared in *Life & Letters Today* (a journal published by H.D.'s lover, Bryher), and that has since become a canonical text in the history of the encounter between psychoanalysis and feminism.

For H.D., this half-buried allusion to Alcott's *Little Women* suggests one of the central problems that has concerned me in the course of this present study. According to conventional recent understanding, as I have noted, insider-outsider work presupposes a dramatic encounter between an embattled individual and a larger and more powerful institution that others her – thus, the argumentative polarity of resistance and complicity that has determined the shape of the recent reception histories of Kahlo, Carrington, Hurston, Deloria, and also, finally, of H.D. I have argued, however, that it is critically important to attend to the way in which insider-outsider texts take shape not simply in an instance of polarized conflict, but by means of a process of *multiple* affiliation; thus, while Deloria's

Waterlily can be (and productively has been) read as an interrogation of specific disciplinary protocols of Boasian anthropology, it matters at least as much that we attend to Deloria's other, perhaps more muted engagements, instanced in my own analysis by her intertextual dealings with Hurston's writings. To see H.D. operating in dialogue with psychoanalysis as well as with other intellectual traditions – Alcott's writing is only one from among many possible examples – is to begin to understand some of the complex determinants of H.D.'s postanalytic textual engagement with Freud.[31]

For example, as I noted before, H.D. approached Freud in part out of frustration over the increasing politicization of many of her poetic contemporaries; she writes in the *Tribute* of her hesitation to air her "morbid ... self-centered and introspective" thoughts in the company of "those who were aware of the trend of political events," and who were, according to H.D., "almost too clever, too politically minded, too high-powered intellectually" (*TF*, 57). With Freud, she set out to construct a comparably "high-powered" model for the process of introspection itself. H.D. also makes reference in the *Tribute* to prominent intellectual connections from her own past: Havelock Ellis, an old acquaintance, makes several cameo appearances in her text; D. H. Lawrence emerges into view in "Advent," the second part of her memoir; both men, of course, had fraught relationships to the developing institution of psychoanalysis. Moreover, H.D. also sustained a correspondence with Bryher during the course of her analysis – against Freud's wishes – that has itself come to constitute a major text in much recent feminist commentary on H.D.'s relationship to Freud, notably Friedman's.[32] Freud, as well, was involved in multiple engagements of his own – including the cross-disciplinary experiments to which I have already referred – and H.D. takes up the possibility of an interdisciplinary engagement with psychoanalysis, explicitly if largely in uncritical ways, from the very first pages of the *Tribute*. Early in the memoir, for instance, she describes her response to the news of the death of J. J. van der Leeuw, the patient whose "hour" preceded hers during the first segment of her analysis in 1933. Van der Leeuw, H.D. explains, was a student of Freud's looking to apply psychoanalytic principles to "general education" (*TF*, 5). She recounts her own remarks to Freud after she has learned of van der Leeuw's death in an airplane accident: " 'I felt all the time,' " she writes, " 'that he was the person who would apply, carry on the torch – carry on your ideas, but not in a stereotyped way' "; she continues, telling Freud that she " 'know[s] there is the great body of the Psycho-Analytical Association, research workers, doctors, trained analysts, and so on! But Dr. van der Leeuw was different'" (*TF*, 6). In this passage H.D. stresses the fact of van der Leeuw's *difference* from Freud's more orthodox disciples as the quality that best prepared him to become Freud's inheritor: the continuity of psychoanalysis will best be assured by its differences from itself – its extensions and expansions – not by endless repetition and narrow refinement of Freud's core ideas. Freud's response to H.D.'s characterization of van der Leeuw is enigmatic: "'You have come,'" she reports that Freud responded, "'to take his place'" (*TF*, 6). Freud recognizes H.D.'s ambitions, but stops short of offering her his inheritance.

Later in the essay H.D. reinforces the notion that psychoanalysis can best be carried on by an outsider, by expressing her anxiety over the notion that many of Freud's better-"trained" disciples – including Hanns Sachs and Marie Bonaparte – will also be writing memoirs of Freud.[33] She protects herself from this "noose of self-criticism" (*TF*, 15) by stressing that her impressions of Freud will differ from the others' – as if that difference itself constituted her worthiness – and goes on in the next paragraph to refer, almost boastfully, to the "uncanonica[l]" quality of her sessions with Freud. (*TF*, 15). Repeatedly, H.D. seems to place herself among the initiates – "One day he said to me, 'You discovered for yourself what I discovered for the race'" (*TF*, 18) – only to stress concurrently her own separation from the psychoanalytic community, including Freud himself: "the Professor," according to her now-famous assessment, "was not always right" (*TF*, 18).

Again, late in her memoir, when H.D. specifically addresses the question of the future of psychoanalysis, she backs away from direct praise of Freud's written words: she writes, with understated dismissiveness, that "he would live in his books, of course" (*TF*, 63). Praising him in this way, guarding his reputation by adopting an attitude of unqualified reverence toward psychoanalytic doctrine and decorum, would be (as she writes that Freud himself is) "so tribal, so conventionally Mosaic" (*TF*, 62). Simple reiteration, for H.D., would constitute a gesture "too formal, too prim and precise, too conventional, too banal, too *polite*" (*TF*, 63); she means, instead, to develop new strategies for the dissemination of psychoanalysis, strategies at variance with those of more "conventiona[l]" followers like Sachs or Bonaparte.

In light of H.D.'s repeated stress upon difference – upon avoidance of the "conventional," the "banal," or the "polite" – it is understandable that most of her contemporary feminist commentators locate her at the margins of the psychoanalytic institution.[34] At the same time, however, it is notable that Ernest Jones (as well as certain other, much more recent commentators on the *Tribute*[35]) described H.D.'s memoir with sets of adjectives paralleling H.D.'s own: in Jones's view, for example, her work was "lovely," "enchanting," even "precious."[36] Above and beyond its obvious reductiveness, what Jones's commentary does disclose, in its inadvertent echo of H.D.'s own dismissal of canonical forms of psychoanalytic continuity, is the extraordinarily narrow breadth within which H.D., as student-analysand, was made to operate; rejecting a canonical relationship to Freud, she was nonetheless positioned, by Jones, as a largely unthreatening and thoroughly dutiful institutional daughter.[37] In the light of Freud's own experimental impulses during the mid-thirties, this is itself, in part, comprehensible: part of what I will go on to emphasize is the manner in which H.D.'s "uncanonica[l]" tendencies worked in important if paradoxical ways to align her texts all the more more closely with those of "the Professor" himself.

Commenting on the future of psychoanalysis, H.D. repeatedly deploys a particular strategy that brings to light her contradictory position within the theory and practice of psychoanalysis: using lyric poems from various European and American traditions in order to examine her own position *vis-à-vis* the psychoanalytic institution, H.D. produces a complex dramatization of the difficulties entailed in resisting more conventional institutional imperatives at a time when the discipline was itself mutating and expanding its own applications. A significant instance of this form of "lyrical interrogation" (*TF*, 110) occurs near the conclusion of the memoir, and takes the form of H.D.'s brief translation of and commentary upon Mignon's aforementioned lyric from Goethe's *Wilhelm Meister's Apprenticeship*. Some pages after she has quoted the lyric – first briefly, and then at length – H.D. begins her commentary on Goethe's text with a brief prose interlude wherein she associates herself, through a series of autobiographical details, with the character of Mignon: H.D. recalls how she was once "a girl between two boys," whose soul "found itself in a song" (*TF*, 107).

The lyric contains Mignon's supplication to Wilhelm, her "protector" and surrogate "father," to take her with him when he departs. Mignon, singing to the accompaniment of the harpist, embodies a quite traditional conception of lyricality – lyric that is pure, immediate, naive, oral rather than written. In the novel, Mignon sings the words, presumably in the same hybrid French and Italian in which she speaks (the original language of her song goes unspecified in the novel), and they are translated by Wilhelm, who then transcribes them in German. The narrator then comments on Wilhelm's transcription of the lyrics (here, I quote from Carlyle's widely read translation of the novel):

> [Wilhelm] made [Mignon] once more repeat the stanzas, and explain them; he wrote them down, and translated them into his native language. But the originality of its turns he could imitate only from afar; its childlike innocence of expression vanished from it in the process of reducing its broken phraseology to uniformity, and combining its disjointed parts. The charm of the tune, moreover, was entirely incomparable.[38]

The difference between Mignon's reiterated song and Wilhelm's formal rendering of it is akin to the distinction that Freud makes, in his case histories, between the raw, immediate event of the therapeutic exchange and its eventual transformation into pristine scientific document. While in Freud's account of the therapy, the analyst's rational narrative prevails over the analysand's unfiltered account, in H.D.'s, the lyric provides a kind of order to her account of her own analysis. H.D. uses Mignon's lyric as a guide through the final sections of her memoir, gradually putting it into English in a layered process of translation that echoes the translation already enacted by Wilhelm in Goethe's novel.[39] Mignon's proposal – "Let's go ... " – is for a leave-taking. As Mignon does with Wilhelm, H.D. transforms the occasion of Freud's anticipated departure into its opposite: she is the one who issues the invitation, who casts herself in the role of guide, and who thus, in temporary but significant ways, reverses the hierarchy implicit in the analyst/analysand relationship.

This process of questioning, of *interrogation by lyric*, is present both in Goethe's poem – "the lyrical interrogation and the implication that the answer is given with it" (*TF*, 110) – and in the memoir itself, where H.D. uses lyric to interrogate Freud's notion of psychoanalytic continuity. In part, H.D. references Goethe's/Mignon's lyric in order to analyze her own analysis: she allows the poems to structure her flow of associations, to give sequence to the associative rhythms of her memoir. At the same time, however, her commentary on the lyric in some sense also gives the analyst's side of the story: it contains both question and answer, and speaks in two voices. Dianne Chisholm, in a rich reading of these passages, has argued that the interlocutionary dynamic of Mignon's lyric, redeployed by H.D., places the analysand in a position of authority; Chisholm suggests that "the student, not the master, initiates the process of self-discovery."[40] My own sense, however, is that the bivocal quality of H.D.'s "lyrical interrogation" dramatizes, above all, the contradictoriness of H.D.'s situation. Indeed, as Chisholm notes, H.D. elsewhere in the memoir describes Freud's strategies for eliciting questions as well as answers from the analysand: "The question must be propounded by the [analysand] himself," H.D. writes; "he must dig it out from its buried hiding-place, he must find the question before it could be answered" (*TF*, 84). I would argue, however, that the "question" – as H.D. implies in her repeated use of the verb "must" – is inevitably a question that has already been scripted or "initiate[d]" by Freud, enunciated by the analysand in response to an unspoken imperative. While the *Tribute* successfully engages (Freud's) representation and (H.D.'s) self-representation in a volatile relation, its clear affirmations of the expressive possibilities of therapeutic dialogue are thus vitiated by H.D.'s more understated sense that the parameters of the dialogic exchange have been established, well in advance, by the Professor himself. Interrogating Freud with lyric – and by extension, interrogating the disciplinary limits of psychoanalysis itself – H.D. was at the same time participating in an effort of interdisciplinary expansion within which Freud was himself engaged.

The limits of H.D.'s specifically literary intervention into psychoanalysis are thus marked, albeit negatively, by the intertextual dynamics of her references to Goethe's Mignon. Recontextualized from Goethe's novel to H.D.'s memoir, Mignon's song calls attention to the mutual interrogation of H.D. and Freud. Read otherwise, however – as a more veiled allusion to Alcott's *Little Women* – the significance of Mignon's lyric within H.D.'s memoir begins briefly to open outward, pointing toward a third term in H.D.'s interlocutionary process: that is, toward her concurrent engagement with a longer tradition of women writers in the process of interrogating their own "Professor[s]."

It would of course be possible to read H.D.'s well-hidden textual exchange with Alcott's *Little Women* as an understated gesture of specifically feminist intervention. At least as telling, however, are the ways in which the subversive possibilities of H.D.'s intertextual dialogue with Alcott are largely contained, later in the *Tribute*, in the course of H.D.'s only explicit reference to *Little Women*. In "Advent," the journal entries published alongside "Writing on the Wall" in 1974, H.D. recounts how her half-brother Eric – whom, she notes, was "known generally as the 'young Professor'" (*TF*, 144) – had given her a copy of *Little Women* when she as a girl. Eric had also, H.D. points out in that same passage, "nursed [her] over [her] 'resistance' to long-division" (*TF*, 144) What might appear as a secret shared between women is thus transformed into a gift given by a brother to a sister – a brother who, by virtue of his nickname, his scientific capabilities, and his talent for overcoming H.D.'s "'resistance[s],'" is clearly linked to Freud himself.

Although H.D. took pride in the "uncanonica[l]" aspects of her sessions with Freud, and emphasized in her memoir the moments when poet and scientist broke free from disciplinary decorum, I have suggested as well that H.D. intermittently betrays a sense that she was haunted by the possibility that her utterances were scripted in advance by Freud: his observations, as she writes, left her at times feeling trapped, as if she were caught in "the confined space of a wicker cage, or useless under the mesh of a bird net" (*TF*, 30). Freud's therapeutic technique held within it the possibility of dialogue, of mutual interlocution, but collapsed all too often into monologue, with the patient dutifully fulfilling the analyst's expectations. This alternation between resistance, on one hand, and neutralization of resistance, on the other, marks many aspects of H.D.'s psychoanalytic practice. As I will argue in the following pages, however, H.D. goes on to position herself more critically towards these issues in the context of her late long poem *Helen in Egypt*.

3

H.D.'s response to Freud assumed a revised form in *Helen in Egypt*, published shortly before her death in 1961.[41] In that poem, H.D. constructs a dialogue between a series of first-person lyric tercets and prose commentaries in order to test the permeability of the boundary between the psychoanalytic institution and the objects of its investigation, as well as to allegorize her own situation as a woman intellectual working between disciplines. *Helen in Egypt*, as such, contains her final and perhaps her most self-conscious reconsiderations of both the possibilities and the limitations of the interlocutionary dynamic of therapy. In it, H.D. adapts her plot from a classical countertradition, established by Stesichorus and Euripides, in which Helen waited out the Trojan war in Egypt while a phantom

Helen remained in Troy. In the apocryphal version of the events, H.D.'s prose commentator tells the reader, "the Greeks and the Trojans alike fought for an illusion."[42]

Helen in Egypt, as several critics have recently noted, contains as well an implicit interrogation of Freud's notion that a primal act of violence, generated by rivalry over a woman, could be seen as civilization's originary gesture.[43] *Moses and Monotheism,* of course, includes Freud's final elaboration of his "primal horde" myth, wherein he postulates an Egyptian Moses, murdered by envious and rebellious male followers. A dense web of speculation and self-admittedly "arbitrar[y]" uses of source material (*MM,* 27, note 2), Freud's study contains perhaps his most extravagant effort to expand the applications of his discipline – a process that worked simulta-neously to interrogate psychoanalysis from within, and to extend its boundaries outwards. Notably, as in *Totem and Taboo* (published, as François Roustang argued, in response to Freud's feuding with Jung[44]), Freud recapitulates his myth of the primal horde at a time when the continuity of his own discipline is in crisis. In *Moses and Monotheism,* moreover, he develops in detail the notion that civiliza-tions are guided by conflicts among men; for the most part, the position of women in Freud's narrative – as countless recent feminist commentators have observed – is blank. Women exist primarily as objects of exchange or of desire, and have little active influence upon larger processes of cultural change.

In her own response to classical myths of masculine violence and valor – myths premised upon the setting up of an illusory woman who is then scapegoated – and in her reinstatement of women as historical agents, H.D. in *Helen in Egypt* provides a historical inven-tory that parallels Freud's own. In doing so, part of what she accomplishes is to investigate an absence that Freud created when, as Elizabeth Abel has recently explained, he erased the matrilineal kinship models favored by his British anthropological predecessors, replacing them with patrilineal ones.[45] Moreover, H.D. achieves a second and in many respects more meaningful effect by recontextua-lizing Freud's writings: she links his theories of cultural development not to the social-scientific research that he details in a manner both painstaking and cavalier, but to a series of classical legends. This move suggests a great deal about H.D.'s own notion of herself as a bearer of Freud's intellectual legacy. Implicitly proposing classical legend as an intertext for Freud's *Moses,* she displaces Freud into the epic tradition, showing how her own negotiations between psychoanalytic, literary, and social-scientific discourses operate both against and within Freud's own late-era textual experimentation. Her heroine Helen, shifting between lovers, between geographical settings, and between conflicting accounts of her own history, thus enacts a negotiation comparable to H.D.'s own.

Because *Helen in Egypt* is such a generic oddball (Virginia Woolf knew, after all, that women do not write epic[46]), descriptions of the poem have tended, with good reason, to emphasize H.D.'s upstart role in the process of the development of modernist epic.[47] Why choose the thematics and techniques of epic (or "pseudo-epic," as Elizabeth Hirsch has usefully classified *Helen in Egypt*[48]) as a way of commenting on psychoanalysis? When H.D. chooses a plot (the story of Helen) and a form (the long poem) which recall the tradition of classical epic, she responds both pointedly and elliptically to several arguments crucial to *Moses and Monotheism*. I have noted that H.D.'s choice of plot, the story of the Egyptian Helen, enables her to criticize particular aspects of Freud's cultural theory. At the same time, her subject matter also responds in vigorous ways to Freud's efforts – in evidence at specific moments in the text of *Moses and Monotheism* – to terminate the epic tradition. In a bizarre interpolation into an already bewildering series of essays, Freud in the *Moses* text launches into a brief polemic on the irrelevance of epic poetry in the modern world. During his attempt to consolidate his arguments for the "Egyptian Moses" theory, Freud briefly makes an analogy between the genesis of epic poetry and the genesis of religious institutions (*MM*, 71–72). Both, according to Freud, emerge from dissatisfaction with the present; in both instances, moreover, the "artist" invents a "golden age" based upon the "incomplete and blurred memories" that Freud calls "tradition" (*MM*, 71). Paralleling the individual psychic process of the family romancer, the epic poet invents a story of cultural origins that includes an ideal lineage. Of course, in his "primal horde" narrative, Freud creates a myth of cultural beginnings whose grandeur is vastly diminished; he attempts to demonstrate how "culture" derives from a horrendous act of violence and the communal guilt generated by it – in effect, correcting the epic tradition and positing in its place a sharply critical notion of what heroism means.

In a somewhat superfluous prefatory argument, however, Freud has already discussed the possibility – more precisely, the impossibility – of modern epic poetry. He writes that the "determining cause [for epic] no longer exists." (*MM*, 71), because the work of the epic poet has been subsumed by historians (with their ideal of objectivity): "the old material was used up," Freud argues, "and, for all later events historical writing took the place of tradition" (*MM*, 71). Freud attempts to checkmate the epic impulse with this argument, first by describing somewhat unflatteringly the psychic mechanisms that arouse it, and then by putting an endpoint on the tradition and handing it over to historians. He diminishes it and closes it off in a single, digressive move.

Despite his dismissal of the possibility of modern epic poetry, however, Freud makes some tantalizing observations – asides to his own asides – that in some sense place *Moses and Monotheism* squarely within the tradition that he seems to be attempting to end. In the context of his own dismissal of epic, for example, Freud states that "the vaguer a tradition has become the more serviceable it becomes for a poet" (*MM*, 71). *Moses and Monotheism*, as Freud himself periodically acknowledges, is comprised in large part of scholarly shadow play, bound up as it is with early twentieth-century archaeological speculation about the history of Egypt. By recontextualizing Moses, suggesting that he was Egyptian, Freud transforms himself into a lay Egyptologist, participating in a field that in the early decades of this century remained wildly inventive.[49] Despite Freud's painstaking and occasionally somewhat amusing efforts to document his own research – at one point, he goes so far as to call his own methods "autocrati[c]" (*MM*, 27, note 2) – Freud goes on to inform his readers that his investigations center on "obscure centuries which are scarcely accessible to historical research" (*MM*, 46, note).

Reaching back into this "obscure" and "scarcely accessible" history, Freud develops an argument that the traditional story of the Hebrew Moses evolved from a series of repressions and distortions of the historical "fact" of the Egyptian Moses and his murder by his followers. Describing the consolidation of more conventional Mosaic legend, Freud writes:

> in its implications the distortion of a text resembles a murder: the difficulty is not in perpetrating the deed, but in getting rid of its traces. We might well lend the word "*Entstellung* [distortion]" the double meaning to which it has a claim but of which to-day it makes no use. It should mean not only "to change the appearance of something" but also "to put something in another place, to displace." (*MM*, 43)

Freud's own quasi-epic creation – his "distortion" of the conventional Mosaic legends – partakes of each of these elements: in Freud's own, new story, the father is murdered and his traces removed; he is then "put ... in another place," as Freud transforms Moses' conventionally Hebrew origins into Egyptian ones. Thus, Freud's purported exposure of the psychic mechanisms underlying the invention of the Hebrew Moses – the sequence of "distortions" – parallels in remarkable ways the new plot that Freud invents to replace the old one.

The sorts of Egyptological distortions that prop up Freud's argument are not by any means absent from H.D.'s efforts to reconceive the significance of *Moses and Monotheism*;[50] she shares with Freud a tendency to render the history of Egypt in near-fantastical ways, ways reminiscent of contemporaneous productions of Richard Strauss's opera *Die Aegyptische Helena* (1928), which was performed throughout Germany during the late twenties and early thirties. (Photographs and sketches from early performances of the opera disclose – among other things – enormous, gilded chaises, billowing palm fronds, and dazzling costumes.[51]) As she responds to *Moses and Monotheism* in a reconceived epic form, one of H.D.'s most notable achievements is nonetheless to underscore the fictive qualities of Freud's own 1938 text. She follows Freud by putting her heroine in another place, although in H.D.'s writing this movement from one place to another is more often referred to as translation – the shift from one language or register or set of tropological conventions into another. Moreover, she appropriates the skeleton of Freud's plot – the violence between men resulting from rivalry over a woman – this time situating that plot within literary rather than anthropological or historical traditions. Her argument with Freud then takes a further turn in that she mounts a counterhistory for the woman who figures so minimally in Freud's scheme of cultural development, the woman who (as Abel pointed out) was elided in the course of Freud's revision of the British anthropological tradition.[52] In H.D.'s own revision, men's history is grounded in illusion, in misapprehension – women's in a continual process of entwinement with and separation from that of the men who continually represent them.

While H.D.'s poem makes cross-disciplinary revisions of Freud's narrative of cultural history, its form complicates her relation to psychoanalysis, dramatizing her repeated engagements with and disengagements from it. If the thematics of the poem serve to situate Freud's cultural theory in a literary tradition by recalling its epic lineage, the form of *Helen in Egypt* – its combination of poetry and prose – brings to light the tense relations between analyst and analysand. Friedman, whose most recent work on H.D. has comprised an extended consideration of the problematics of textual revision in H.D.'s work, has made brief observations about the mixed form of *Helen in Egypt* that, for the broader purposes of this present project, are richly suggestive. Noting that the prose passages were added to the poem after the verse portions were complete, Friedman writes that "[t]he prose insets in *Helen in Egypt* ... do not provide authoritative readings of the lyrics, but rather, in their rhetoric of indeterminacy, emphasize the Penelopean endlessness of (re)interpretation and reinscription".[53]

I agree with Friedman's claim that the prose commentaries are not in any sense "authoritative." Rather than emphasizing their "Penelopean endlessness," however, I will proceed by suggesting ways in which H.D. in *Helen in Egypt* works within and against conventional distinctions between prose commentary and lyric: the commentaries, one is led to expect, will be linear and rational, while the lyrics will be immediate, intuitive, atemporal, and confessional. To recontextualize this relation, the prose commentaries resemble Freud's written case histories, while the lyrics resemble the voice of the analysand in the therapeutic situation. Put in yet another way, the commentaries will bear a relation to psychoanalytic literary criticism produced by Freud's more "conventional" disciples – Marie Bonaparte, for example – while the lyrics, to the contrary, will resemble the work of Bonaparte's privileged subject, Edgar Allan Poe. In setting up and then failing to meet these sorts of expectations, H.D. generates some of the poem's most important tensions.

A delicate and complicated layering of competing accounts of the story of Helen, *Helen in Egypt* traces Helen's efforts to recollect her past through a series of encounters with former lovers, chiefly Achilles and Paris. At the center of the poem, Helen meets with the sage-like Theseus on the mysterious island of Leuké. Their conversations comprise an effort to order and explain the often bewildering array of information that precedes and follows their meeting: Helen pleads with Theseus to "teach [her] to remember ... teach [her] not to remember" (*HE*, 207). Theseus, obviously (and according to critical consensus) a stand-in for Freud, carries on a dialogue with Helen that lasts through several books in the second part of the poem. In the interplay between prose and lyric, as well as in the shifting relation between Helen's and Theseus's lyrics, H.D. transforms the therapeutic analyst/analysand relation into a model for poetic composition. Indeed, the scene of Helen's meeting with Theseus brings to culmination an argument that begins to unfold as early as the opening lines of the poem.

At the start of *Helen in Egypt*, the two competing genres – prose and poetry – do seem at first to meet the most conventional expectations for commentary and lyric. Even in these earliest passages, however, the distinction between the two has already begun to shift and blur. In her opening statement, for example, the prose commentator aligns herself not with Helen but with a reader familiar with the canonical (Homeric) story of the Trojan War, a story "we all know" (*HE*, 1). She is a pedagogue, an explicator, who poses questions and then answers them. She provides definition, boundaries, context. To introduce the lyric speaker's first intervention, she introduces also the shadowy, uncanonical tradition of the Egyptian Helen. As in Freud's apocryphal narrative of the Egyptian Moses, the underground legend of the Egyptian Helen takes center stage in the new version.

In her first lyric, however, Helen begins by creating doubt not only about her own substantiality, but also about the substantiality of the events of the Trojan War. Although locating herself specifically in Egypt – "in this Amen-temple" – she states that "the hosts / surging beneath the walls" (the invading Greek armies in Troy) are "(no more than I) . . . ghosts" (*HE*, 1). While the commentator locates the "real" Helen in Egypt at some distance from the "real" war in Troy, Helen casually undermines both those observations, creating a space in which all solid formulations of identity or history seem to dissolve. While Helen describes the temple in Egypt, using theatrical metaphors, as a scene emptied of contents or actors, she simultaneously observes and inhabits this purported emptiness: "the scene is empty and I am alone" (*HE*, 1). Moreover, although she places herself in Egypt, she can hear the sounds of the battle in Troy, the voices of her own detractors. She states that "there is no veil between us" (*HE*, 2), between Egypt and Troy, between the spurious legends of the Trojan Helen and the increasingly indeterminate counter-legend of the Egyptian Helen.

From the earliest lines of the poem, then, the seemingly authoritative voice of the narrator fails adequately to explain this new manifestation of Helen. Ironically, the efforts of the narrator to *locate* Helen – in literary history, in Egypt – are met chiefly by Helen's refusal to situate herself in any distinct way. Thus, what appears at first as a fairly clean separation of commentary and lyric is even in this early stanza a distinction that begins to muddy itself. This is, moreover, not merely a case of commentary subverted by lyric; in certain important ways, the prose passages also seep into the poetry. Although speaking to no one, for example, Helen the lyric speaker delivers a series of imperatives, of authoritative readings of her own about the history of the Trojan War. The narrator had observed that "the Greeks and the Trojans alike fought for an illusion" (*HE*, 1), an observation that Helen substantiates, however uncertainly, in her lyric. Moreover, Helen's lyric, though spoken from a position separate from the conflict, seems at the same time to be conditioned by the historical events going on about her. The war leaks in constantly, finally closing off her first lyric: "here there is peace / for Helena," she states, seemingly oblivious to the bloodshed; she concludes, however, by acknowledging that she is "hated of all Greece" (*HE*, 2).

Clearly, then, rather than simply presenting an authoritative commentary that precisely locates Helen, the narrator–commentator allows the lyric voice periodically to escape. At the same time, however, the narrative presents information that is not clearly available to the lyricist; thus, the speaker in the tercets is hardly more authoritative than the commentator. More and more as the poem continues, the two voices interpenetrate: first by the inclusion of quotations from the lyrics within the commentaries, then by the intervention of secondary interlocutors – Achilles, Paris, and Theseus – and finally by means of the narrator's growing dependence upon the authority of Helen the lyric speaker–singer.

The interplay of commentary and lyric is most compressed in *Leuké*, during the dialogue between Helen and Theseus. While one might expect the narrator to align herself with Theseus, the surrogate therapist who attempts to provide order to Helen's conflicting reminiscences of her own experience, this does not turn out to be the case. The narrator begins the sequence by following the direction of Theseus, but ends by capitulating to Helen. Theseus, the narrator tells us, is "another lover" of Helen's; he kidnapped her when she was a child, but allowed her to escape. When Helen appears to Theseus, she temporarily cedes control of the lyric passages to him. Hardly seeming older and wiser than Helen, however, Theseus launches into an immediate stream of reminiscences of his own, asking somewhat pathetically whether Helen didn't love him – "a little, / frail maiden that you still were" (*HE*, 148) – at the time of her escape from him. Far from being the authoritative figure one might expect – he was, after all, the slayer of the Minotaur – he is self-absorbed and uncertain of who she is. This uncertainty is mirrored in the prose paragraphs, which utterly displace the figure of Helen. The reader is only able to picture her part in this dialogue by means of Theseus's remarks about her clothing and her attitude – to see her through Theseus's narrowly delimited perspective.

With his assurance to Helen that "all myth, the one reality / dwells here" (*HE*, 151), Theseus appears briefly, genuinely authoritative. At precisely this point, however, Helen reenters the dialogue, and with her, the narrator temporarily takes sides (*HE*, 153). Helen discusses her desire to return home, rather than continually to search for the "mysteries," by repeating the story of the Fall of Troy (*HE*, 153–54). The clipped dialogue that follows merits quotation at some length:

> "laugh if you are Theseus,
> and I think you are,
>
> for you laughed once,
> finding a Maiden
> (Helena she was)
>
> entangled in the nets
> your huntsmen spread";
> "you spoiled our quarry –"
>
> "– but to free the birds –"
> "– and found yourself entangled –"
> "– that is Love."
>
> (*HE*, 154)

This image of violation and entrapment – Helen's kidnapping by Theseus – is used in order to define "Love," and to articulate precisely the problem in H.D.'s consideration of female entanglement in masculinist discourse; it is a process, like Helen's "Love," that entails continual, restless shifting between complicity and resistance. Helen then echoes Freud in his own most pessimistic moments (for example, the Freud of "Analysis Terminable and Interminable"), posing a problem that haunts both H.D. and Freud: "do the mysteries untangle / but to re-weave?" (*HE*, 155). In her poem, each solution that Helen reaches is provisional.

By now the prose narrator gives herself over entirely to Theseus, displacing Helen near-completely from the action of the poem. Theseus's suggestions become more and more coercive, his questions more and more leading. Helen's voice is only audible when it is filtered through his quotations (*HE*, 160–61). Finally, as his instruction becomes incoherent – he at once soothes and tranquillizes her and tries to revitalize her – she talks back, arguing against his defense of Paris, reasserting her own memory of Achilles (*HE*, 171). Theseus resists briefly, attempting to answer her questions for her. By this time, however, even the prose commentator, up to now sympathetic to Theseus, grows impatient: "He seems," she observes, "deliberately to have stepped out of the stream of our and of Helen's consciousness" (*HE*, 172). Helen then corrects Theseus's recollection (*HE*, 173) and regains control of the poem. When she begins to talk back in earnest, the narrator finally regains sympathy for Helen, reading her mind. Helen evokes the therapeutic ideal of two unconsciousnesses speaking to one another:

> draw near, draw nearer;
>
> do you hear me? do I whisper?
> there is a voice within me,
> listen – let it speak for me.   (*HE*, 175)

When Helen speaks, she speaks as a series of different Helens: the heroic Helen of Sparta, and the lyrical songstress (*HE*, 176–81). One is grounded in history; the other emits pure sound. One's speech is bombastic, littered with apostrophe; the other's is purely musical. One "passed the frontier, the very threshold," while the other reconciles opposites, ignoring all boundaries. Although H.D.'s poem creates a counternarrative for the woman misrepresented in canonical versions of the fall of Troy, she presents not a unified self, but a multiplicity.

4

I have thus far emphasized the ways in which H.D. manages to complicate Freud's masculinist claims about cultural origins by reinstating the woman erased from Freud's social script, and by displacing Freud's work into a series of imaginative traditions; I have argued further that H.D. uses these techniques in order to elaborate a female character – the Egyptian Helen – whose feminine psyche is itself richly variegated and fragmented. While this reading matters, however, it matters only as a starting point, one that requires further problematization.

When H.D. referred, in the *Tribute*, to her anxiety about the relation between her memoir and those being written by institutional "insiders" like Bonaparte and Sachs, she inadvertently echoed Freud's own anxieties about his position as an "outsider" to professional anthropology. As Freud had done with the social-scientific traditions

that most informed *Moses and Monotheism*, H.D. in *Helen in Egypt*
produced a text that served at once as a critique and a reclamation of
the discrete intellectual practice – in her case, Freud's psychoanalysis
– to which it was so tenuously attached. *Helen in Egypt* does,
however, bear at least one crucial resemblance to the sorts of psychoanalytic orthodoxies that she was more often inclined to resist.

H.D.'s well-known comment that her relationship to Freud was
fractured by an "argument implicit in [their] very bones" is immediately preceded in the *Tribute* by a less familiar, irretrievably ambiguous claim that "[a]bout the greater transcendental issues, [they]
never argued" (*TF*, 13). On one hand, this comment might well serve
as a marker of important disagreements that H.D. chose *not* to
articulate in the context of her conversations with Freud; on the
other, however, it might also mark out broader ranges of consensus
between them. In the paragraph that precedes these remarks, for
example, H.D. sums up the basic tenets of Freud's own version of
speculative anthropology, with which she largely concurs:

> [Freud] had opened up, among others, that particular field of
> the unconscious mind that went to prove that the traits and
> tendencies of obscure aboriginal tribes, as well as the shape
> and substance of the rituals of vanished civilizations, were
> still inherent in the human mind – the human psyche, if you
> will.
> (*TF*, 13)

While H.D., in order to consolidate their points of agreement, puts
her own spin on Freud in this passage, she nonetheless gets him right
in certain crucial ways: she rearticulates, clearly and uncritically,
Freud's habitual equation between "obscure aboriginal tribes," "van-
ished civilizations," and the traces of infantile conflict that psychoanalysis purports to disclose in the "human psyche."

In her above-cited reiteration of Freudian primitivism, H.D. makes
use of metaphors that indicate an acute responsiveness to the
boldness of Freud's cross-disciplinary experimentation: "[Freud] had
opened up," she writes, " ... that particular field of the unconscious
mind" (*TF*, 12), even as the openings between his own "field" into
the fields of anthropological and literary practice were being explored in his own and in H.D.'s writings. In a manner characteristic
of interwar insider-outsider activity, H.D.'s work stands at the point
of overlap; it serves, to use a privileged term from H.D.'s own poetic
lexicon, as a "medium" (*TF*, 13). Also in the manner of Kahlo,
Carrington, *et al.*, H.D. goes on to allegorize these forms of institutional unsituatedness in her text: as she discloses Helen's negotiations

between Paris, Achilles, and Theseus, she recalls her own transformational negotiations between the literary, the psychoanalytic, the
anthropological, and the Egyptological.

Helen in Egypt, however, pins its feminist rereading of the opera-
tions of female exchange to a logic that enables its individual
protagonist to articulate a richly varied and multiple subjectivity –
audible in the shifting voices and locations of Helen – by erasing
many of the cultural complexities contained within the category of
"women," for which Helen stands as exemplar. Thus, in her groundbreaking 1994 reading of *Helen in Egypt*, "Hysteria, Montage, and
Revolution in *Helen in Egypt*," Susan Edmunds has noted how H.D.'s
Helen becomes at various points in the poem "a black woman," a
white woman in the act of "assuming blackface," and a woman who
is "rac[ially] ambiguous."[54] Although noting how these sorts of
shifts serve in part to "alig[n]" Helen with "the hysteric, who
recklessly acquires the traits, gestures, and symptoms of other
people," Edmunds goes on to show how they also serve to align
H.D. with Freud's own tendency to draw "associations between
[white] women, people of color, ancient and/or primitive societies,
and unconscious thinking."[55] As I argued in chapter 1, with regard
to Gayle Rubin's "The Traffic in Women," I will suggest here as well
that H.D.'s universalizing poetic argument needs to be read against
its own grain – not as a text that makes a global, transhistorical point
about the position of women within the broader forces that work to
produce "culture," but instead, as a decidedly local consideration of
the problem of her own shifting intellectual affiliations. To read
H.D.'s postanalysis texts in this way, of course, is to sharply limit the
claims that one can make about her work as an exemplary examination of the relationship between feminism and psychoanalysis.
Instead, it encourages a more local, somewhat more modest consideration of the specific circumstances that led H.D. to her own
encounter with Freud, one whose determinants were multiple and
complex.

Indeed, the earlier *Tribute to Freud* contains what might be H.D.'s
most resonant depiction of her own transformational practice.
Describing the "writing on the wall" that she and Bryher had
envisioned on their hotel room wall in Corfu, H.D. focuses on one
particular inscription that she had witnessed, an image of a tripod:

> Religion, art, and medicine, through the latter ages, became
> separated; they grow further apart from day to day. These three
> working together, to form a new vehicle of expression or a new

form of thinking or living, might be symbolized by the tripod, the third of the images on the wall before me, the third of the "cards" I threw down, as it were on the table, for the benefit of the old Professor. (*TF*, 50–51)

Rachel Blau DuPlessis has demonstrated how H.D.'s tripod "suggests H.D.'s desire to unite, in a post-Freudian synthesis, the three modes of thought or scientia to which Freud had so definitively contributed – religion, art, and medicine."[56] H.D., as medium of "occult or hidden knowledge," *and* as mediator between "religion, art, and medicine," traces out in this figure the dual function of the insider-outsider, caught at once within epistemological and within institutional entanglements, negotiating between the desire for mimesis (as a woman student-analyst writing about feminine subjectivity), and mimetic desire (as a woman vacillating among a range of competing intellectual "fields"). H.D. continues: "The tripod, we know, was the symbol of prophecy, prophetic utterance or occult or hidden knowledge; the Priestess or Pythoness of Delphi sat on the tripod while she pronounced her verse couplets, the famous Delphic utterances which it was said could be read two ways" (*TF*, 51). H.D.'s title, "The Writing on the Wall," as many readers have noted, points in clear ways to the prophetic function that she assigned to her own postanalysis texts, to their projection of a possible future for psychoanalysis after Freud. Like the "Delphic utterances" to which she refers, however, her title can also "be read two ways."

It is a fascinating coincidence that H.D.'s memoir shares its title with one of the earliest full-length studies of the graffiti that adorned the walls of Pompeii, Helen Weiand Cole's 1931 volume *The Writing on the Wall: or Glimpses from Pompeian Graffiti into the Daily Life of the Ancient Romans*. H.D.'s *Tribute* is filled with references to writings on walls of various kinds: from the light-pictures in her Corfu hotel, to the hieroglyphic symbolism that H.D. locates within some of the dreams that she recounts to Freud, to the swastikas chalked on the public sidewalk leading to Freud's Vienna office. In H.D.'s postanalytic texts, inscriptions made upon architectural boundaries – whether ephemeral or permanent, profane or sacred, vernacular or oracular – are profoundly significant, providing her with one of her governing metaphors.[57] In part, they indicate her awareness of her own place as a writer on the boundaries that separate a range of conflicting, even competing intellectual formations and traditions.[58] Moreover, though generally understood to denote the future, "writing on the wall" can also communicate a range of competing messages about the distant past, whether that past be constituted in the "everyday" messages scratched into stucco surfaces by Pompeiian graffiti writers whose work Helen Cole examined, or (in an entirely different temporal, cultural, and geographical setting) in the formal hieroglyphic tracings that preoccupied a range of Egyptologists who were also at work during the early decades of this century.

With regard to H.D.'s place within academic feminism's sense of its own, less-distant past, Edmunds has written of the need to "break open the almost allegorical power of the pairing of Freud and H.D., disrupting the impulse to read the H.D.–Freud debates as a discrete, uncanny foretelling of the subsequent encounter between academic feminism and psychoanalysis."[59] Rather than reading H.D.'s encounter with Freud as an "almost allegorical ... foretelling" of the present intellectual context, I have instead looked backward, toward the condition of cross-disciplinary unsituatedness that was itself allegorized within H.D.'s postanalysis writings, chiefly *Helen in Egypt*. Looking back, however, enables us as well to refocus upon the present moment, and to pose a new set of questions about the sorts of present-day institutional forces that are allegorized within a range of much more recent feminist–theoretical writings. These are questions that I will address in my concluding chapter.

Conclusion: broken form

P.S. 2. I don't wonder the office staff were struck by the valuation I put on the MS! It must have seemed conceited in the extreme . . . I am sure nobody insures so highly. But you know, I thought if anything happened to the package, and I had to rewrite it, I'd have to have that much money before I'd attempt it. On second thought, that might have been a good thing – rewrite it! But it is a wearying thought, anyway.

Ella Deloria to Ruth Benedict, 7 April, 1947[1]

After insuring for several thousand dollars her unique copy of the enormous "Camp Circle Society" manuscript draft, then mailing the draft from Sisseton, South Dakota to Ruth Benedict in New York City, Ella Deloria – embarrassed by the news that members of the Columbia office staff had raised their eyebrows at her immodest estimation of the manuscript's worth – briefly toyed with the fantasy of starting all over again, from scratch. This, however, was too "wearying" a prospect even for a self-reviser as relentless as Deloria was, a fact that takes on a harshly ironical cast when one considers that this manuscript, like that of her novel *Waterlily*, never did see print during her own lifetime.

Much as Deloria disliked the prospect of closing off her research, the fact that she finally did made no concrete, material difference. As such, the resistance to closure that constitutes such an important philosophical premise in all of Deloria's work cannot be celebrated in wholly unambiguous ways, as a triumph over or subversion of the positivistic tendencies of Boasian method. Deloria arguably got what she wanted: a text that refused to complete itself. She got it, however, not by means of some pointed, willful intervention of her own, but instead because Benedict's sudden 1948 death and a fickle postwar publishing industry worked together to create conditions within which Deloria's major scholarly achievement, a text designed to enact her resistance to closure in explicit, public ways, would finally fail to find its own way to publication.

The problematical "valuation" of insider-outsider activity during the interwar years will concern me throughout this final chapter, a chapter whose conclusions will bear marks of provisionality and tentativeness that have been imprinted on my own method by long engagement with work by a series of women who, with varying degrees of tenacity, refused ever to let a subject go. Following this process through the course of their interwar careers, I have made my way across the shifting terrains of Kahlo's succession of mutating or masked self-images; Carrington's pointed revisions of "Down Below," Hurston's repeated recastings of field findings, Deloria's early feminist interrogation of Hurston's *Their Eyes Were Watching God*, and H.D.'s repetitive reengagement of the problematics of psychoanalysis during the final phases of her career.

I have argued that in these cases, the women's practice of self-revision – their willful inconclusiveness, inscribed within the textual sequences that they produced – constituted a serious, sustained challenge to the reductive expectations of authenticity with which they continually met in the context of metropolitan intellectual life. At the same time, however, I have attempted to extend and complicate these claims by insisting throughout the preceding chapters that their self-revisionary activity must also be viewed as an indicator of their enforced accommodation to a series of shifting and often burdensome circumstances that circumscribed their work. The relationship between the abstract and self-resistant philosophical resonances of interwar insider-outsider activity and its concrete (if highly complex) historical determinants was always, I have suggested, a reciprocal one – a problem illustrated in graphic ways by the image of Deloria's voluminous archive of unpublished writings.

The most important of these determinants that I have described was the heterogeneity of these women's intellectual affiliations, and in these concluding pages, I will go on to make a series of suggestions about the utility of attending to multiple affiliation as a determinant of present-day academic feminist practice. For the "valu[e]" of interwar insider-outsider activity, I have argued, consisted not only in the theoretical challenges that it posed, despite the fact that recent feminist commentators have understandably focused – in both affirmative and critical ways – upon this particular measure of its worth. Throughout the recent reception histories of Kahlo, Carrington, *et al.*, as such, scholars have implicitly used their interwar texts as positive or negative standards against which to evaluate privileged contemporary feminist-theoretical methods – methods that operate, as I have repeatedly noted, according to a similar "insider-outsider" logic. I have argued as well, however, that during the interwar period, the "valu[e]" of insider-outsider activity could also be calculated, far more problematically, in the fact that these women often served (or were made to serve) as mediators between distinct intellectual formations at the center, as well as on the peripheries, of metropolitan culture.

I contended in my introductory chapter that Gayle Rubin's mid-seventies theorization of the "traffic in women" contains a powerfully suggestive metacommentary on the heterogeneous affiliations that metropolitan women intellectuals have maintained throughout this century – a process whose reverberations are as palpable in Deloria's fiction as they were in her intellectual biography. My point here, again, is not to underscore Rubin's far-reaching (and since-repudiated) claims that the "traffic in women" should be understood transhistorically and globally; the diversity of examples that I have given within the relatively narrow purview of this present volume – in which the significances of female "traffic" have constantly shifted – should adequately illustrate the vanity of this sort of conclusion. My more modest point, to the contrary, is that the "traffic in women" is a hypothesis that has repeatedly been *allegorized* within texts produced by twentieth-century women intellectuals precisely because of the powerful analysis that it provides of the narrow, specific, and local conditions that alternately enable and disable their work.

On one hand, therefore, we can measure and affirm the philosophical reverberations of Deloria's refusal to "self-nativise" (Geertz's phrase) when we observe her irreducibly complex, self-revisionary negotiations among a diverse range of audiences: scholars, friends, ministers, relatives, social workers, and informants in the field. On the other, however, we can also see how the more concrete difficulties of multiple affiliation were emplotted within her novel *Waterlily*, in Deloria's sustained focus on the communicative thickets traversed by fictional heroines determined to observe proper avoidance etiquettes as they moved to the unfamiliar surroundings of their husbands' camp circles, and back again to their own. In a manner akin to those of Kahlo's revamped courtesans, Carrington's lapsed

debutantes, Hurston's conjure women, and H.D.'s culturally displaced Helen, Deloria's fictional heroines enacted a series of mediations that served to reference Deloria's own deeply unstable but
profoundly necessary position within Boasian anthropology – whose
expansive tendencies she helped to enforce, even as she was in the
process of violating some of its narrower disciplinary protocols.

It is no accident, I think, that the early decades of this century –
when women intellectuals were in the process of achieving unprecedented visibility in the metropolitan public sphere as they circulated
among male-governed formations – was also a time when rudimen-
tary (prefeminist) versions of Rubin's mid-seventies arguments about
the role played by female "traffic" in the consolidation of "culture"
were being set down by British anthropologists and then widely
disseminated by their interpreters, including Freud. Nor does it seem
coincidental that the multiply affiliated texts of Kahlo, Carrington,
et al. were rediscovered during a decade – the nineteen-eighties –
when academic analyses of gender came to be dominated by post-
"Traffic" arguments about the triangulation of women "between
men."[2] In recent years, theorist Susan Fraiman has asked difficult,
pointed questions about the "tremendous explanatory force of this
three-sided figure" – the "erotic triangle."[3] In a necessarily tentative
effort to respond to Fraiman's crucial queries, I will suggest here that
the "force" of the figure is not "explanatory," but rather symptomatic. In other words, its attractiveness rests in part in its ability to
disclose tensions within the contemporary academic context: a
context within which difficult interdisciplinary maneuvers performed by "area studies" scholars during the sixties and seventies –
scholars who were caught between competing departments, commitments, philosophies, methods, and linguistic imperatives – have
more recently been enlisted in the services of a new academic center.
Thus, for example, we have bell hooks's 1990 remarks (cited more
extensively in chapter 1) about the "prestige and acclaim" currently
accorded to cultural studies in the US academy, a prestige that
stands in stark contrast to the reception of "area studies" methodologies, in their own heyday as in the present moment.[4] My point is
not to that we should return to a golden age of "area studies";
according to many of those who were there at the time, that is a
golden age that never was. My point, instead, is that amidst
contemporary celebrations of interdisciplinarity and scholarly formal
experimentation, it is crucial to attend, carefully and at all points, to
the ways in which "intellectual labor" (hooks's phrase) performed by

marginalized subjects working in "area studies" fields has been taken up and used, often sympathetically, but often, as well, at those subjects' own expense. As such, by looking closely at the multiple determinants and significances of insider-outsider activity, I have attempted to perform my own strategic mediations between "area studies" and "cultural studies" – in a practice related to what Mae G. Henderson has recently called "border" scholarship.[5]

In his 1986 essay "On Ethnographic Allegory," James Clifford made the harshly illuminating claim that "ethnographic texts are inescapably allegorical, and [that] a serious acceptance of this fact changes the ways they can be written and read."[6] There, in his final example, Clifford suggested that Marcel Mauss's *The Gift* be read *not* as "a classic comparative study of exchange," as was the common practice, but instead, as a commentary upon the time and place of its own composition, and thus, as "an admirable example of science deploying itself *in* history."[7] While Clifford suggested that Mauss's "classic" text might more productively be treated as a "response to the breakdown of European reciprocity in World War I" than as an analysis of intercultural processes of exchange, I am suggesting here that a range of twentieth-century writings dealing explicitly and implicitly with problems of "exchange," "reciprocity," and mediation might well be read with an eye towards their "allegori[cal]" considerations of the shifting position of women in metropolitan intellectual life. This kind of "allegorical" focus might enable a hard (though admittedly sidelong) look at the uses to which work by metropolitan women intellectuals has been put throughout this century. Moreover, and at least as important, it might contribute to a more complex and self-critical consideration of the ways in which women intellectuals working in the West have displaced their own concerns onto the figure of the "Third World Woman" – a problem that I considered in my brief juxtaposition of H.D.'s *Helen in Egypt* with Rubin's "The Traffic in Women" at the close of chapter 6.[8] It is not, however, the purpose of this book to provide a feminist-critical genealogy of ideas about the exchange of women; that is a topic that would require a book of its own. Instead, what I mean to suggest is that by attending closely to the tense dynamics and power differentials encompassed within the process of multiple affiliation, we can observe more clearly some of the institutional determinants and effects not only of interwar, but also of contemporary feminist debate.

These sorts of processes, however, tend largely to be overlooked in the dominant recent understanding of the development of academic-feminist methodology. Although official histories of academic feminism have only just begun to unfold, unofficial histories have been inscribed within various forms of feminist scholarship since the earliest phases of "Women's Studies" during the late sixties. From the start, certain towering figures – Virginia Woolf, Simone de Beauvoir, Margaret Mead – seemed destined to serve as central (if relentlessly contested) characters within academic feminism's narrativization of its own past, and the rises and dips in these women's reputations have in fact already provided occasion for fascinating commentary on the cultural history of intellectual feminism.[9] The women whose texts have concerned me in this present study are less deeply entrenched because they have more recently been incorporated in this emerging story, but despite this, most of them seem likely to endure the evaluative shifts with which their works are bound to meet, or have in fact already met; among them, only Deloria, whose reputation remains unsupported by any but the most fragile of institutional apparati, seems vulnerable to renewed neglect.[10]

More important, perhaps, than the rotating cast of characters is the overarching shape that these historical narratives have assumed. Despite the newness of the genre, certain conventions have already been formalized within it, the most notable being a two-part, sequential scheme within which the "experiential" moment of early seventies "Women's Studies" advances to the "theoretical" moment of the mid-seventies and beyond. Jane Gallop, in the 1992 essay "Writing About Ourselves," commented critically on academic feminism's tendency to cast its own history in terms of "progress narrative[s]"; my two-part sequence is suggested by the tendencies marked within Gallop's formulation.[11] The hallmark of the first phase is a monolithic and essentialized categorization of "women," which is then enlisted in the services of a "woman-centered" curriculum; the second phase defines itself against the first, and comprises a more skeptical and self-resistant effort to read privileged theoretical texts against their own grain, a process that brings to light both the instability and the complex heterogeneity of the category of "women."[12] In retrospect, the rediscovery of Kahlo, Carrington, *et al.* during this second phase – and the rapid containment of their work within polarized debates over resistance and complicity – seems nearly inevitable: as I have suggested throughout this volume, interwar insider-outsider activity, which operated within and against dominant cultural frameworks for the understanding of "difference," bears a more than passing resemblance to feminist theory as it has been practiced during the last decade and a half.

By stressing the prevalence of this "progress narrative," I do not mean to suggest that much of the most innovative recent feminist commentary does not consist (as it in fact does) of a delicate, multilayered interrogation of the now-conventional polarization of "experiential" and "theoretical" feminisms – a fact that suggests to me a widespread, long-simmering dissatisfaction with the ways in which major debates in the field have habitually been framed.[13] Despite their philosophical complexity, however, some of these same commentaries work to reenforce, rather than to interrogate, the more concrete *historiographical* distinctions that I have just noted – to present themselves, in other words, as fresh syntheses of dialectically opposed feminisms characteristic of the earlier and later phases.[14] Nor by making these claims do I mean to enforce some new kind of homogeneity within the extravagantly varied field of recent feminist commentary; it is important to note that the values assigned to each of these two feminist moments are continually shifting and transforming, in fascinating and frequently unpredictable ways. Lately, for example, several key components and practitioners of "seventies feminism," once routinely maligned, have finally been accorded long-overdue respect.[15] I suspect, however, that an unfortunate consequence of these subtle, recent interventions might well be that a much less nuanced turn towards the repudiation of "eighties theory" will follow in their wake.

My basic point is that amidst these variations, distinct as they are, the defining historical polarity remains intact, providing a pivot point in the dominant contemporary understanding the development of academic-feminist methodology, and a way of authorizing present-day feminist-theoretical activity. As one possible alternative, I would suggest a history of academic feminism that emplots itself not in a "progress narrative" that moves towards the happy ending of increasingly nuanced interrogations of the relationship between "theory" and its "others," but instead, one that makes its difficult analytical way across the swerving trajectories of multiple affiliation, attending at all points to the reciprocal relationship between scholarly commentary and the varied conditions within which it develops, and to the ways in which that relationship discloses itself. I have attempted in the preceding chapters to demonstrate how these methods might operate in analyses of texts from the interwar period;

they would work as well, I think, in our readings of texts from a much more recent past. This process would of course require a sharp alteration of focus, and a new emphasis upon critical gestures that might previously have appeared only marginally significant. At the same time, however, it would also work to unravel certain tensions and problems that I have noted within conventional current understanding of the evolution of feminist scholarship.

A pair of admittedly cursory readings of recent texts, deliberately stark in the contrasts that they pose, might demonstrate the utility of this altered focus. The first, Gayatri Spivak's 1988 essay "Can the Subaltern Speak?" will be positioned, provisionally, as an exemplary enactment of the kinds of "theoretical" methodologies that defined academic-feminist commentary throughout the eighties. At the other end of the methodological continuum, Barbara Christian's 1993 essay, "Being the Subject and the Object: Reading African–American Women's Fiction," can be located – equally tentatively – as a text that privileges the "experiential."

Spivak's central arguments (as well as the central critical disputes that have followed in her essay's wake) are encompassed within her unsparing conclusions about the problematical representability of "Third World Woman" within metropolitan discourse. In her aforementioned essay, Spivak performs a clear and detailed interrogation of what I have been calling the *desire for mimesis*, which she concludes with her famous claim that "the subaltern cannot speak," a declaration that she supports with a lengthy but narrowly focused defense of the interpretive protocols of deconstruction.[16] In less clear ways, however, what her article allegorizes are a series of affiliative relationships wherein Spivak herself negotiates between Foucault and Derrida, between the Subaltern Studies group and the French intellectual left, between Marxism and psychoanalysis; her relentless "shuttling" (a privileged term in her critical lexicon) between competing disciplinary formations and their distinct interpretive modes might well be read as an implicit commentary on the workings of *mimetic desire*, dramatized in her repeated gesture of situating herself as a woman intellectual working between (but inevitably in the services of) male-governed formations.[17] Finally, Spivak's multiplication of self-descriptive qualifiers – the hyphenated litanies that are a hallmark of her critical style: postcolonial-Marxist-feminist-deconstructionist-etc. – further illuminates the process of multiple affiliation, in a manner both focused and diffuse.

Meanwhile, at the opposite end of the methodological continuum of recent scholarly work, we find Barbara Christian's "Being the Subject and the Object," a 1993 memoir of her activities during the phase in which Black Studies programs were being developed in the late-sixties US academy. This essay serves primarily and most explicitly as an account of Christian's gratitude in finding for the first time novels by black women writers that reflected back to her complex versions of her own experience; in a manner directly opposed to Spivak's, Christian's essay seems at first to serve as an argument *for* the pure representability of marginalized subjects, and thus as a defense of early "Black Studies" methodologies against newer and more skeptical theoretical interventions in the field. She encourages her readers – via her own literary interpretations – to "dar[e] to remember the recent past,"[18] rather than repudiating that past. While the article begins by drawing direct equations between Paule Marshall's fictional plots and her emplotment of her own memories, however, Christian goes on to complicate these equations by communicating an understated distrust of the transparent meaningfulness of either fiction or of personal experience. Again and again, she asserts and then qualifies her own identification with the subjects of Marshall's and other black women writers' fictions; she even qualifies, in the essay's opening sentence, her trust in her own recollections of the period. Although less systematic and severe by far than Spivak, Christian nonetheless does proceed by referencing a profound (if deliberately understated) skepticism towards the possibility of pure, transparent representability of black women. What she seeks out, instead, are fictional voices that are "authentically like" hers: "authentic[ity]" suggesting wholistic identification; "like[ness]" suggesting separation and distinction.[19] Moreover, she sets her memoir up by discussing her negotiation between her activities as a graduate student at Columbia, her work with the SEEK program at the City College of New York, and her forays into used-bookstores in Harlem, where she was first able to find out-of-print copies of novels written by black women; as Spivak does in "Can the Subaltern Speak?," Christian depicts a complex scholarly negotiation enacted in the interstices of a series of formations to which she herself is only intermittently attached.

I bring together such radically distinct examples not in order to blot out the philosophical and methodological differences between them, which remain important, serving as they do as indicators of the energetic conflicts contained within the extraordinarily diverse category of "academic feminism." What I mean to demonstrate, to the contrary, is the manner in which a too-cursory polarization of "theoretical" and "experiential" feminisms works in order to simplify both, to reduce complex critical performances to mere, broad gestures. I mean to propose, instead, that we read these texts not on some sliding scale of value that alternately privileges theoretical intensity and empirical weightiness – as if those two terms were themselves fully separable – but with a sharp focus upon the manner in which affiliative issues tend at all times to be embedded within broader discussions of difference and representation.

As such, recent feminist commentary across a range of positions has tended to allegorize the conditions of its own production in the process of multiple affiliation, a process that involves being always unsettled and in-between, acted on by and then acting out against particular formations to which the feminist critic may claim only partial and temporary connections. I do not necessarily see this as a matter for uncritical celebration; as I have argued repeatedly in a series of divergent contexts, my own sense is that innovative interformational "intellectual labor" (hooks) by women tends, in many if not all cases, to be performed largely at women's own expense. I do see some reason for optimism, however, in the fact that new, highly *explicit*, and richly critical articulations of the manifold reverberations of contemporary forms of scholarly "mediation" – in particular, Lana Mati's work on "multiple mediations" in the field of postcolonial ethnographic theory, and Deborah Gordon's on the fraught relations between the "political," the "textual," and the "ethnographic" in the recent history of feminist anthropology – are beginning to exert influence that will, I hope, be felt for some time across a range of feminist disciplinary and interdisciplinary practices.[20] I would hope as well that interventions like Mati's and Gordon's might enable the production of even newer theoretical vocabularies through which to reassess the history of academic feminism in a way that is less neatly polarized and more messily "multiple" (Mati's privileged term), as feminist affiliations and their worldly ramifications have in fact always been.

By way of concluding, however, I want to return briefly to my own point of departure, considering once again the 1994 debate between Elizabeth Grosz and Teresa de Lauretis about the utility and the limits of feminist-theoretical practices that work to demonstrate (in Grosz's words) "the capacity of every text (however phallocentric or patriarchal it may be) to be read otherwise."[21] As I noted in my introduction, de Lauretis responded to Grosz's "interrogation" of de Lauretis's own interrogation of psychoanalytic discourse by describing how she

> build[s her] argumentation with reference to and in dialogue
> with works by other lesbians and feminists with which [she]
> engage[s] directly, sometimes critically, often painstakingly,
> and always explicitly because [she] want[s] to acknowledge that
> the writings of these women – be they theorists or poets,
> novelists or critics – constitute the epistemological terrain of
> [her] own thinking no less than do the more prestigious
> writings of Freud, Lacan, or Foucault.[22]

I have suggested throughout these pages that the polarized, power-laden relationship between the insider-outsider and the institution within which she works needs to be reconceived, in the interwar context, as a more complex field of activity within which Kahlo, Carrington, *et al.* were made to serve as points of contact between marginal and centrist cultural formations. While my retrospective analysis was fueled by a large measure of pessimism about the manner in which these women's works were put to use in the contexts that gave rise to them, I have been interested to observe the ways in which recent commentators – in a manner akin to de Lauretis's – have worked to complicate the verticality and the reductive binarism of the "inside-outside" model by enacting a citational practice that operates, to the contrary, both horizontally and multiply.

In her 1994 collection *Fictions of Feminist Ethnography*, for example, Kamala Visweswaran's theoretical interventions are situated in complex and occasionally conflictual relation to the activity of deconstruction. Rather than engaging in direct ways with de Man or Derrida, however, Visweswaran confronts deconstruction through the medium of Derrida's women translators; her title takes the form of an improvisatory reinscription of Peggy Kamuf's 1982 title *Fictions of Feminine Desire*; her working definition of "deconstruction," moreover, is attributed to Gayatri Spivak.[23] Visweswaran does not explain these pointed gestures of exclusion and inclusion, and my reading of their effects is necessarily speculative. My sense, however, is that her complex practice of citation and allusion – which includes, perhaps most suggestively, prefatory acknowledgments addressed to Zora Neale Hurston and Ella Deloria – is meant to redefine the conventional theoretical decorums that Elizabeth Grosz criticizes in her arguments about the limited utility of feminist and lesbian confrontations with psychoanalysis. Visweswaran describes her volume, in her opening sentence, as "a collective project,"[24] and acknowledges the various ways in which her textual experiments have "broken form" – have departed, in other words, from a variety of professional etiquettes and expectations surrounding the activity of theorizing in recent years. For the purposes of my own, present analysis, the salient aspect of Visweswaran's deliberately indecorous commentary is her insistence upon communicating in explicit ways with peers who are at work on related issues; this aspect of her work, I believe, bears an important relationship to Deloria's and H.D.'s largely implicit responses to other women working in related institutional contexts. With this gesture, Visweswaran opens up possibilities for reconceiving the mediative function that was so often assigned to women intellectuals in the interwar contexts that I have examined.

In *This Sex Which Is Not One* (1977), Luce Irigaray made the broad claim that "[w]oman exists only as an occasion for mediation, transaction, transition, transference, between man and his fellow man, indeed between man and himself."[25] She went on to ask, however, what would happen if women *"refused to go to 'market,'"* and managed somehow to "maintai[n] 'another' kind of commerce, among themselves?"[26] Part of the force of de Lauretis's response to Grosz, I think, is that it brings into view possibilities for an alternative way of reading the recent history of academic feminism, one in which we would attend to the ways in which women intellectuals have responded not only to the "prestigious writings of Freud, Lacan, or Foucault," but also, though sometimes in muted and often in conflictual ways, to each other. What Irigaray sets forth as a "utopia[n]" possibility might more productively be construed as practice that has continually *been* enacted – albeit not in some space of unfettered self-inventiveness, apart from the forces of what Irigaray calls the "'market'" – but instead, within the sharply delineated limits of women's intellectual affiliations, practices, and protocols.

Notes

Introduction

1 I focus in this project upon a small and recently delineated canon of interwar women intellectuals whose activities have been repeatedly compared to contemporary feminist-critical practice. It is important to note, however, that during the last decade, critics and theorists have grown increasingly insistent in the broader parallels that they draw between the interwar period and the present moment. This is a contemporary historiographical habit that is itself worthy of more detailed analysis. See especially George E. Marcus and Michael M. J. Fischer, *Anthropology as Cultural Critique: an Experimental Moment in the Human Sciences* (Chicago, 1986), pp. 9–10; and Hazel Carby, "The Politics of Fiction, Anthropology, and the Folk: Zora Neale Hurston," in Michael Awkward (ed.), *New Essays on Their Eyes Were Watching God* (Cambridge, 1990), p. 73.

2 Teresa de Lauretis, "Habit Changes," in *differences* 6:2–3 (1994), p. 298.

3 bell hooks, *Talking Back: Thinking Feminist, Thinking Black* (Boston, 1989), pp. 5–9. Euroethnic feminist theory is itself, of course, a primary recipient of hooks's oppositional back talk throughout this 1989 volume.

4 James Clifford, for example, gives pride of place to Benjamin's essay in his influential 1981 study "On Ethnographic Surrealism," revised and reprinted in *The Predicament of Culture: Twentieth-Century Ethnography, Literature, and Art* (Cambridge, Mass., 1988), p. 119, taking Benjamin's remarks as a general commentary on interwar cultural life, whereas I will be reading them as local and specific in their significance. Giorgio Agamben's 1978 volume *Infancy and History: Essays on the Destruction of Experience*, trans. Liz Heron (London, 1993), uses "The Storyteller" as a point of departure for a broad-based historical and philosophical consideration of what Benjamin calls the "declin[e] in value" of experience.

5 Walter Benjamin, "The Storyteller: Reflections on the Works of Nikolai Leskov" (1936), in *Illuminations*, trans. by Harry Zohn, ed. Hannah Arendt (New York, 1969). Passages from "The Storyteller" cited in these paragraphs appear on pp. 83–85.

6 Eugene Lunn, *Marxism and Modernism: an Historical Study of Lukács, Brecht, Benjamin and Adorno* (London, 1985), p. 37.
7 Benjamin, "Storyteller," p. 83.
8 Nancy Hartsock, "Rethinking Modernism: Minority vs. Majority Themes," in Abdul R. JanMohamed and David Lloyd (eds.), *The Nature and Context of Minority Discourse* (Oxford, 1990), p. 26.
9 Benjamin, "Storyteller," p. 85.
10 Ibid., p. 84.
11 The phrase is Andreas Huyssen's, from "Mass Culture as Woman: Modernism's Other," in his *After the Great Divide: Modernism, Mass Culture, Post-Modernism* (Bloomington, 1986).
12 Chandra Talpade Mohanty, "Under Western Eyes: Feminist Scholarship and Colonial Discourses," in *Boundary 2* 12:3/13:1 (1984), p. 344.
13 E. H. Carr, *What is History?* (1961; New York, 1972), p. 29.
14 Deborah McDowell, "Transferences: Black Feminist Discourse: the 'Practice' of 'Theory,'" in Diane Elam and Robyn Wiegman (eds.), *Feminism Beside Itself* (New York, 1995), p. 105; see pp. 95ff., for an incisive analysis of the "pervasiveness of the theory/practice division." See also Judith Butler and Gayle Rubin, "Sexual Traffic," in *differences* 6:2–3 (1994), p. 92–93, for a suggestive discussion of the specious divisions between "theoretical" and "empirical" oppositional scholarship.
15 Teresa de Lauretis, "The Violence of Rhetoric," in *Technologies of Gender: Essays on Theory, Film, and Fiction* (Bloomington, 1987), p. 32.
16 Raymond Williams's blisteringly ironical *Keywords* entry on the "intellectual" demonstrates the importance of attending to the long history of shifting, unstable relations between and valuations of "experience" and "intelligence." *Keywords: a Vocabulary of Culture and Society*, revised edn (Oxford, 1984), pp. 169–71.
17 Elizabeth Grosz, "The Labors of Love. Analyzing Perverse Desire: an Interrogation of Teresa de Lauretis's *The Practice of Love*," in *differences* 6:2–3 (1994), pp. 287 and 278.
18 De Lauretis, "Habit Changes," p. 307.
19 Ibid., p. 297.

1 "Familiar strangeness"

1 Zora Neale Hurston, *Their Eyes Were Watching God* (New York, 1990), p. 45.
2 Ibid., p. 45.
3 Ibid., p. 45, emphasis added.
4 This litany of adjectives appears in Franz Boas's preface to Hurston's 1935 ethnography *Mules and Men* (New York, 1990), pp. xii–xiv.
5 Alice Walker's 1975 essay "Looking for Zora" contains the classic configuration of Hurston as an ancestral presence for African-American women writers; since the publication of Walker's essay, a diverse range of women critics and writers have claimed Hurston as an intellectual ancestor. See "Looking for Zora," in *In Search of Our Mothers' Gardens* (New York, 1983).

6 This increasing pessimism, I believe, signaled the beginnings of a turn, marked in my introductory discussion of Elizabeth Grosz and Teresa de Lauretis, towards a reevalution of dominant feminist-theoretical strategies of the seventies, eighties, and early nineties. The schematic three-part history that I have given here, however, has the virtue of clarity, coupled with the vice of reductiveness. While it accurately depicts general trends in recent Hurston criticism, it avoids acknowledgment of the frequent overlap among these positions – to some extent apparent in all three examples listed below – as well as the somewhat thornier issue (worthy of far more extensive analysis) of the varying significances that Hurston's ethnographies hold for commentators based in literature and in anthropology departments. For examples of the three modes at work, see Deborah Gordon's "The Politics of Ethnographic Authority: Race and Writing in the Ethnography of Margaret Mead and Zora Neale Hurston," in Marc Manganaro (ed.), *Modernist Anthropology: From Fieldwork to Text* (Princeton, 1990) for an argument that Hurston's ethnographic writings resist the institutional imperatives of Boasian Anthropology; bell hooks's "Saving Black Folk Culture: Zora Neale Hurston as Anthropologist and Writer," in her *Yearning: Race, Gender, and Cultural Politics* (Boston, 1990) for a more divided view; and Hazel Carby's "The Politics of Fiction, Anthropology, and the Folk: Zora Neale Hurston," for a much more skeptical take on Hurston's investment in the Boasian logic of cultural "salvage." Apart from the specific realm of Hurston's ethnographic publications, Mary Helen Washington's various essays on Hurston's novels, published between the early seventies and the early nineties, comprise an eloquent and highly self-conscious example of the unfolding of the three phases that I have noted.

7 See Michele Wallace, "Who Owns Zora Neale Hurston? Critics Carve up the Legend," in her *Invisibility Blues: From Pop to Theory* (London, 1990); Carby, "Politics of Fiction,"; Mary Helen Washington, Foreword to the HarperPerennial edition of *Their Eyes Were Watching God* (New York, 1990); and Ann duCille, "The Occult of True Black Womanhood: Critical Demeanor and Black Feminist Studies," in *Signs* 19:3 (1994).

8 I will discuss critical response to these separate figures in the chapters that follow. The parallels between Hurston's reception history and those of H.D. and Kahlo are particularly striking. Carrington and Deloria, whose work did not become widely available until the late eighties, are currently being praised for the resistant capacities disclosed in their work; more critical future assessments of their work are, I think, inevitable.

9 Wallace, "Who Owns Zora Neale Hurston?," p. 181. Wallace notes that the "role model" model is "too narrow."

10 Kamala Visweswaran, "Defining Feminist Ethnography" (1988) in her *Fictions of Feminist Ethnography* (Minneapolis, 1994), p. 32. Visweswaran's "alternate *ethnographic* canon" (emphasis added) includes Hurston and Deloria.

Notes to pages 12–16

11 Gyan Prakash, "Science 'Gone Native' in Colonial India," in *Representations* 40 (Fall 1992), p. 172.
12 Williams's work on "formations" was brought to my attention by Edward W. Said's reapplication of Williams in *Culture and Imperialism* (New York, 1993), pp. 243–45.
13 For general discussions of these issues in the context of the social sciences, see John L. Aguiar, "Insider Research: an Ethnography of a Debate," in Donald A. Messerschmidt (ed.), *Anthropologists at Home in North America: Methods and Issues in the Study of One's Own Society* (Cambridge, 1981); Hussein Fahim and Katherine Helmer, "Themes and Counter-Themes: the Burg Wartenstein Symposium," in Hussein Fahim (ed.), *Indigenous Anthropology in Non-Western Countries* (Durham, 1982); Peter Rose, "Problems in Conveying the Meaning of Ethnicity: the Insider/Outsider Debate," in *Mainstreams and Margins: Jews, Blacks, and Other Americans* (New Brunswick, 1983).
14 Rose, "Insider/Outsider Debate," p. 211.
15 Abdul R. JanMohamed, "Worldliness-Without-World, Homelessness-As-Home: Toward a Definition of the Specular Border Intellectual," in Michael Sprinker (ed.), *Edward Said: a Critical Reader* (Cambridge, Mass., 1992), p. 97.
16 Teresa de Lauretis, "The Technology of Gender," in her *Technologies of Gender: Essays on Theory, Film, and Fiction* (Bloomington, 1987), p. 10.
17 Teresa de Lauretis, "Habit Changes," in *differences* 6:2–3 (1994), p. 298.
18 For a detailed account of Boasian "cultural critique," see Richard Handler, "Boasian Anthropology and the Critique of American Culture," in *American Quarterly* 42:2 (1990), pp. 252–73.
19 Clifford Geertz, "Us/Not Us: Benedict's Travels," in *Works and Lives: the Anthropologist as Author* (Stanford, 1988), p. 106.
20 Gayle Rubin, "Sexual Traffic" (interview with Judith Butler) in *differences* 6:2–3 (1994), p. 66.
21 While I am discussing this issue in the context of the 1930s and 1940s, I have been influenced by parallel discussions of the present moment: see Teresa de Lauretis, "The Violence of Rhetoric," in her *Technologies of Gender*, which contains her influential discussion of the relation between "woman" and women in poststructuralist theory; Gayatri Spivak's earlier, related analysis in "Displacement and the Discourse of Woman," in Mark Krupnick (ed.), *Displacement: Derrida and After* (Bloomington, 1983); and Elspeth Probyn's recent critique of James Clifford's work in "Moving Selves and Stationary Others: Ethnography's Ontological Dilemma," in *Sexing the Self: Gendered Positions in Cultural Studies* (New York, 1993).
22 I mean for this passage to echo and to recontextualize Teresa de Lauretis's oft-cited remark about women in poststructuralist theory: "If Nietzsche and Derrida can occupy and speak from the position of woman, it is because that position is vacant and, what is more, cannot be claimed by women." See de Lauretis, "Violence of Rhetoric," p. 32.

198

23 Alternative histories of very different forms of insider-outsider activity can be found in Robert Stepto's *From Behind the Veil: a Study of Afro–American Narrative* (Urbana, 1991), where Stepto makes an apt comparison between narratives of slavery and "participant-observation" activity; Wayne Koestenbaum's *Double Talk: the Erotics of Male Literary Collaboration* (New York, 1989), which includes commentary on gay men who worked with early twentieth-century sexologists on the categorization of gay male sexualities; and Gyan Prakash's "Science 'Gone Native' in Colonial India," which takes up the role played by Indian peasants in pageants staged by British museum administrators in colonial India.

24 Behar's exemplary history, "Introduction: Out of Exile," appeared in print as I was completing final revisions on this current volume. See Ruth Behar and Deborah Gordon (eds.), *Women Writing Culture* (Berkeley, 1995). Feminist responses to mid-eighties writings by Clifford and other cultural-studies-based analysts have themselves been wide-ranging and internally conflictual; my concern at this point, however, is to foreground the institutional tension between "cultural studies" and "area" studies, a tension most clearly and concisely addressed in hooks's brief essay. For flashpoints in these debates, see bell hooks, "Culture to Culture," in *Yearning: Race, Gender, and Cultural Politics* (Boston, 1990); Lila Abu-Lughod, "Can There Be A Feminist Ethnography?," in *Women and Performance* 5:1 (1990), pp. 7–27; Deborah Gordon, "Writing Culture, Writing Feminism," in *Inscriptions* 3–4 (1988), pp. 7–24; Frances Mascia-Lees *et al.*, "The Postmodernist Turn in Anthropology: Cautions from a Feminist Perspective," in *Signs* 15:1 (1989), pp. 7–33; Judith Newton and Judith Stacey, "Learning Not to Curse, or, Feminist Predicaments in Cultural Criticism by Men," in *Cultural Critique* (Winter 1992/93), 51–79; Probyn, "Moving Selves"; and Visweswaran, "Defining Feminist Ethnography."

25 James Clifford, "Introduction: Partial Truths," in James Clifford and George Marcus (eds.), *Writing Culture: the Poetics and Politics of Ethnography* (Berkeley, 1986), p. 21.

26 In that footnote, Clifford writes that he is "uneasy with a general notion that privileged discourse indulges in esthetic or epistemological subtleties, whereas marginal discourse 'tells it like it is.'" See "Introduction: Partial Truths," p. 21, n.11.

27 In a major 1989 essay, Valerie Smith noted how these same difficulties have also surfaced in recent years *within* feminism. Smith notes a tendency among white feminist theorists to "rematerialize their discourse" by referring to works by black women. In a passage that has since been quoted many times, Smith writes that

> This association of black women with reembodiment resembles rather closely the association, in classic Western philosophy and in nineteenth-century cultural constructions of womanhood, of women of color with the body and therefore with animal passions and slave labor. Although in these theoretical contexts the impulse to rehistoricize produces insightful readings and

illuminating theories, and is politically progressive and long overdue, nevertheless the link between black women's experiences and "the material" seems conceptually problematic. See Valerie Smith, "Black Feminist Theory and the Representation of the 'Other,'" in Cheryl Wall (ed.), *Changing Our Own Words: Essays on Criticism, Theory, and Writing by Black Women* (New Brunswick, 1989), p. 45.

28 hooks, "Culture to Culture," p. 125.

29 Ibid., p. 126.

30 Visweswaran, in "Defining Feminist Ethnography," made a slightly earlier and largely congruent case for this archival gap in Clifford's analysis.

31 James Clifford, "Traveling Cultures," in Lawrence Grossberg, Cary Nelson, and Paula A. Treichler (eds.), *Cultural Studies* (New York, 1992), p. 97.

32 For much more extensive commentary on the "form"/"content" distinction in Clifford's essay, see Gordon, "Writing Culture/Writing Feminism," pp. 15–17.

33 James Clifford, "On Ethnographic Surrealism," in *The Predicament of Culture: Twentieth-Century Ethnography, Literature, and Art* (Cambridge, Mass., 1988), p. 145, emphasis added.

34 In "Traveling Cultures," Clifford notes his "embarassment" upon discerning these sorts of gaps in his earlier work. See p. 104.

35 Raymond Williams, "Metropolitan Perceptions and the Emergence of Modernism," in his *The Politics of Modernism: Against the New Conformists*, edited by Tony Pinkney (London, 1989), p. 45.

36 Edward W. Said, "Secular Criticism," in his *The World, the Text, and the Critic* (Cambridge, Mass., 1983), p. 19.

37 Ibid., pp. 19 and 20.

38 Lillian Faderman, *Odd Girls and Twilight Lovers: a History of Lesbian Life in Twentieth-Century America* (New York, 1991), pp. 37–61.

39 Said, "Secular Criticism," p. 22.

40 Nina Miller, "The Bonds of Free Love," in *Genders* 11 (Fall 1991), pp. 37–57.

41 Said, *Culture and Imperialism* p. 244. Much of James Clifford's commentary in "Traveling Cultures" is also pertinent to these issues.

42 Sandra Gilbert and Susan Gubar, "'Forward into the Past': the Female Affiliative Complex," in *No Man's Land: the Place of the Woman Writer in the Twentieth Century*, vol. I, *The War of the Words* (New Haven, 1988).

43 See Susan Stanford Friedman, "Against Discipleship: Collaboration and Intimacy in the Relationship of H.D. and Freud," in *Literature and Psychology* 33:3–4 (1987), pp. 89–108; Gordon, "Politics of Ethnographic Authority."

44 For a stunning analysis of a career circumscribed by these kinds of shifting affiliations, see Biddy Martin's 1989 book on Lou Andreas-Salomé, *Woman and Modernity: the (Life)Styles of Lou Andreas-Salomé* (Ithaca, 1991). There are, of course, exceptions to this pattern of multiple affiliation, but they tend to fall into the category of idiosyn-

cratic cases involving inheritance, whether institutional (as in Anna Freud's case) or financial (as in Marie Bonaparte's).
45 Gordon, "Politics of Ethnographic Authority," p. 162.
46 Friedman, "Against Discipleship," p. 94.
47 Klaus Theweleit, *Object–Choice (All You Need is Love . . .)* (1990), trans. by Malcolm R. Green (London, 1994), pp. 65 and 57. I will address Theweleit's commentary in more detail in chapter 6 below.
48 Gayle Rubin: "The Traffic in Women: Notes on the 'Political Economy' of Sex," in Ilene J. Philipson and Karen V. Hansen (eds.), *Women, Class, and the Feminist Imagination: a Socialist–Feminist Reader* (Philadelphia, 1990).
49 Ibid., p. 81.
50 Ibid., p. 82.
51 Ibid., p. 81.
52 See Nancy K. Miller, *Getting Personal: Feminist Occasions and Other Autobiographical Acts* (New York, 1991), p. 125, where Miller cites the widespread influence of "The Traffic in Women" as an example of how, during the "apocalyptically illuminating" decade of the 1970s, it was "hard to resist the appeal of the monolith." Chandra Talpade Mohanty's "Under Western Eyes: Feminist Scholarship and Colonial Discourses, in *Boundary* 2 12:3/13:1 (1984), pp. 333–58, and Susan Fraiman's "Geometries of Race and Gender: Eve Sedgwick, Spike Lee, Charlayne Hunter-Gault," in *Feminist Studies* 20:1 (1994), pp. 67–84, include careful critical responses to the universalism of kinship models based upon uninflected arguments about the brutality and oppressiveness of the exchange of women.
53 Rubin, "Traffic in Women," p. 87.
54 Rubin and Butler, "Sexual Traffic," p. 65.
55 Ibid., p. 88.
56 Rubin would be likely to raise sharp objections to my admittedly "exigetical" (her term) reading of her mid-seventies essay; she makes careful social-scientific distinctions in her own more recent commentary between "kinship" arrangements (which are involuntary) and "voluntary" forms of association (among which, no doubt, she would include specifically *intellectual* affiliation). I'm not so persuaded that "voluntary" forms of association are actually all that "voluntary." What I am after, moreover, is what Chandra Mohanty calls the "latent self-presentation" of Rubin's essay: in other words, the way in which, in Rubin's analysis of kinship structures, the workings of the academic institution are allegorized and problematized. In this respect, Judith Butler's pointed 1994 interrogation of Rubin's strict application of the notion of "kinship" is extremely useful. See Mohanty, "Under Western Eyes," p. 344; Rubin and Butler, "Sexual Traffic," pp. 86–87.
57 See Carby, "Politics of Fiction," and Gordon, "Politics of Ethnographic Authority." Carby and Gordon both focus on Hurston's mediations between the cultural context of the Harlem Renaissance and the community of anthropologists at Columbia: Carby, in order to examine Hurston's implicatedness in the colonialist crosscurrents

that were palpable in both formations; Gordon, as I've already noted, in order to celebrate Hurston's interdisciplinary experimentation in *Tell My Horse*. Although my strategies, methods, and conclusions diverge sharply from Carby's and Gordon's own very different readings of Hurston, their turn towards the issue of Hurston's split engagements – which I term here "multiple affiliation," and which I elaborate in my examination of disciplinary expansion and incorporation – was a crucial one in Hurston's recent reception history.

58 H.D., *Tribute to Freud* (New York: New Directions, 1974), p. 107.

59 Tania Modleski, "Doing Justice to the Subjects," (forthcoming, 1997); Gayatri Spivak, "Acting Bits/Identity Talk," in *Critical Inquiry* 18 (Summer 1992), pp. 770–803.

60 Edward Said, "Representing the Colonized: Anthropology's Interlocutors," in *Critical Inquiry* 15 (Winter 1989), pp. 222–23.

61 Susan Stanford Friedman, "The Return of the Repressed in Women's Narrative," in *Journal of Narrative Technique* 19 (Winter 1989), p. 145.

62 Brenda R. Silver, "Textual Criticism as Feminist Practice: Or, Who's Afraid of Virginia Woolf Part II," in George Bornstein (ed.), *Representing Modernist Texts: Editing as Interpretation* (Ann Arbor, 1991).

63 Nathaniel Mackey, "Other: From Noun to Verb," in *Representations* 39 (Summer 1992), p. 52. It is worth noting here that important aspects of Mackey's theoretical argument are attributed to Zora Neale Hurston's prior work.

64 De Lauretis, "Technology of Gender," p. 10.

65 Paul De Angeles, "Interview with Leonora Carrington," in *Leonora Carrington: the Mexican Years* (San Francisco, 1991), p. 42.

66 As was the case in my earlier reading of Rubin's "'The Traffic in Women,'" this reading of Abu-Lughod's work is also largely "exegetical," and is not meant as a faithful summary of her own, clearly stated positions.

67 Lila Abu-Lughod, *Writing Women's Worlds: Bedouin Stories* (Berkeley, 1993), pp. xii-xiii.

68 Ibid., p. xii.

69 Ibid., p. xv.

70 See Lila Abu-Lughod, "Fieldwork of a Dutiful Daughter" in Soraya Altorki and Camillia El-Solh (eds.), *Arab Women in the Field*, (Syracuse, 1988).

71 Lila Abu-Lughod, "Preface" to *Writing Women's Worlds*, p. xvii. For more extensive theoretical consideration of the problem of multiple address, see Lata Mani's "Multiple Mediations: Feminist Scholarship in the Age of Multinational Reception," in *Feminist Review* 35 (Summer 1990), 24–41, and Barbara Johnson's "Thresholds of Difference: Structures of Address in Zora Neale Hurston," in her *A World of Difference* (Baltimore, 1987).

72 Abu-Lughod, "Preface," p. xvii.

73 Abu-Lughod, "Can There Be A Feminist Ethnography?," p. 19.

74 Lila Abu-Lughod, "Introduction" to *Writing Women's Worlds*, p. 3.

75 Abu-Lughod, "Can There Be A Feminist Ethnography?," p. 26n.

2 A courtesan's confession: Frida Kahlo and Surrealist entrepreneurship

1 It was, however, repeated posthumously, and in much the same terms. For analyses of Kahlo's recent celebrity, see Oriana Baddeley, " 'Her Dress Hangs Here': De-Frocking the Kahlo Cult," in *The Oxford Art Journal* 14:1 (1991), and Janis Bergman-Carton, "Strike a Pose: the Framing of Madonna and Frida Kahlo," in *Texas Studies in Language and Literature* 35:4 (1993).

2 André Breton and Diego Rivera, "Manifesto: Towards a Free Revolutionary Art," trans. Dwight Macdonald, in *Partisan Review* 6:1 (Fall 1938), pp. 49–53; "Leon Trotsky to André Breton," in *Partisan Review* 6:2 (Winter 1939), pp. 126–27.

3 The brief history of the Kahlo/Breton exchange has been recounted repeatedly; the standard biographical sources – from which I draw throughout this chapter – are Hayden Herrera's *Frida: a Biography of Frida Kahlo* (New York, 1983); Raquel Tibol's *Frida Kahlo: una vida abierta* (1983), translated by Elinor Randall as *Frida Kahlo: an Open Life* (Albuquerque, 1993); Sarah Lowe's *Frida Kahlo* (New York, 1991); and Hayden Herrera's "Beauty to His Beast: Frida Kahlo and Diego Rivera," in Whitney Chadwick and Isabelle de Courtivron, *Significant Others: Creativity and Intimate Partnership* (London, 1993). For important commentary on feminist resistances in Kahlo's work, see Oriana Baddeley and Valerie Fraser, *Drawing the Line: Art and Cultural Identity in Contemporary Latin America* (London, 1989), and Jean Franco, *Plotting Women: Gender and Representation in Mexico* (New York, 1989), pp. 102–112. Finally, Claudia Schaefer's *Textured Lives: Women, Art, and Representation in Modern Mexico* (Tucson, 1992), while largely unconcerned with Kahlo's involvement with Surrealism, is full of important cultural–historiographical detail and analysis.

4 See, for example, Whitney Chadwick, *Women Artists and the Surrealist Movement* (Boston, 1985); and the essays collected in *Surrealism and Women*, ed. Mary Ann Caws, Rudolf Kuenzli, and Gwen Raaberg (Cambridge, Mass., 1991).

5 Kahlo biographer Hayden Herrera, for example, writes in *Frida: a Biography of Frida Kahlo* that Kahlo found Breton "pretentious, feckless, and boring" (p.227), and we have no reason to suspect otherwise.

6 Sarah M. Lowe, "Essay," in *The Diary of Frida Kahlo: an Intimate Self-Portrait* (New York, 1995), p. 27. Lowe gives a clear and concise description of "Breton's compulsive need to arbitrate what exactly might be considered Surrealism – ironic in light of his movement's anarchic founding ideas" (p. 27).

7 James Clifford, "On Ethnographic Surrealism," in his *The Predicament of Culture: Twentieth-Century Ethnography, Literature, and Art* (Cambridge, Mass., 1988), p. 145. For more recent articulations and extensions of Clifford's positions, see Sidra Stich's catalog texts for the University Art Museum, Berkeley's 1990 exhibition *Anxious Visions: Surrealist Art* (New York, 1990) and Martica Sawin's "El surrealismo etnográfico y la América indígena," included in the catalog for the

1989/90 exhibition *El surrealismo entre viejo y nuevo mundo* (Centro Atlantico de Arte Moderno, 1990).

8 James Clifford, "Traveling Cultures," in Lawrence Grossberg, Cary Nelson, and Paula A. Treichler (eds.), *Cultural Studies* (New York, 1992), pp. 104–5.

9 Kenneth Burke, "Surrealism," in *New Directions in Prose and Poetry* (Norfolk, Conn., 1940), p. 563.

10 Breton, "Manifesto of Surrealism" (1924), in *Manifestoes of Surrealism*, trans. Richard Seaver and Helen R. Lane (Ann Arbor, 1972), p. 35.

11 Sidra Stich, *Anxious Visions: Surrealist Art* (University Art Museum, Berkeley, California; New York, 1990), p. 11.

12 Edward W. Said, "Representing the Colonized: Anthropology's Interlocutors," in *Critical Inquiry* 15 (Winter 1989), p. 210.

13 Julien Levy, *Surrealism* (1936) (New York, 1995). In an appendix to Levy's *Memoir of an Art Gallery* (New York, 1977), Levy includes a list of exhibitions held at his gallery, including Max Ernst, Dali, Man Ray, and other prominent figures associated with the movement; de Chirico, Picasso, and other painters who influenced Surrealism; and (toward the end of the decade) younger artists from the Bretonian second wave including Kahlo and Leonor Fini.

14 Levy, *Memoir of an Art Gallery*, p. 203.

15 Ibid., p. 203.

16 Ibid., p. 13.

17 Kahlo's objections to Breton's French catalog essay are documented in Herrera, *Frida*, p. 232, and Tibol, *Frida Kahlo*, p. 69. The review to which I refer appeared in *Time* magazine, 14 November 1938, p. 29.

18 The linguistic stratification to which I here refer reflects more largely upon Surrealist practice in the late 1930s. Suleiman notes in *Subversive Intent* (p. 31) that "women from other countries" than France tended to be especially welcome, and suggests that as *writers*, they were "less threatening to the French male Surrealists' egos." British writer Leonora Carrington's first book, it should be recalled here, was published in French, complete with uncorrected errors.

19 My account of the 1938 exhibition draws upon a variety of sources that will be noted in the course of my discussion. Special mention, however, goes to Hayden Herrera, who reproduces in her 1983 biography of Kahlo the sequence of paintings listed in the catalog, and identifies many of the works that were displayed under different titles than those by which they are now known. Herrera, *Frida*, pp. 230–31 and p. 471 n. 230.

20 Herrera notes in *Frida* that the identity of the painting entitled *Eye* is uncertain, hypothesizing that "it could be the *Portrait of Diego*, whom we know she thought of as having a particularly acute eye. Or it could be a self-portrait, with the title a pun on the word 'I' " (p. 471 n). My necessarily speculative conclusion was drawn in this way: *Portrait of Diego* was lent to Levy, as Herrera points out, by its owner Edward G. Robinson; it was also one of the paintings reproduced in *Vogue*'s 11/1/38 coverage of the exhibition; thus, its appearance in the show is near-certain. Moreover, only one other title

in the exhibition catalog, *Passionately in Love*, could fit the portrait, and Hayden points out that *Passionately in Love* is likely to be the ironical exhibition title for the violent painting now known as *A Few Small Nips*.

21 Herrera, *Frida*, p. 417 n. 230.

22 In the 1993 essay "Beauty to His Beast: Frida Kahlo and Diego Rivera," p. 120, Hayden Herrera reinforces this resilient reading of Kahlo's work by contrasting her self-portraits to Rivera's murals: "[Rivera] painted monumental murals embracing broad historical and political subjects on vast public walls. By contrast, the majority of Kahlo's paintings are small, extraordinarily personal self-portraits. Although her focus was narrow, she probed deep, and her self-portraits capture universal feelings so vividly that they pull out all our empathy and reveal us to ourselves."

23 André Breton, "Frida Kahlo de Rivera," in *Surrealism and Painting*, translated by Simon Watson Taylor (New York, 1972), pp. 143 and 144.

24 Ibid., p. 144.

25 For useful commentary on the cultural crosscurrents flowing through early twentieth-century Mexico City, see the biographical sources noted above. Sarah Lowe, in particular, performs a blistering critique of Breton's critical presumption. See Lowe, *Frida Kahlo*, pp. 77–80.

26 Clifford, "On Ethnographic Surrealism."

27 I am quoting here from Simon Watson Taylor's translation of the catalog essay; Breton's autoallusion in the Kahlo essay – "Je suis la pensée sur le bain dans la pièce sans glaces" – matches exactly the text of his 1928 novel.

28 Bertram Wolfe, "Rise of Another Rivera," *Vogue*, (November 1938), p. 66.

29 See Baddeley, " 'Her Dress Hangs Here.' "

30 Tibol, *Frida Kahlo*, p. 67.

31 Wolfe, "Rise of Another Rivera," p. 64.

32 Ibid., p. 66.

33 Diego Rivera, "Frida Kahlo y el arte mexicano," quoted in Tibol, *Frida Kahlo*, p. 124.

34 Baddeley, " 'Her Dress Hangs Here'"; Bergman-Carton, "Strike a Pose." See also Schaefer's *Textured Lives*, p. 13, for a comparison of Kahlo's artifice to that of contemporaneous film stars; and Sarah M. Lowe's 1995 "Essay," where Lowe makes the pointed and extremely useful observation that "there is an uncanny restraint evident in Kahlo's self-portraits, a false honesty, an omission in every one" (p. 26).

35 Herrera, "Beauty to His Beast," p. 126.

36 Elspeth Probyn, "Moving Selves and Stationary Others: Ethnography's Ontological Dilemma," in *Sexing the Self: Gendered Positions in Cultural Studies* (New York, 1993).

37 Franco, *Plotting Women*, p. 107.

38 Barbara Johnson, "My Monster/My Self," in her *A World of Difference* (Baltimore, 1987), p. 146.

39 Lowe, "Essay," p. 26.

40 Eugene Lunn, *Marxism and Modernism: an Historical Study of Lukács, Brecht, Benjamin and Adorna* (London, 1985), p. 36.
41 "The New Julien Levy Gallery," in *Harper's Bazaar*, November 1937, p. 138, emphasis added.
42 Mark Polizzotti, "Introduction" to Julien Levy's *Surrealism*, p. vii.
43 Ibid., p. vii.
44 Coco Fusco, in a joint 1993 interview with Guillermo Gómez-Peña, observes that

> the Frida Kahlo venerated by American feminists is a very different Frida Kahlo to the one people learn about in Mexico, in the Chicano community. In her country, she is recognized as an important artist and a key figure in revolutionary politics of early twentieth century Mexico. Her communist affiliations are made very clear. Her relationship with Trotsky is underscored. All her political activities with Diego Rivera are constantly emphasized. The connection between her art and her politics is always made.

See Anna Johnson, interview with Guillermo Gómez-Peña and Coco Fusco in *Bomb* (Winter 1993), p. 38. My reading of the politics of the Levy Gallery show is meant to provide a history for the sorts of "venerat[ions]" that Fusco criticizes here.
45 Quoted in Tibol, *Frida Kahlo*, p. 102.
46 Ibid., p. 101.
47 Franco, *Plotting Women*, p. 102.
48 Detailed commentaries on the significance of *La Malinche* appear throughout the recent critical literature on gender and sexuality in Mexican culture; see Baddeley and Fraser, *Drawing the Line*; Franco, *Plotting Women*; and Mary Louise Pratt, "'Yo soy La Malinche': Chicana Writers and the Poetics of Ethnonationalism," in *Callaloo* 16:4 (1993), 859–73, in which Pratt discusses recent efforts by Chicana writers to reexamine her culpability.
49 Breton and Rivera, "Manifesto," p. 49.
50 Trotsky, "Leon Trotsky to André Breton," p. 126.
51 Breton, "Frida Kahlo de Rivera," p. 144.
52 Ibid., p. 144.
53 Ibid.
54 Ibid.
55 Frances Toor, *A Treasury of Mexican Folkways* (New York, 1947), p. 64.
56 Ibid., p. 64.
57 For an important discussion of Kahlo's complex relatedness to Mexican popular traditions, see Schaefer, *Textured Lives*, pp. 32–36.
58 James Clifford's "Histories of the Tribal and the Modern," in *The Predicament of Culture*, p. 192, has influenced me here: Clifford notes that while "[a]bstraction and conceptualism, are, of course, pervasive in the arts of the non-Western World," nonetheless "[t]o say that they share with modernism a rejection of certain naturalist projects is not to suggest anything like an affinity." Thus, what is clear in *Demoiselles* is that Picasso means to encode this questionable "affinity."

59 Breton, "Frida Kahlo de Rivera," p. 143.

60 Breton, *L'art magique* (Paris, 1957), quoted by William S. Rubin in *Dada, Surrealism, and Their Heritage* (1968; New York, 1982), p. 80.

61 Nancy Deffebach Breslow, "Frida Kahlo's 'The Square is Theirs': Spoofing Giorgio de Chirico," in *Arts* magazine 56 (January 1982), pp. 120–23.

62 Rubin, *Dada, Surrealism*, p. 82.

63 Franco, *Plotting Women*, p. 107.

64 Teresa de Lauretis, "The Technology of Gender," in her *Technologies of Gender: Essays on Theory, Film, and Fiction* (Bloomington, 1987), p. 25.

65 Ibid., p. 26.

3 Leonora Carrington's self-revisions

1 Carrington is now in her eighties, living part-time in the United States and in Mexico. The publication history given in this first paragraph is derived from Marina Warner's extensive editorial commentary in Carrington's *The House of Fear: Notes From Down Below* (New York, 1988), which I will discuss in some detail later in the chapter. Biographical information on Carrington derives from Warner's "Introduction," and from other sources that will be acknowledged during the course of the chapter.

2 Leonora Carrington, "The Debutante," trans. Marina Warner with Kathrine Talbot in *The House of Fear: Notes from Down Below*, p. 47.

3 Carrington, "The Debutante," p. 48. Carrington's reference to the mother's "pale"-faced "rage" might well be read as an indictment of the forms of racism embedded in the metaphorics of debutante culture. Historian Angela Lambert, for example, points out that the expression "blue blood" is derived from *"sangre azul,* claimed by certain families of Castile, as being uncontaminated by Moorish, Jewish or other admixture; probably founded on the blueness of the veins of people of fair complexion (*Shorter Oxford Dictionary*). Thus racism and anti-Semitism are also inherent in the idea of blue-bloodedness." See Lambert, *1939: the Last Season of Peace* (London, 1989), p. 15.

4 Christopher Ogden, *Life of the Party: the Biography of Pamela Digby Churchill Hayward Harriman* (Boston, 1994), p. 58. Harriman's debut was in 1938, two years after Carrington's.

5 Lambert, *1939*, p. 18. For a distinct but related perspective, see Jessica Mitford's memoir *Hons and Rebels* (London, 1978).

6 These racialist dynamics can also be detected in contemporaneous popular-cultural uses of images of young aristocratic British women. In a cold cream advertisement printed in the April 1937 issue of the international fashion journal *Harper's Bazaar* (p. 131), "high-born women" who would participate in the coronation ceremonies for George VI were praised for the "fragile, transparent beauty of their exquisitely cared for skins."

7 In the early decades of this century, with increasing popular awareness of developments within the discipline of anthropology, a series
of smugly self-mocking "debutante jokes" – which compared debutante rituals to puberty rites among non-Western peoples – started to
emerge among the upper classes. Edith Wharton's *The Age of Innocence* (1920), for example, is filled with jokes of this kind. While these
jokes successfully mocked the pretensions of those who presumed
that their activities stood for the height of "civilization," they also
required a generic (and utterly problematical) hypothesis of a "primitive" cultural "other" to serve as the ultimate butt of the joke. Thus,
while Carrington's short story bears some resemblance to this kind of
humor, her tone is quite different: she undermines its smugness by
foregrounding violence in an extremely disruptive way.

8 The "marriage market" is a blunt, sardonic term that appears
throughout the literature on British debutante culture, used by
debutantes and non-debutantes alike. Carrington's comments about
her own debutante season appear in her interview with Paul De
Angeles, published in the exhibition catalog ("Interview with
Leonora Carrington") for *Leonora Carrington: the Mexican Years (1943–
1985)* (San Francisco, 1991), p. 34. Other major interviews are repro-
duced in interview essays: see Susan Rubin Suleiman, "The Bird
Superior Meets the Bride of the Wind: Leonora Carrington and Max
Ernst," in *Significant Others: Creativity and Intimate Partnership*, ed.
Whitney Chadwick and Isabelle de Courtivron, (London, 1993); and
Warner, "Introduction".

9 De Angeles, "Interview with Leonora Carrington," p. 34.

10 See, for example, Renée Riese Hubert's "Beyond Initiation: Leonora
Carrington and Max Ernst," in *Magnifying Mirrors: Women, Surrealism, and Partnership* (Lincoln, Neb., 1994), p. 131. Hubert, who reads
the story much more optimistically than me, argues that in order
"[t]o create the desired rift between the child and her parents,
between freedom and social conventions, the author joins together
without cause, explanation, or transition the human and the bestial."

11 Kenneth Burke, "Surrealism," in *New Directions in Prose and Poetry*
(Norfolk, Conn., 1940), p. 563.

12 See "Bomb Beribboned," an unsigned *Time* magazine review of
Kahlo's 1938 show at the Julien Levy Gallery. There, the anonymous
critic wrote about "scholarly, pale-faced, silken-voiced Herbert Read,
who occupies the magnificently ambiguous position of arch Surrealist
apologist and editor of the *Burlington Magazine*, England's most
conservative art publication." *Time* magazine, 14 November 1938,
p. 29.

13 De Angeles, "Interview with Leonora Carrington," p. 40.

14 Mitford, *Hons and Rebels*, p. 34. Huxley's writing (along with Gide's
and Lawrence's) was, for Mitford, bound up with an "art school"
milieu that she treats almost as sardonically as she does the more
conventional debutante set. Elizabeth Bowen's essay appeared in
Spectator 2 (December 1936), and is quoted in Donald Watt's *Aldous
Huxley: the Critical Heritage* (Boston, 1975), p. 275.

15 Aldous Huxley, *Eyeless in Gaza* (1936; London, 1950), p. 290.
16 Ibid., p. 291.
17 Ibid., p. 291.
18 Sandra Gilbert and Susan Gubar have commented on Huxley's "sense of a literary apocalypse set in motion by the changing literary relations of the sexes," and I think it is appropriate to understand Carrington's "Down Below," in part, as a feminist recasting of the gendered metacommentary that runs throughout *Eyeless in Gaza*. Sandra Gilbert and Susan Gubar, *No Man's Land: the Place of the Woman Writer in the Twentieth Century*, vol. I, *The War of the Words* (New Haven, 1988), p. 133.
19 Huxley, *Eyeless in Gaza*, pp. 304–5.
20 Warner, "Introduction," p. 18.
21 Ibid., p. 16.
22 Walter Benjamin, "The Storyteller" (1936), translated by Harry Zohn in *Illuminations*, edited by Hannah Arendt (New York, 1969), pp. 83–84.
23 Susan Rubin Suleiman, *Subversive Intent: Gender, Politics, and the Avant-Garde* (Cambridge, Mass., 1990), p. 172; Hubert, "Beyond Initiation," p. 115.
24 Leonora Carrington's "Down Below" appeared first in English, with translation by Victor Llona, in *VVV* 4 (February 1944), pp. 70–86.
25 The photograph appears in a small reproduction on the final page of the essay. Ibid., p. 86.
26 Ogden, *Life of the Party*, p. 58.
27 "Down Below," in *VVV* 4, p. 70.
28 Pierre Mabille, "Le Paradis," in *VVV* 4, p. 33.
29 Ibid., p. 33. The "paradise complex" and the "edenic myth" – operating in the services of an attainment of "les délices infinies du Paradis" – are diagnosed by Mabille in terminology that is self-consciously and somewhat sardonically pedantic and clinical.
30 Ibid., pp. 33 and 36.
31 Carrington, "Down Below" (1944), p. 70.
32 Ibid.
33 Ibid., p. 73, emphasis in original.
34 Ibid.
35 Warner, "Introduction," p. 215, emphasis added.
36 See "Down Below" (1944), p. 71: "I jammed in my anguish beyond all power of description. I jammed in the motions of my body"; "Down Below" (1988), p. 168, "My anguish jammed me completely." See "Down Below" (1944), p. 77: "I was penetrated by all of this as by a foreign body and such a torture was beyond any attempt at description"; and "Down Below" (1988), p. 186: "I was penetrated by all of this as by a foreign body. This was torture."
37 In her "Introduction" to *The House of Fear*, p. 15, Marina Warner notes that the first edition of *La Maison de la peur* (1938) was published "with its original spelling and grammar intact," and thus, with Carrington's errors.
38 Suleiman, "The Bird Superior Meets the Bride of the Wind," p. 115.

39 Carrington, "Down Below," in *VVV* 4, p. 77; "Down Below," in *The House of Fear*, p. 185.
40 Carrington, "Down Below," in *VVV* 4, p. 83; "Down Below," in *The House of Fear*, p. 199.
41 Carrington, "Down Below," in *VVV* 4, p. 70; "Down Below," in *The House of Fear*, p. 164.
42 Carrington, "Down Below," in *VVV* 4, pp. 72–73.
43 Carrington, "Down Below," in *The House of Fear*, pp. 171–72.
44 Carrington, "Down Below," in *VVV* 4, p. 74; "Down Below," in *The House of Fear*, p. 175.
45 Hubert, "Beyond Initiation," p. 114.
46 Hubert does remark upon one fascinating but minor change that appeared in the intermediate editions of the text; see ibid., p. 115.
47 Marina Warner, "A Note on the Texts," in *The House of Fear*, p. 215.
48 Paul Fussell, *Abroad: British Literary Traveling Between the Wars* (New York, 1980), p. 36.
49 Carrington, "Down Below," in *VVV* 4, p. 73; "Down Below," in *The House of Fear*, p. 172.
50 Patricia Joplin, "The Voice of the Shuttle is Ours" (1984) in *Rape and Representation*, ed. Lynn A. Higgins and Brenda R. Silver (New York, 1991); Susan Fraiman, "Geometries of Race and Gender: Eve Sedgwick, Spike Lee, Charlayne Hunter-Gault" in *Feminist Studies* 20:1 (Spring 1994), pp. 67–84.
51 Suleiman, *Subversive Intent*, p. 110.
52 Breton writes that Nadja took pleasure in refusing him, and qualifies her pleasure with the adjective "malin," denoting cunning and calculation. Interestingly, Richard Howard's 1960 Grove Press translation of the novel glosses "malin" as the relatively understated "sly," while Suleiman's scholarly translation of the passage in *Subversive Intent* transforms "malin" into the much more pointed and vivid "nasty." See André Breton, *Nadja* (Paris, 1964), p. 134; Breton, *Nadja*, trans. Richard Howard (New York, 1960), p. 113; Suleiman, *Subversive Intent*, p. 110.

4 Hurston among the Boasians

1 Nathaniel Mackey: "Other: From Noun to Verb," in *Representations* 39 (Summer 1992), pp. 53–54.
2 Barbara Johnson, "Thresholds of Difference: Structures of Address in Zora Neale Hurston," in *A World of Difference* (Baltimore, 1987), p. 172.
3 Trinh T. Minh-Ha, "Outside In Inside Out," in *When the Moon Waxes Red: Representation, Gender, and Cultural Politics* (New York, 1991).
4 Oriana Baddeley discusses the telegraphing of Frida Kahlo's concerns into the present moment in " 'Her Dress Hangs Here': De-Frocking the Kahlo Cult," in *The Oxford Art Journal* 14:1 (1991); for other examples of this critical strategy at work, see Susan Rubin Suleiman's juxtaposition of Leonora Carrington's work with work by contemporary novelist Jeanette Winterson in *Subversive Intent: Gender, Politics, and the Avant-Garde* (Cambridge, Mass., 1990), p. 163; and Elizabeth Hirsch's

discussion of H.D.'s anticipations of more recent psychoanalytic theory in "New Eyes: H.D., Modernism, and the Psychoanalysis of Seeing," in *Literature and Psychology* 32:3 (1986).

5 Robert Hemenway's *Zora Neale Hurston: a Literary Biography* (Urbana, 1977) remains the standard account of Hurston's life, from which I draw throughout this essay.

6 Quandra Prettyman Stadler, "Learning What She Wanted: Zora Neale Hurston '28," *Barnard College Alumnae Magazine* (Winter 1979), p. 16.

7 Melville J. Herskovits, *The Anthropometry of the American Negro* (1930; New York, 1970), p. xiv.

8 Hurston mentions Benedict briefly in her autobiography and in letters to Boas, and the two women shared a brief correspondence that is preserved with Benedict's papers at Vassar. Although Hurston's transcripts contain no record of courses taken with Benedict, a letter in the Barnard archives from Benedict to the registrar indicates that Hurston submitted an essay to Benedict in January 1927 for academic credit. (Benedict to A. E. Meyer, 23 December 1926). Benedict was editor of the *Journal of American Folk-Lore* when Hurston published "Hoodoo in America" there in 1931.

9 Arnold Krupat, "Ethnography and Literature: a History of Their Convergence," in his *Ethnocriticism: Ethnography, History, Literature* (Berkeley, 1992), p. 67.

10 My extremely brief and selective overview of Boasianism in the twenties and thirties comes from a number of sources. In addition to records from Columbia and Barnard, I have depended upon the following sources: Ruth Benedict, *An Anthropologist at Work*, edited by Margaret Mead (Boston, 1959); Margaret Caffrey, *Ruth Benedict: Stranger in This Land* (Austin, 1989); Melville J. Herskovits, *Franz Boas: the Science of Man in the Making* (New York, 1953); Margaret Mead, "Apprenticeship Under Boas," in Walter Goldschmidt (ed.), *The American Anthropologist, Memoir No. 89: the Anthropology of Franz Boas: Essays on the Centennial of His Birth* (New York, 1959); Margaret Mead, *Blackberry Winter: My Earlier Years* (New York, 1972); Margaret Mead, *Ruth Benedict* (New York, 1974); Judith Modell, *Ruth Benedict: Patterns of a Life* (Philadelphia, 1983); George Stocking, *Race, Culture, and Evolution: Essays in the History of Anthropology* (New York, 1968); George Stocking, "Introduction" to *A Franz Boas Reader: the Shaping of American Anthropology, 1883–1911* (New York, 1974). Finally, Ann Douglas's *Terrible Honesty: Mongrel Manhattan in the 1920s* (New York, 1995), contains useful and detailed commentary on the cultural overlap between "Harlem" and "Columbia"; see chapter 8, "Taking Harlem," pp. 303–45; particular comments on the Boasians appear on pp. 305–6.

11 Boas, quoted in *The World*, 14 February 1926 (clipping, Columbiana Library, Columbia University).

12 Mead, "Apprenticeship Under Boas," p. 30.

13 David Levering Lewis, *When Harlem Was in Vogue* (New York, 1981), p. 116.

14 Melville J. Herskovits, "The Negro's Americanism," in his *The New Negro* (1925), ed. Alain Locke (New York, 1986), p. 353.

15 bell hooks, in *Yearning* (Boston, 1990) and Hazel Carby, in "The Politics of Fiction, Anthropology, and the Folk," in Michael Awkward (ed.), *New Essays on Their Eyes Were Watching God* (Cambridge, 1990) have both commented on Hurston's implicatedness in the Boasian logic of salvage; I will go on to discuss their specific positions later in the chapter.

16 For a much fuller discussion of the *varieties* of Boasian irony, see Arnold Krupat, "Modernism, Irony, Anthropology: the Work of Franz Boas" in *Ethnocriticism*.

17 Herskovits, "The Negro's Americanism," p. 353.

18 Ibid., p. 353.

19 Richard Handler, "Boasian Anthropology and the Critique of American Culture," in *American Quarterly* 42:2 (1990), pp. 255–57.

20 Clifford Geertz, "Us/Not-Us: Benedict's Travels," in his *Works and Lives: the Anthropologist as Author* (Stanford, 1988), pp. 106–7.

21 James Clifford, "On Ethnographic Surrealism," in his *The Predicament of Culture: Twentieth-Century Ethnography, Literature, and Art* (Cambridge, Mass., 1988).

22 My interpretations here have been influenced by Elspeth Probyn's readings of similar tactics of self-ironization in contemporary "Cultural Studies"-based analyses. See Probyn, "Moving Selves and Stationary Others: Ethnography's Ontological Dilemma," in her *Sexing the Self: Gendered Positions in Cultural Studies* (New York, 1993). Deborah Gordon gives a related analysis of the limits of Boasian self-irony in her important 1990 comparison of Hurston's *Tell My Horse* to Margaret Mead's *Coming of Age in Samoa*, where Gordon argues that Mead's technique "depended on the setting up of a relationship between self and other in which the other was absorbed within the self, swallowed up by the demand for America's self-scrutiny." See Gordon, "The Politics of Ethnographic Authority: Race and Writing in the Ethnography of Margaret Mead and Zora Neale Hurston," in Marc Manganaro (ed.), *Modernist Anthropology: From Fieldwork to Text* (Princeton, 1990), p. 151. My description of this "swallow[ing]" process is a bit more literal-minded than Gordon's; I suggest that Boasian self-irony ("self-scrutiny") relied upon a *ventriloquistic* technique that bore a subtle relationship to, for example, Joel Chandler Harris's *Uncle Remus* stories.

23 In a 1992 essay "The Occult of Black Womanhood: Critical Demeanor and Black Feminist Studies," in *Signs* 19:3 (1994), pp. 607–12, Ann DuCille wrote about the shortcomings of this strategy in contemporary work by white critics working on African–American literary traditions.

24 Michael North, in *The Dialect of Modernism* (New York, 1994), pp. 180–83, makes important observations about Hurston's responses to white mimicry of African–American cultural forms.

25 Teresa de Lauretis, "The Violence of Rhetoric," in her *Technologies of Gender* (Bloomington, 1987), p. 32.

26 Mary Helen Washington, "Foreword" to Hurston, *Their Eyes Were Watching God* (New York, 1990), p. xiii. This kind of double negation in Hurston's fiction and ethnography has received copious commentary in recent years: see Barbara Johnson's "Threshholds of Difference" and "Metaphor, Metonymy, and Voice," in her *A World of Difference* ; and Michele Wallace's "Who Owns Zora Neale Hurston?" in her *Invisibility Blues: From Pop to Theory* (London, 1990).

27 Franz Boas, "Preface" to Zora Neale Hurston's *Mules and Men* (1935; New York, 1990), p. xiii.

28 Ibid., p. xiii.

29 See Houston A. Baker, Jr., *Workings of the Spirit: the Poetics of Afro-American Women's Writing* (Chicago, 1991), pp. 82–83, and Johnson, "Thresholds of Difference," in *A World of Difference*, p. 182.

30 See Richard Handler "The Aesthetics of Sapir's *Language*," in *Studies in the History of Language Sciences* 41 (1986); and Handler, "Vigorous Male and Aspiring Female: Poetry, Personality, and Culture in Edward Sapir and Ruth Benedict," in George Stocking (ed.), History of Anthropology, vol. IV, *Malinowski, Rivers, Benedict and Others: Essays on Culture and Personality* (Madison, 1986). Handler's work includes a discussion of Sapir's "Symposium of the Exotic," which I will expand upon below. See also Krupat, *Ethnocriticism*, pp. 64–74; and Kamala Visweswaran, "Defining Feminist Ethnography," in her *Fictions of Feminist Ethnography* (Minneapolis, 1994). While Handler, Krupat, and Visweswaran carefully map out the "scientific" contours of Boasian anthropology, they argue in their separate analyses that the "linkage of ethnography and literature" (Krupat, *Ethnocriticism*, p. 69) made itself felt in important ways in works by many of Boas's students. Visweswaran, finally, makes specific observations about experimental ethnographies by women anthropologists.

31 For two important instances of this argument at work, see James Weldon Johnson's introduction to *The Book of American Negro Poetry* (1922; New York, 1969) and Hurston's own "Characteristics of Negro Expression," in Nancy Cunard (ed.), *Negro: an Anthology* (London, 1934). Important analyses of these debates in the late nineteenth and early twentieth centuries appear in Henry Louis Gates, Jr.'s "Zora Neale Hurston and the Speakerly Text," in his *The Signifying Monkey: a Theory of Afro-American Literary Criticism* (New York, 1988), and in North's *Dialect of Modernism*.

32 Johnson's novel was published in 1912, but was reissued in 1927.

33 Franz Boas, "Preface" to Zora Neale Hurston's *Mules and Men*, p. xiii.

34 Walter Jackson, "Melville Herskovits and the Search for Afro-American Culture," in George Stocking (ed.), History of Anthropology, vol. IV, *Malinowski, Rivers, Benedict and Others: Essays on Culture and Personality* (Madison, 1986), p. 107. According to Jackson's notations, Herskovits's letter is dated 6/10/27, and comes from the Melville J. Herskovits Papers at Northwestern University, Evanston, Illinois.

35 Valerie Smith, "Black Feminist Theory and the Representation of the 'Other,'" in Cheryl Wall (ed.), *Changing Our Own Words* (New

Brunswick, 1989), p. 45. For related observations, see DuCille, "The Occult of True Black Womanhood."

36 Hemenway, *Zora Neale Hurston*, p. 213. This contrast mounted by Hemenway has exerted enormous influence over recent readings of Hurston's ethnographies. See bell hooks, "Saving Black Folk Culture," in *Yearning*, and Baker, *Workings of the Spirit* for related examples of this kind of reading.

37 Zora Neale Hurston, "Hoodoo in America," in *Journal of American Folk-Lore* 44:174 (1931), p. 318.

38 Zora Neale Hurston, *Mules and Men* (1935; New York, 1990), p. 183.

39 Gordon, "The Poetics and Politics of Ethnographic Authority." In "Multiple Subjectivities and Strategic Positionality: Zora Neale Hurston's Experimental Ethnographies," in Ruth Behar and Deborah Gordon (eds.), *Women Writing Culture* (Berkeley, 1995), Graciela Hernández makes a series of congruent observations about Hurston's *Mules and Men*.

40 Carby, "The Politics of Fiction." A more recent and more extensive effort to complicate the interdisciplinary relations between "literature" and "anthropology" comes in Kamala Visweswaran's 1994 revision of her 1988 essay "Defining Feminist Ethnography," published in *Fictions of Feminist Ethnography* (Minneapolis, 1994). I will discuss Visweswaran's book in some detail in my concluding chapter.

41 See Krupat, *Ethnocriticism*, pp. 64–74.

42 Edward Sapir, "A Symposium of the Exotic," in *Dial* 73 (1922), 568–71.

43 Ibid., p. 570.

44 Ibid.

45 Ibid.

46 Ibid., p. 571.

47 Kamala Visweswaran, in "Defining Feminist Ethnography," p. 32, notes a contemporary version of these concerns: "Self writing about like selves has thus far not been on the agenda of experimental ethnography. To accept 'native' authority *is* to give up the game."

48 George Stocking, "Ideas and Institutions in American Anthropology: Thoughts Toward a History of the Inter-War Years," in *Selected Papers from "The American Anthropologist," 1921–45* (Washington, 1976), pp. 32–33.

49 George Stocking, "The Ethnographic Sensibilities of the 1920s and the Dualism of the Anthropological Tradition," in George Stocking (ed.), *Romantic Motives: Essays on Anthropological Sensibility* (Madison, 1989).

50 See Claudine Raynaud, " 'Rubbing a Paragraph With a Soft Cloth?' Muted Voices and Editorial Constraints in *Dust Tracks on a Road*," in Sidonie Smith and Julia Watson (eds.), *De/Colonizing the Subject* (Minneapolis, 1992) for a careful exposition of the distinctions between the two versions.

51 Individual tales collected in Hurston's folkloric publications have been anthologized repeatedly; in addition, her scholarly work on New Orleans hoodoo was groundbreaking in its time. To the extent that Hurston's research findings were themselves subjected to

frequent self-revision, it strikes me that an important contribution to Hurston studies would be a consideration of the ways in which her fluid, metamorphic hypotheses and experiments were solidified into uninflected scholarly "facts" as they were put to use by later anthologists and researchers.

52 Mackey, "Other: From Noun to Verb," p. 53. Mackey, in a crucial example, bases aspects of his theorization in Hurston's own discussion of verbal nouns in her well-known essay "Characteristics of Negro Expression."

53 Another critical essay that is highly suggestive in this context is Françoise Lionnet's reading of Hurston's *Dust Tracks on a Road* entitled "Autoethnography: the An-Archic Style of *Dust Tracks on a Road*" (in her *Autobiographical Voices: Race, Gender, Self-Portraiture* [Ithaca, 1989]). Lionnet argues that Hurston's attitudes towards her anthropological fieldwork are reflected throughout the autobiography, noting that Hurston "does not just record, describe, and represent; *she transforms and is transformed by her autobiographical performance*" (104, emphasis added); it is this emphasis upon *transformation* that I underscore in my own reading, via Mackey's methodology, of Hurston's textual self-revisions.

54 hooks, "Saving Black Folk Culture," and Carby, "The Politics of Fiction."

55 Zora Neale Hurston, "Black Death," in *The Complete Stories* (New York, 1995). The second version, discussed in the forthcoming pages, appeared in Hurston's *Journal of American Folk-Lore* monograph "Hoodoo in America" in 1931; a third version, "Aunt Judy Bickerstaff," was published as a segment of Nancy Cunard's *Negro: an Anthology* in 1934; I quote here from its reprint in *The Sanctified Church: the Folklore Writings of Zora Neale Hurston*, (Berkeley, 1981), pp. 37–40. A fourth appeared in the chapter entitled "Figure and Fancy," in Hurston's 1942 autobiography *Dust Tracks on a Road* (1942; New York, 1991), pp. 45–60. A fifth, truncated version of the tale, extracted from work that Hurston produced for the Works Progress Administration (WPA) during the late thirties, was published as an appendix to *The Florida Negro: A Federal Writers' Project Legacy*, ed. Gary W. McDonogh (Jackson, Miss., 1993), pp. 150–52.

56 Hurston, "Black Death," p. 203.

57 Ibid..

58 Ibid.

59 Hurston, "Hoodoo in America," pp. 404–5.

60 Barbara Johnson, "Thresholds of Difference: Structures of Address in Zora Neale Hurston," in her *A World of Difference* (Baltimore, 1987).

61 Hurston, "Black Death," p. 202.

62 Hurston, *Dust Tracks on a Road*, p. 127.

63 Hemenway, *Zora Neale Hurston*, p. 78.

64 Hurston, *Dust Tracks on a Road*, p. 58.

65 Ibid., p. 59.

66 Ibid., pp. 58–59.

67 Raynaud gives a full account of recent responses to *Dust Tracks* in her essay " 'Rubbing a Paragraph With a Soft Cloth'?".
68 Ibid., p. 21.
69 Ibid., p. 28.
70 Marjorie Pryse, "Introduction: Zora Neale Hurston, Alice Walker, and the 'Ancient Power' of Black Women," in Marjorie Pryse and Hortense J. Spillers (eds.), *Conjuring: Black Women, Fiction, and Literary Tradition* (Bloomington, 1985); Baker, *Workings of the Spirit*.
71 Hurston, *Mules and Men*, p. 189.
72 Ibid., p. 243.
73 Ibid., pp. 214–15.
74 Ibid., p. 191.
75 Pryse, "Introduction: Zora Neale Hurston," Baker, *Workings of the Spirit*, p. 99.
76 In the appendix to *The Florida Negro* (p. 151), McDonogh includes this tale as part of a "WPA Guide text attributed to Hurston."

5 Dreaming history: Hurston, Deloria, and insider–outsider dialogue

1 Donald A. Messerschmidt, "On Anthropology 'At Home,' " in Donald A. Messerschmidt (ed.), *Anthropologists at Home in North America: Methods and Issues in the Study of One's Own Society* (Cambridge, 1981), pp. 3–14.
2 Biographical information throughout this chapter is gleaned from a number of sources: Elaine Jahner's "Introduction" to James R. Walker's *Lakota Myth*, ed. Elaine Jahner (Lincoln, Neb., 1983); Agnes Picotte's "Biographical Sketch" and Raymond J. DeMallie's "Afterword" to Ella Deloria's *Waterlily* (Lincoln, Neb., 1988); Julian Rice's *Deer Women and Elk Men* (Albuquerque, 1992); and especially Janette Murray's *Ella Deloria: a Biographical Sketch and Literary Analysis* (Dissertation: University of North Dakota, 1974).
3 Alanna Kathleen Brown, review of *Waterlily* in *Studies in American Indian Literature* 4:2–3 (1992), p. 210 and p. 211.
4 Rice, *Deer Women and Elk Men*, pp. 119–29. A note on terminological complexities in Deloria's work: "Dakota" and "Sioux" appear interchangeably in work by many of the critics whose work I quote in the following pages, a broad designation that covers several more specific ones. I quote here from Rice's overview of the issue of naming and nation (on page 1):

> Like Walker, Wissler, and Boas before her, Deloria used "Dakota" in preference to "Sioux" to generically designate several tribal groups living primarily in Minnesota or South Dakota ... For present purposes it is sufficient to say that the Minnesota and western "Sioux" have mutually intelligible languages, diverging most noticeably in the replacement of *d* with *l* by the western Lakota, as they call themselves. A third dialect spoken by a smaller group in south-central South

Dakota uses *n* where their eastern and western relatives use *d* or *l*. They are Nakota.

5 Arnold Krupat, "Fiction and Fieldwork," in *The Nation*, 2–9 July 1988, p. 23. Krupat's comments on "ethnographic fiction" are expanded in his *Ethnocriticism: Ethnography, History, Literature* (Berkeley, 1992), pp. 70–74.

6 Vine Deloria, Jr., "Revision and Reversion," in Calvin Martin (ed.), *The American Indian and the Problem of History* (New York, 1987), p. 85.

7 George W. Stocking, Jr., "The Ethnographic Sensibility of the 1920s and the Dualism of the Anthropological Tradition," in *Romantic Motives: Essays on Anthropological Sensibility* (Madison, 1989), p. 211.

8 James Clifford, "On Ethnographic Authority," in his *The Predicament of Culture: Twentieth-Century Ethnography, Literature, and Art* (Cambridge, Mass., 1988).

9 Zora Neale Hurston, *Dust Tracks on a Road* (1942; New York, 1991), p. 157.

10 Hazel Carby, "The Politics of Fiction, Anthropology, and the Folk: Zora Neale Hurston," in Michael Awkward (ed.), *New Essays on Their Eyes Were Watching God* (Cambridge, 1990), p. 78.

11 Ella Deloria, *Speaking of Indians* (1944; Vermillion, S. Dak., 1979), p. 14.

12 Franz Boas, letter of recommendation for Ella Deloria (7/7/37), quoted by Murray, *Ella Deloria*, pp. 125–26.

13 For more detailed biographical information about Deloria's anthropological career, see Murray, *Ella Deloria*.

14 Boas to Benedict, 11/24/30. Collected in *Writings of Ruth Benedict: an Anthropologist at Work*, edited by Margaret Mead (Boston, 1959), p. 406.

15 Rice, *Deer Women and Elk Men*, p. 6.

16 Jahner, "Introduction," pp. 16–26. For further analysis of Deloria's correspondence with Boas, see Janet L. Finn's "Ella Cara Deloria and Mourning Dove: Writing for Cultures, Writing Against the Grain," in Ruth Behar and Deborah Gordon (eds.), *Women Writing Culture* (Berkeley, 1995).

17 Ella Deloria to Ruth Benedict, 13 February 1947. Ruth Benedict Papers, Vassar College.

18 Finn, "Ella Cara Deloria," p. 138.

19 Trinh T. Minh-Ha, "Outside In Inside Out," in *When the Moon Waxes Red* (New York, 1991), p. 74.

20 Vine Deloria, Jr., "Revision and Reversion," p. 90.

21 Ella Deloria to Ruth Benedict, 7 April 1947. Ruth Benedict Papers, Vassar College.

22 Ella Deloria to Ruth Benedict, 20 May 1941. Ruth Benedict Papers, Vassar College.

23 Carla Kaplan, "The Erotics of Talk: 'That Oldest Human Longing' in *Their Eyes Were Watching God*," in *American Literature* 67:1 (1995), p. 117.

24 Ibid., p. 118.

25 Ella Deloria to Ruth Benedict, 20 May 1941; 18 June 1947. Ruth Benedict Papers, Vassar College.

26 Quoted by Gerald Vizenor in *Manifest Manners: Postindian Warriors of Survivance* (Hanover, N.H., 1994), p. 87.

27 Ruth Benedict to Ella Deloria, 20 July 1932; Ella Deloria to Ruth Benedict, 14 August 1933. Ruth Benedict Papers, Vassar College.

28 Deloria, *Waterlily*, p. 5; Ella Deloria to Ruth Beredict, 20 May, 1941.

29 Kamala Visweswaran, "Defining Feminist Ethnography," in *Fictions of Feminist Ethnography* (Minneapolis, 1994), p. 37.

30 Murray, *Ella Deloria*, pp. 128–20.

31 Krupat, "Fiction and Fieldwork," pp. 22–23.

32 Visweswaran, "Defining Feminist Ethnography," pp. 36–38.

33 Elaine Jahner, in the introduction to James R. Walker's *Lakota Myth* and Julian Rice, in *Deer Women and Elk Men*, analyze Deloria's contributions to the scholarship on Lakota narrative.

34 Zora Neale Hurston, *Mules and Men* (1935; New York, 1990), p. 41.

35 Barbara Johnson, "Thresholds of Difference," in her *A World of Difference* (Baltimore, 1987), pp. 181–82.

36 Deloria, *Speaking of Indians*, p. 73.

37 Deloria herself makes this point just prior to the above-cited passage in *Speaking of Indians*. For a discussion of the (frequently violent) enforcement of educational policies among the "Sioux" in the late nineteenth and early twentieth centuries, see Murray, *Ella Deloria*, pp. 73–77.

38 Deloria, *Waterlily*, p. 5.

39 Zora Neale Hurston, *Moses, Man of the Mountain* (1939; New York, 1991), p. 1.

40 DeMallie, "Afterword" to Deloria, *Waterlily*, pp. 233–34.

41 Visweswaran, "Defining Feminist Ethnography," p. 37.

42 Mary Helen Washington, "Foreword" to Zora Neale Hurston, *Their Eyes Were Watching God* (1937; New York, 1990), p. xiii.

43 For influential discussions of voice in *Their Eyes Were Watching God*, see Barbara Johnson's "Metaphor, Metonymy, and Voice in *Their Eyes Were Watching God*," in her *A World of Difference*, and Henry Louis Gates, Jr.'s "Zora Neale Hurston and the Speakerly Text," in his *The Signifying Monkey* (New York, 1988).

44 Washington, "Foreword," p. xi.

45 Ibid., p. xii. Washington's own " 'I Love the Way Janie Crawford Left Her Husbands': Zora Neale Hurston's Emergent Female Hero," in Henry Louis Gates, Jr. and K. A. Appiah (eds.), *Zora Neale Hurston: Critical Perspectives Past and Present* (New York, 1993), also contains extensive consideration of Hurston's ambivalent treatment of the issue of female voice.

46 Vizenor, *Manifest Manners*, p. 16

47 Lila Abu-Lughod, "Fieldwork of a Dutiful Daughter," in Soraya Altorki and Camillia Fawzi El-Solh (eds.), *Arab Women in the Field: Studying Your Own Society* (Syracuse, 1988).

48 King-Kok Cheung, *Articulate Silences: Hisaye Yamamoto, Maxine Hong Kingston, and Joy Kogawa* (Ithaca, 1993), p. 1.
49 Kaplan, "The Erotics of Talk," p. 127.
50 For a discussion of the "romantic" tendencies in Hurston's work – which I have here encapsulated within the issue of individualism – see Carby's "The Politics of Fiction."
51 Hurston, *Their Eyes Were Watching God*, p. 15.
52 Ibid., p. 10.
53 Deloria, *Waterlily*, p. 6.
54 Hurston, *Their Eyes Were Watching God*, p. 10.
55 Deloria, *Waterlily*, pp. 6–7.
56 Kaplan, "The Erotics of Talk," p. 115.
57 Hurston, *Their Eyes Were Watching God*, p. 10.
58 Deloria, *Waterlily*, p. 152.
59 Martha Garcia, in her 1990 review of *Waterlily*, makes important observations about the function of " 'good' girls" in Waterlily, noting that "they were agreeable, not rebellious. Many girls fell into the pattern, but not all of them." Review of *Waterlily* in *American Indian Quarterly* 14:1 (1990), pp. 70–71.
60 Kaplan, "The Erotics of Talk," p. 118.
61 Ella Deloria to Ruth Benedict, 18 June 1947. Ruth Benedict Papers, Vassar College.
62 Hurston, *Their Eyes Were Watching God*, p. 7.
63 Deloria, *Waterlily*, p. 165.
64 Ibid., p. 37.
65 In the nonfiction book *Speaking of Indians*, Deloria elaborates the issue of the female "dreamer":

> In the old Dakota culture that we have been observing the same things went on in the same way from generation to generation, leaving nothing to be desired. For the Dakota people, theirs was *the* way to live; there was no other. This does not imply that there was not a continuous change in thought, but it was imperceptible; and, because it was rooted in the culture, it offered no threat. New ideas of art, especially in the matter of design, were always appearing, "dreamed" by certain women whom the tribe regarded as being supernaturally endowed.' (p. 49)

It is worth noting that in *Waterlily*, new ideas "[*not*] rooted in the culture" are also incorporated in a near-"imperceptible" way, especially by means of fabric that the women obtain from white traders and use to make new and highly prized styles of clothing; late in the novel, however, this fabric begins to assume a somewhat sinister quality, by means of its implicit connection to a bundle of blankets, left by the US army and used by Waterlily's relatives, that is contaminated by the smallpox virus and eventually generates an epidemic among her family.
66 Hurston, *Their Eyes Were Watching God*, p. 1.
67 Ibid., p. 20.
68 Deloria, *Waterlily*, p. 50.
69 Ibid., p. 51.

70 Ibid.

71 Ibid.

72 "Stolen Pages: Erdrich and Dorris in the Library," unpublished paper given at the California American Studies Association Conference, May, 1992.

73 Deloria, *Speaking of Indians*, p. 57.

74 bell hooks, "Revolutionary 'Renegades,'" in *Black Looks: Race and Representation* (Boston, 1992), p. 187.

6 "Lyrical interrogation": H.D.'s training–analysis

1 For examples, see Lisa Appignanesi and John Forrester, *Freud's Women: Family, Patients, Followers* (New York, 1992); Dianne Chisholm, "Postscript" to her *H.D.'s Freudian Poetics: Psychoanalysis in Translation* (Ithaca, 1992), pp. 214–27; Lucy Freeman and Herbert S. Strean, *Freud and Women* (New York, 1987); Stephen Heath, "Joan Riviere and the Masquerade," in *Formations of Fantasy*, ed. Victor Burgin, James Donald, and Cora Kaplan (London, 1986), pp. 45–61; John Kerr, *A Most Dangerous Method: The Story of Jung, Freud, and Sabina Spielrein* (New York, 1993); and Klaus Theweleit, *Object-Choice (All You Need is Love . . .)* (1990), translated by Malcolm R. Green (London, 1994).

2 For examples, see Wayne Koestenbaum, "Privileging the Anus: Anna O. and the Collaborative Origin of Psychoanalysis," in his *Double Talk: the Erotics of Male Literary Collaboration* (New York, 1989), pp. 17–42; William J. McGrath, *Freud's Discovery of Psychoanalysis: the Politics of Hysteria* (Ithaca, 1986); Elaine Showalter, *The Female Malady: Women, Madness, and English Culture, 1830–1980* (New York, 1985).

3 See Kamala Visweswaran, *Fictions of Feminist Ethnography* (Minneapolis, 1994), p. 73. Visweswaran notes that "psychoanalysis rescripts the anthropologist–'informant' relationship into a doctor–patient scenario," and cites Gananath Obeyesekere's *The Work of Culture: Symbolic Transformation in Psychoanalysis and Anthropology* (Chicago, 1990) as an authority. Obeyesekere stresses that the two fields are "analog[ical]," and not selfsame (p. 231). Following Visweswaran and Obeyesekere, I don't mean to mute the significant differences between the two fields. Instead, what I mean to suggest is that both are techniques for collecting and disseminating the testimony of marginalized subjects, techniques that were refined and professionalized during the cultural moment of "modernism." In this light, John Forrester's work on Freud as a collector – of antiquities as well as of his analysands' stories – is suggestive. See Forrester, " 'Mille e tre': Freud and Collecting," in John Elsner and Roger Cardinal (eds.), *The Cultures of Collecting* (Cambridge, Mass., 1994).

4 For further commentary on the preclusion of the writing informant in professional ethnographic practice, see James Clifford, "Traveling Cultures," in Lawrence Grossberg *et al.* (eds.), *Cultural Studies* (New York, 1992), p. 100.

5 In this emphasis upon the psychoanalytic insider-outsider as a "mediating" figure, my work overlaps with Theweleit's commentary on

"medial women," from his book *Object–Choice*. I will return to Theweleit's arguments, filling in our points of agreement and disagreement, later in this chapter.

6 Sigmund Freud, "Femininity" (1933), from *New Introductory Lectures on Psycho-Analysis*, translated by James Strachey, in *The Standard Edition of the Complete Psychological Works of Sigmund Freud*, vol. XXII (London, 1964), p. 103.

7 Luce Irigaray, *Speculum of the Other Woman* (1974), trans. Gillian C. Gill (Ithaca, 1985), p. 23. See also Sarah Kofman, *The Enigma of Woman: Woman in Freud's Writings* (1980), trans. Catherine Porter (Ithaca, 1985), pp. 18–19.

8 Walter Benjamin, "The Storyteller," in his *Illuminations* (New York, 1969), p. 83.

9 The term is Robert B. Stepto's; see "I Rose and Found My Voice: Narration, Authentication, and Authorial Control in Four Slave Narratives," in his *From Behind the Veil: a Study of Afro-American Narrative* (1979; Urbana, 1991).

10 The biographical particulars of H.D.'s training–analysis with Freud have been recounted many times, in sources that will be mentioned throughout the notes to this chapter. Of particular importance is Susan Stanford Friedman's account in chapter 5 of *Penelope's Web: Gender, Modernity, H.D.'s Fiction* (Cambridge, 1991), pp. 281–354.

11 Sigmund Freud, *Moses and Monotheism* (1939) in *The Standard Edition of the Complete Psychological Works of Sigmund Freud*, vol. XXIII, ed. James Strachey (London, 1964), p. 55. Subsequent quotations from *Moses and Monotheism* will be acknowledged by page number in the text.

12 Quoted by Stephan Salisbury, "In Dr. Freud's Collection, Objects of Desire" in *New York Times*, 3 September 1989, p. 23H.

13 H.D., *Tribute to Freud* (New York, 1974), p. 13.

14 Ibid., p. 57. See also Barbara Guest, *Herself Defined* (Garden City, 1984), p. 235. Subsequent references to *Tribute to Freud* will be acknowledged by page number in the text.

15 Susan Stanford Friedman, "Against Discipleship: Collaboration and Intimacy in the Relationship of H.D. and Freud," in *Literature and Psychology* 33:3–4 (1987), p. 92.

16 Freud to Max Eitingon (1936), quoted by Ernest Jones in *The Life and Work of Sigmund Freud* (1953), edited and abridged by Lionel Trilling and Steven Marcus (New York, 1961), p. 501.

17 Freud to Lou Andreas-Salomé (6 January 1935), quoted by Peter Gay in *Freud: a Life for Our Time* (1988; New York, 1989), p. 605.

18 Much of this commentary has grown out of work by Friedman, who has argued in numerous contexts – and set the agenda for subsequent discussions of H.D. and Freud – that a feminist critique runs throughout the *Tribute* that takes issue with Freud's hypotheses about female psychosexual development. See Susan Stanford Friedman, *Psyche Reborn: the Emergence of H.D.* (Bloomington, 1981); Friedman and Rachel Blau DuPlessis, "Woman is Perfect: H.D.'s Debate With Freud," in *Feminist Studies* 7 (1981), pp. 417–30; Friedman, "Against

Discipleship," pp. 89–108; and the above-cited *Penelope's Web*. For critical and theoretical extensions of Friedman's arguments about H.D.'s oppositionality, see Elizabeth A. Hirsch, "'New Eyes': H.D., Modernism, and the Psychoanalysis of Seeing," in *Literature and Psychology* 32:3 (1986), pp. 1–10; Claire Buck, *H.D. and Freud: Bisexuality and a Feminine Discourse* (New York, 1991); Chisholm, *H.D.'s Freudian Poetics*; Deborah Kelly Kloepfer, *The Unspeakable Mother: Forbidden Discourse in Jean Rhys and H.D.* (Ithaca, 1989). For a more skeptical take, see Paul Smith, "H.D.'s Flaws," in *Iowa Review* 16:3 (1986), pp. 77–86. Finally, Susan Edmunds, whose work negotiates delicately between claims for or against H.D.'s oppositionality, provides an exemplary reception history in *Out of Line: History, Psychoanalysis, and Montage in H.D.'s Long Poems* (Stanford, 1994), pp. 2–5.

19 Friedman, "Against Discipleship," p. 100.
20 See François Roustang, *Dire Mastery: Discipleship from Freud to Lacan* (1976), translated by Ned Lukacher (Baltimore, 1982).
21 Friedman, "Against Discipleship," p. 95.
22 See also Kerr, *A Most Dangerous Method*; Heath, "Joan Riviere and the Masquerade"; and Appignanesi and Forrester, *Freud's Women*, for accounts of triangulated relationships between women analysands and their male analysts.
23 Theweleit, *Object-Choice*, p. 57.
24 Ibid.
25 Ibid., pp. 94–95. Theweleit's commentary, it is important to note, does not respond specifically to Friedman or to other recent feminist commentators on H.D. and Freud. The counterpoint between his readings and Friedman's, however, is striking; see in particular their contrasting assessments of the Bryher relationship and its effects on H.D.'s analysis: Theweleit, *Object-Choice*, pp. 92–93; Friedman, *Penelope's Web*, pp. 313–29.
26 Kofman, *The Enigma of Woman*, pp. 46–48.
27 Theweleit, *Object-Choice*, p. 67.
28 For example, Friedman proposes (most usefully for my own purposes) that H.D.'s literary practice might well have been viewed by Freud as a potential defense against the creeping medicalization of psychoanalysis. "Against Discipleship," p. 95.
29 Louisa May Alcott, *Little Women* (1868; New York, 1993), pp. 394–97.
30 H.D., *Tribute to Freud*, pp. 90 and 107. Susan Stanford Friedman has noted H.D.'s own recollections of discussions with her mother about Louisa May Alcott. See *Psyche Reborn*, p. 138.
31 Susan Edmunds's *Out of Line: History, Psychoanalysis, and Montage in H.D.'s Long Poems* (Stamford, 1994), which I will turn to later in this chapter, makes related efforts to complicate the polarity of "H.D. and Freud" by engaging the work of Melanie Klein. For much more extensive commentary on H.D.'s postanalysis engagement with US literary traditions, see Chisholm, *Psychoanalysis in Translation: H.D.'s Freudian Poetics*, pp. 43–49.
32 See Friedman, *Penelope's Web*, chapter 5 for extensive commentary on the significance of the Bryher correspondence.

33 Bonaparte appears repeatedly in the memoir, and her presence generates peculiar tensions; many of them, I think, might be explained via consideration of Bonaparte's role in the invention of particularly orthodox forms of psychoanalytic literary criticism in her enormous 1933 study *Edgar Poe: Etude Psychanalytique*, whose publication coincided with H.D.'s analysis. That volume, notoriously tedious, dogmatic, and in recent years ritually maligned, is nonetheless a classic of sorts that stands near the start of a long critical tradition.

34 In addition to Friedman's aforementioned commentary, see Chisholm, *H.D.'s Freudian Poetics*, p. 217.

35 See Appignanesi and Forrester, *Freud's Women*, for an account of H.D.'s analysis that sharply downplays her resistances to Freud; "Freud," they write, "would have had reason to be grateful for H.D.'s gratitude" (p. 387), and they describe the analysis as an "analytic love affair" with Freud (p. 388).

36 Ernest Jones, review of *Tribute to Freud* in *International Journal of Psycho-Analysis* (1957), quoted in *Tribute to Freud*, p. vi.

37 Both in their tone and in their complex ramifications, Jones's remarks bear an interesting relationship to Boas's prefatory commentary in Hurston's *Mules and Men*; while in obvious ways both commentaries are patronizing and reductive, they nonetheless point towards the manner in which Hurston's and H.D.'s apparent violations of disciplinary decorum conform in broader ways to the cross-disciplinary, experimental tendencies of Boasian anthropology and Freud's psychoanalysis during the thirties.

38 Goethe, *Wilhelm Meister's Apprenticeship*, trans. Thomas Carlyle (New York, 1839), p. 111.

39 See Chisholm's *H.D.'s Freudian Poetics* for nuanced and extensive commentary on the significance of "translation" in H.D.'s post-analysis writings.

40 Chisholm, *H.D.'s Freudian Poetics*, p. 14.

41 Like the other women whose work I have discussed in the course of this volume, H.D. was also a relentless self-reviser, an issue that has assumed increasing importance in recent H.D. scholarship. For extended considerations of the activity of self-revision in H.D.'s writings, see Friedman, *Penelope's Web*, and her "The Return of the Repressed in Women's Narrative," in *Journal of Narrative Technique* 19 (Winter 1989), pp. 141–56.

42 *Helen in Egypt* (New York, 1961), p. 1. Subsequent quotations from this volume will be acknowledged in the text by page number.

43 While the earliest feminist readings of the poem (for instance, Susan Stanford Friedman's in *Psyche Reborn*) stressed the relationship between *Helen in Egypt* and Freud's narratives of individual development, more recent readings (including Dianne Chisholm's in *H.D.'s Freudian Poetics* and Susan Edmunds's in *Out of Line*) have attended to the relationship between *Helen* and Freud's narratives of cultural history, including *Totem and Taboo* and *Moses and Monotheism*. My reading, though different in its emphases from Chisholm's and Edmunds's, reflects this latter tendency.

44 Roustang, *Dire Mastery*, p. 11.
45 Elizabeth Abel, *Virginia Woolf and the Fictions of Psychoanalysis* (Chicago, 1989), pp. 24–25. In the conclusion to *H.D.'s Freudian Poetics*, pp. 223–25, Dianne Chisholm makes a related point, arguing that in *Helen in Egypt*, "[t]hat the mother should be recovered and revalued ... [makes for] a significant rejoinder to the study of the archetypal hero in *Moses and Monotheism*."
46 Virginia Woolf, *A Room of One's Own* (1929; New York, 1957), p. 80.
47 See Albert Gelpi, "Hilda in Egypt," in *The Southern Review* 18:2 (Spring 1982); Susan Stanford Friedman, "Gender and Genre Anxiety: Elizabeth Barrett Browning and H.D. as Epic Poets," in *Tulsa Studies in Women's Literature* 5:2 (Fall 1986).
48 Hirsch, "New Eyes," p. 6.
49 Edward W. Said has noted, with regard to an earlier phase in the discipline's development, that "Egyptology is Egyptology and not Egypt." See Said, *Culture and Imperialism* (New York, 1993), p. 117. Playwright John Heath-Stubbs, whose own dramatic version of *Helen in Egypt* was published in 1958, reflects this inventiveness in his introduction to the play: "Ancient Egypt and other early civilizations *have, or must seem to us to have, no history*. They were bound by magic and ritual, and their story is a mere chronicle of cycles which repeat themselves." *Helen in Egypt and Other Plays* (London, 1958), p. xi, emphasis added.
50 For contrasting arguments on H.D.'s uses of Egypt, see Dianne Chisholm's *H.D.'s Freudian Poetics*, chapter 4, for an argument that *Helen in Egypt* constitutes a series effort to interrogate the idea of "Greece" as a point of civilizational "origin"; and Susan Edmunds's more skeptical position, mapped out in *Out of Line*, chapter 2, which I will take up at the conclusion of this present chapter.
51 While there is much in the staging and the plot to suggest H.D.'s deliberate intertextual engagement of Strauss's opera in *Helen in Egypt*, I leave this merely as a suggestion, because I have been unable to document the connection between the two texts; H.D., as biographer Barbara Guest has noted, credits Eliza M. Butler's *The Fortunes of Faust* as the source of H.D.'s interest in the countertradition of the Egyptian Helen. See Guest, *Herself Defined*, pp. 290–91. On *Die Aegyptische Helena*, see Charles Osborne, *The Complete Operas of Richard Strauss* (North Pomfret, Vt., 1988), pp. 139–53; Rudolf Hartmann, *Richard Strauss: the Staging of His Operas and Ballets* (New York, 1981).
52 Abel, "(En)gendering History," in her *Virginia Woolf and the Fictions of Psychoanalysis*, pp. 1–29.
53 Friedman, *Penelope's Web*, p. 358.
54 Edmunds, *Out of Line*, p. 120.
55 Ibid. pp. 120–22.
56 Rachel Blau DuPlessis, *H.D.: the Career of that Struggle* (Bloomington, 1986), p. 87. DuPlessis's analysis, as can be seen in this passage, is sensitive throughout to the ways in which, "[t]o all agendas given by others, H.D. is characteristically both complicit and resistant," p. 5.

57 In *Crimes of Writing: Problems in the Containment of Representation* (Oxford, 1991), p. 223, Susan Stewart argues, with regard to the regulation of contemporary graffiti, that "[g]raffiti writers have put their subjectivity in the wrong place; it must be properly reassigned by disciplinary measures." In light of H.D.'s triple preoccupation – with "graffiti" of various kinds; with "subjectivit[ies]," like the Egyptian Helen's, that are "in the wrong place"; and with the maintenance and mutation of a range of "disciplinary" formations – Stewart's remark is richly suggestive.

58 Elizabeth Abel writes persuasively about the relationship between interwar psychoanalysis and anthropology as a "disciplinary *contest*" (emphasis added). See Abel, *Virginia Woolf*, pp. 24–25.

59 Edmunds, *Out of Line*, p. 9.

Conclusion: broken form

1 Ella Deloria to Ruth Benedict, 7 April 1947, from the Ruth Benedict Papers, Vassar College.

2 I refer here, of course, to Eve Kosofsky Sedgwick's vastly influential *Between Men: English Literature and Male Homosocial Desire* (New York, 1985).

3 Susan Fraiman, "Geometries of Race and Gender: Eve Sedgwick, Spike Lee, Charlayne Hunter-Gault," in *Feminist Studies* 20:1 (1994), p. 67.

4 bell hooks, "Culture to Culture," in her *Yearning: Race, Gender, and Cultural Politics* (Boston, 1990), p. 124.

5 *Borders, Boundaries, and Frames: Cultural Criticism and Cultural Studies*, ed. Mae G. Henderson (New York, 1995), pp. 25–26, on the fraught contemporary relationship between cultural studies and African–American studies, has influenced me here. In "Introduction: Borders, Boundaries, and Frame(works)," Henderson writes that

> [i]f ethnic studies (like Women's Studies) continues to be associated with the notions of essentialism and particularism, then the notions of postmodern transnationalism or global culture also carry with them an equally suspect universalism. It is the aim of border studies ... precisely to mediate between the dangers of particularism embodied in the ideas of nationalism and ethnicity (or class and gender) on the one hand and the perils of universalism embodied in transnationalism on the other.

6 James Clifford, "On Ethnographic Allegory," in James Clifford and George Marcus (eds.), *Writing Culture: the Poetics and Politics of Ethnography* (Berkeley, 1986), p. 99.

7 Ibid., p. 120.

8 Elspeth Probyn's "Moving Selves and Stationary Others: Ethnography's Ontological Dilemma," in her *Sexing the Self: Gendered Positions in Cultural Studies* (New York, 1993), has influenced me here; Probyn mounts an important critique of Clifford's "allegorical" strategy that stresses these issues.

9 See Nancy C. Lutkehaus, "Margaret Mead and the 'rustling-of-the-wind-in-the-palm-trees-school' of Ethnographic Writing," in Ruth Behar and Deborah Gordon (eds.), *Women Writing Culture* (Berkeley, 1995); Toril Moi, *Feminist Theory and Simone de Beauvoir* (Cambridge, Mass., 1990); and Brenda Silver, "Mis-fits: The Monstrous Union of Virginia Woolf and Marilyn Monroe," in *Discourse* 16:1 (1993), pp. 71–108.

10 This, of course, is not meant to be indicative of the quality or depth of the extant scholarship on Deloria, which I discussed in some detail in chapter 5. It is, however, indicative of the fact that Native American Studies is perhaps the most severely marginalized and underfunded of any "area studies" field, a condition that has shown no sign of amelioration during the years I have spent working on this current project.

11 Jane Gallop, "Writing About Ourselves," in *Around 1981: Academic Feminist Literary Theory* (New York, 1992), p. 98.

12 The shortcomings of this sort of narrative are demonstrated at some length in Gallop's essay; here, I will specify a pair of difficulties that bear directly on my own argument. First, and most obviously, texts that blur the clarity of the time line tend to be cast aside and forgotten. Thus, for example, we have a little-known essay like June Jordan's "On Richard Wright and Zora Neale Hurston: Notes Toward a Balancing of Love and Hatred" (*Black World*, August 1974, pp. 4–9), which contains a witty but dead-serious, protodeconstructive rereading of the habitual critical distinctions between "protest" and "affirmation" that had been used to cast Hurston's writings into thirty years' oblivion. Jordan's argumentative subtlety makes her essay chronologically inconvenient, thus forgettable. Second, and perhaps more subtle in its effects, is the manner in which variants of the "progress narrative" tend at times, wholly inadvertently, to divert attention from the cultural heterogeneity of feminist discussion *prior* to the early eighties. Thus, for example, *This Bridge Called My Back: Writings by Radical Women of Color* (1981), edited by Cherríe Moraga and Gloria Anzaldúa (New York, 1983), is habitually located by contemporary commentators on an early eighties pivot point in the historical "progress" of feminist debate towards a more diverse and richly conflictual understanding of the meanings of the category of "women." My point here is by no means to question the volume's importance within recent debate, which is undeniable. To the contrary, I am troubled by the way in which *This Bridge*, which contains an extensive bibliography (and some reprints) of texts produced by women of color during the seventies and earlier, is so rarely treated as an indicator of the complex heterogeneity of feminist discussion during the years *before* its publication – merely *after*.

13 For the most explicit and suggestive efforts in this regard, see Deborah McDowell's "Transferences," in Diane Elam and Robyn Wiegman (eds.), *Feminism Beside Itself* (New York, 1995), and Gayle Rubin, "Sexual Traffic" (interview with Judith Butler) in *differences* 6:2–3 (1994). Both McDowell and Rubin are acutely sensitive to what

McDowell calls the "chronopolitics" (p. 99) – i.e., the historiographical nuances – of much recent feminist discussion.

14 See, for example, Nancy K. Miller, *Getting Personal: Feminist Occasions and Other Autobiographical Acts* (New York, 1991), pp. 124–27.

15 See, for example, Deborah Gordon's "Border Work: Feminist Ethnography and the Dissemination of Literacy," in Behar and Gordon (eds.), *Women Writing Culture*; in addition, the October 1993 issue of the *Voice Literary Supplement* contained an important series of reconsiderations of second-wave figures including Solanis and Firestone.

16 Gayatri Spivak, "Can the Subaltern Speak?," in Lawrence Grossberg and Cary Nelson (eds.), *Marxism and the Interpretation of Culture* (Urbana, 1988), p. 308.

17 For a slightly less implicit commentary on these issues, see Spivak's commentary on "identity as commodity" in "Acting Bits/Identity Talk," in *Critical Inquiry* 8 (1992), pp. 798–99.

18 Barbara Christian, "Being the Subject and the Object: Reading African–American Women's Novels," in Gayle Greene and Coppélia Kahn (eds.), *Changing Subjects: the Making of Feminist Literary Criticism* (New York, 1993), p. 200.

19 Ibid.

20 See Lata Mani, "Multiple Mediations: Feminist Scholarship in the Age of Multinational Reception," in *Feminist Review* 35 (Summer 1990), pp. 24–41; Gordon, "Border Work."

21 Elizabeth Grosz, "The Labors of Love. Analyzing Perverse Desire: an Interrogation of Teresa de Lauretis's *The Practice of Love*," in *differences* 6:2–3 (1994), p. 275.

22 Teresa de Lauretis, "Habit Changes," in *differences* 6:2–3 (1994), p. 297.

23 Kamala Visweswaran, *Fictions of Feminist Ethnography* (Minneapolis, 1994), p. 73.

24 Ibid., p. ix and p. 11.

25 Luce Irigaray, *This Sex Which Is Not One* (1977), translated by Catherine Porter (Ithaca, 1985), p. 193.

26 Ibid., p. 196.

Bibliography

Abel, Elizabeth. *Virginia Woolf and the Fictions of Psychoanalysis* (Chicago, 1989).

Abu-Lughod, Lila. *Writing Women's Worlds: Bedouin Stories* (Berkeley, 1993).

"Can There Be a Feminist Ethnography?," in *Women and Performance: a Journal of Feminist Theory* 5:1 (1990).

"Fieldwork of a Dutiful Daughter," in Soraya Altorki and Camillia Fawzi El-Solh (eds.), *Arab Women in the Field: Studying Your Own Society* (Syracuse, 1988).

Agamben, Giorgio. *Infancy and History: Essays on the Destruction of Experience*, translated by Liz Heron (London, 1993).

Aguiar, John L. "Insider Research: an Ethnography of a Debate," in Donald A. Messerschmidt (ed.), *Anthropologists at Home in North America: Methods and Issues in the Study of One's Own Society* (Cambridge, 1981).

Alcott, Louisa May. *Little Women* (New York, 1993).

Allen, Paula Gunn. *The Sacred Hoop: Recovering the Feminine in American Indian Traditions* (Boston, 1986).

Angeles, Paul De. "Interview with Leonora Carrington," in Paul de Angeles, *Leonora Carrington: the Mexican Years (1943–1985)* (San Francisco, 1991).

Appignanesi, Lisa and Forrester, John. *Freud's Women: Family, Patients, Followers* (New York, 1992).

Baddeley, Oriana. " 'Her Dress Hangs Here': De-Frocking the Kahlo Cult," in *The Oxford Art Journal* 14:1 (1991).

Baddeley, Oriana, and Fraser, Valerie. *Drawing the Line: Art and Cultural Identity in Contemporary Latin America* (London, 1989).

Baker, Houston A., Jr. *Workings of the Spirit: the Poetics of Afro-American Women's Writing* (Chicago, 1991).

Benjamin, Walter. *Illuminations*, edited by Hannah Arendt, translated by Harry Zohn (New York, 1969).

Bergman-Carton, Janis. "Strike a Pose: the Framing of Madonna and Frida Kahlo," in *Texas Studies in Language and Literature* 35:4 (1993).

Bonaparte, Marie. *The Life and Works of Edgar Allan Poe* (1933), translated by John Rodker (New York, 1971).

Breslow, Nancy Deffebach. "Frida Kahlo's *The Square is Theirs*: Spoofing Giorgio de Chirico," in *Arts* magazine 56 (January 1982).

Breton, André. *Manifestoes of Surrealism*, translated by Richard Seaver and Helen R. Lane (Ann Arbor, 1972).

Surrealism and Painting, translated by Simon Watson Taylor (New York, 1972).

Breton, André and Rivera, Diego. "Manifesto: Towards a Free Revolutionary Art," translated by Dwight MacDonald, in *Partisan Review* 6:1 (Fall 1938).

Brown, Alanna Kathleen. Review of *Waterlily*, in *Studies in American Indian Literature* 4:2–3 (1992).

Buck, Claire. *H.D. and Freud: Bisexuality and a Feminine Discourse* (New York, 1991).

Burgin, Victor, Donald, James, and Kaplan, Cora (eds.). *Formations of Fantasy* (London, 1986).

Burke, Kenneth. "Surrealism," in *New Directions in Prose and Poetry* (Norfolk, Conn., 1940).

Caffrey, Margaret M. *Ruth Benedict: Stranger in This Land* (Austin, 1989).

Carby, Hazel. "The Politics of Fiction, Anthropology, and the Folk: Zora Neale Hurston," in Michael Awkward (ed.), *New Essays on Their Eyes Were Watching God* (Cambridge, 1990).

Carr, E. H. *What is History?* (1961; New York, 1972).

Carrington, Leonora. *The House of Fear: Notes From Down Below*, edited by Marina Warner, translated by Marina Warner with Kathrine Talbot (New York, 1988).

"Down Below," translated by Victor Llona, in *VVV* 4 (February 1944).

Caws, Mary Ann, Kuenzli, Rudolf, and Raaberg, Gwen (eds.). *Surrealism and Women* (Cambridge, Mass., 1991).

Chadwick, Whitney. *Women Artists and the Surrealist Movement* (Boston, 1985).

Cheung, King-Kok. *Articulate Silences: Hisaye Yamamoto, Maxine Hong Kingston, and Joy Kogawa* (Ithaca, 1993).

Chisholm, Dianne. *H.D.'s Freudian Poetics: Psychoanalysis in Translation* (Ithaca, 1992).

Christian, Barbara. "Being the Subject and the Object: Reading African–American Women's Novels," in Gayle Greene and Coppélia Kahn (ed.), *Changing Subjects: The Making of Feminist Literary Criticism* (New York, 1993).

Clifford, James. *The Predicament of Culture: Twentieth-Century Ethnography, Literature, and Art* (Cambridge, Mass., 1988).

"Partial Truths: Introduction," in James Clifford and Marcus, George E. (eds.), *Writing Culture: the Poetics and Politics of Ethnography* (Berkeley, 1986).

"Traveling Cultures," in Lawrence Grossberg, Cary Nelson, and Paula A. Treichler (eds.), *Cultural Studies* (New York, 1992).

Deloria, Ella Cara. *Speaking of Indians* (Vermillion: S.D., 1979).

Waterlily (Lincoln, Neb., 1988).

Deloria, Vine, Jr. "Revision and Reversion," in Calvin Martin (ed.), *The American Indian and the Problem of History* (New York, 1987).

Douglas, Ann. *Terrible Honesty: Mongrel Manhattan in the 1920s* (New York, 1995).

duCille, Ann. "The Occult of True Black Womanhood: Critical Demeanor and Black Feminist Studies," in *Signs* 19:3 (1994).

DuPlessis, Rachel Blau. *H.D.: the Career of that Struggle* (Bloomington, 1986).

Edmunds, Susan. *Out of Line: History, Psychoanalysis, and Montage in H.D.'s Long Poems* (Stanford, 1994).

Edmundson, Mark. *Towards Reading Freud: Self-Creation in Milton, Wordsworth, Emerson, and Sigmund Freud* (Princeton, 1990).

Elsner, John and Cardinal, Roger, eds. *The Cultures of Collecting* (Cambridge, Mass., 1994).

Faderman, Lillian. *Odd Girls and Twilight Lovers: a History of Lesbian Life in Twentieth-Century America* (New York, 1991).

Fahim, Hussein and Helmer, Katherine. 1982. "Themes and Counter-Themes: the Burg Wartenstein Symposium," in Hussein Fahim (ed.), *Indigenous Anthropology in Non-Western Countries* (Durham, 1982).

Fraiman, Susan. "Geometries of Race and Gender: Eve Sedgwick, Spike Lee, Charlayne Hunter-Gault," in *Feminist Studies* 20:1 (1994).

Franco, Jean. *Plotting Women: Gender and Representation in Mexico* (New York, 1989).

Freeman, Lucy and Strean, Herbert S. *Freud and Women* (New York, 1987).

Freud, Sigmund. *Moses and Monotheism*, vol. XXIII of *The Standard Edition of the Complete Psychological Works of Sigmund Freud*, edited and translated by James Strachey (London, 1964).

"Femininity," in *New Introductory Lectures on Psycho-Analysis*, vol. XXII of *The Standard Edition* (see previous entry).

Friedman, Susan Stanford. *Penelope's Web: Gender, Modernity, H.D.'s Fiction* (Cambridge, 1991).

Psyche Reborn: the Emergence of H.D. (Bloomington, 1981).

"Against Discipleship: Collaboration and Intimacy in the Relationship of H.D. and Freud," in *Literature and Psychology* 33:3–4 (1987).

"Gender and Genre Anxiety: Elizabeth Barrett Browning and H.D. as Epic Poets," in *Tulsa Studies in Women's Literature* 5:2 (Fall 1986).

"The Return of the Repressed in Women's Narrative," in *Journal of Narrative Technique* 19 (Winter 1989).

Friedman, Susan Stanford, and DuPlessis, Rachel Blau, "Woman is Perfect: H.D.'s Debate With Freud," in *Feminist Studies* 7 (1981).

Fusco, Coco and Guillermo Gómez-Peña, Interview with Anna Johnson, in *Bomb* (Winter 1993).

Fussell, Paul. *Abroad: British Literary Traveling Between the Wars* (New York, 1980).

Gallop, Jane. *Around 1981: Academic Feminist Literary Theory* (New York, 1992).

Garcia, Martha. Review of *Waterlily*, in *American Indian Quarterly* 14:1 (1990).

Gates, Henry Louis, Jr. *The Signifying Monkey: a Theory of Afro-American Literary Criticism* (New York, 1988).

Gates, Henry Louis, Jr. and Appiah, K. A. (eds.). *Zora Neale Hurston: Critical Perspectives Past and Present* (New York, 1993).

Gay, Peter. *Freud: a Life for Our Time* (New York, 1989).

Geertz, Clifford. *Works and Lives: the Anthropologist as Author* (Stanford, 1988).

Gelpi, Albert. "Hilda in Egypt," in *The Southern Review* 18:2 (Spring 1982).

Gilbert, Sandra and Gubar, Susan. *No Man's Land: the Place of the Woman Writer in the Twentieth Century*, vol I, *The War of the Words* (New Haven, 1988).

Goethe, Johann Wolfgang von. *Wilhelm Meister's Apprenticeship*, translated by Thomas Carlyle (New York, 1839).

Gordon, Deborah. "The Politics of Ethnographic Authority: Race and Writing in the Ethnography of Margaret Mead and Zora Neale Hurston," in Marc Manganaro (ed.), *Modernist Anthropology: From Fieldwork to Text* (Princeton, 1990).

"Writing Culture, Writing Feminism," in *Inscriptions* 3–4 (1988).

Gordon, Deborah and Ruth Behar (eds.). *Women Writing Culture* (Berkeley, 1995).

Grosz, Elizabeth. "The Labors of Love. Analyzing Perverse Desire: an Interrogation of Teresa de Lauretis's *The Practice of Love*", in *differences* 6:2–3 (1994).

Guest, Barbara. *Herself Defined: the Poet H.D. and Her World* (Garden City, 1984).

H.D. *Helen in Egypt* (New York, 1961).

Tribute to Freud (New York, 1974).

Handler, Richard. "The Aesthetics of Sapir's *Language*," in *Studies in the History of Language Sciences* 41 (1986).

"Boasian Anthropology and the Critique of American Culture," in *American Quarterly* 42:2 (1990).

"Vigorous Male and Aspiring Female: Poetry, Personality, and Culture in Edward Sapir and Ruth Benedict," in George W. Stocking, Jr. (ed.), *History of Anthropology*, volume IV, *Malinowski, Rivers, Benedict and Others: Essays on Culture and Personality* (Madison, 1986).

Harper's Bazaar. Unsigned review of "The New Julien Levy Gallery," November 1937.

Hartmann, Rudolf. *Richard Strauss: the Staging of His Operas and Ballets* (New York, 1981).

Hartsock, Nancy. "Rethinking Modernism: Minority vs. Majority Themes" in Abdul R. JanMohamed and David Lloyd (eds.), *The Nature and Context of Minority Discourse* (Oxford, 1990).

Heath-Stubbs, John. *Helen in Egypt and Other Plays* (London, 1958).

Hegeman, Susan. "Native American 'Texts' and the Problem of Authenticity," in *American Quarterly* 2:41 (1989).

Hemenway, Robert. *Zora Neale Hurston: a Literary Biography* (Urbana, 1977).

Henderson, Mae G. "Introduction: Borders, Boundaries, and Frame-

(work)s," in Mae G. Henderson (ed.), *Borders, Boundaries, and Frames: Cultural Criticism and Cultural Studies* (New York, 1995).

Herrera, Hayden. *Frida: a Biography of Frida Kahlo* (New York, 1983).

"Beauty to His Beast: Frida Kahlo and Diego Rivera," in Whitney Chadwick and Isabelle de Courtivron (eds.), *Significant Others: Creativity and Intimate Partnership* (London, 1993).

Herskovits, Melville J. *The Anthropometry of the American Negro* (New York, 1970).

Franz Boas: The Science of Man in the Making (New York, 1953).

"The Negro's Americanism," in Alain Locke (ed.), *The New Negro* (New York, 1986).

Hirsch, Elizabeth A. " 'New Eyes': H. D., Modernism, and the Psycho-analysis of Seeing," in *Literature and Psychology* 32:3 (1986).

hooks, bell. *Black Looks: Race and Representation* (Boston, 1992).

Talking Back: Thinking Feminist, Thinking Black (Boston, 1989).

Yearning: Race, Gender, and Cultural Politics (Boston, 1990).

Hubert, Renée Riese. *Magnifying Mirrors: Women, Surrealism, and Partnership* (Lincoln, Neb., 1994).

Hurston, Zora Neale. *Dust Tracks on a Road* (New York, 1991).

Moses, Man of the Mountain (New York, 1991).

Mules and Men (New York, 1990).

Their Eyes Were Watching God (New York, 1990).

The Sanctified Church: the Folkore Writings of Zora Neale Hurston (Berkeley, 1981).

"Black Death" (1925), in *The Complete Stories* (New York, 1995).

"Characteristics of Negro Expression," in *Negro: an Anthology*, ed. Nancy Cunard (London, 1934).

"Hoodoo in America," in *Journal of American Folk-Lore* 44:174 (1931).

Huxley, Aldous. *Eyeless in Gaza* (1936; London, 1950).

Huyssen, Andreas. *After the Great Divide: Modernism, Mass Culture, Post-Modernism* (Bloomington, 1986).

Irigaray, Luce. *Speculum of the Other Woman*, translated by Gillian C. Gill (Ithaca, 1985).

This Sex Which Is Not One, translated by Catherine Porter (1977; Ithaca, 1985).

Jackson, Walter. "Melville Herskovits and the Search for Afro-American Culture," in George W. Stocking, Jr. (ed.), *History of Anthropology*, volume IV, *Malinowski, Rivers, Benedict, and Others: Essays on Culture and Personality* (Madison, 1986).

Jahner, Elaine. "Introduction" to James R. Walker's *Lakota Myth*, edited by Elaine Jahner (Lincoln, Neb., 1983).

JanMohamed, Abdul R. "Worldliness-Without-World, Homelessness-As-Home: Toward a Definition of the Specular Border Intellectual," in Michael Sprinker (ed.), *Edward Said: a Critical Reader* (Cambridge, Mass., 1992).

Johnson, Barbara. *A World of Difference* (Baltimore, 1987).

Johnson, James Weldon (ed.). *The Autobiography of an Ex-Coloured Man* (New York, 1990).

The Book of American Negro Poetry (New York, 1969)

Jones, Ernst. *The Life and Work of Sigmund Freud*, abridged, edited by Lionel Trilling and Steven Marcus (New York, 1961).

Joplin, Patricia Klindienst. "The Voice of the Shuttle is Ours," in Lynn A. Higgins and Brenda R. Silver (eds.), *Rape and Representation* (New York, 1991).

Jordan, June. "On Richard Wright and Zora Neale Hurston: Notes Toward a Balancing of Love and Hatred," in *Black World* (August 1974).

Kaplan, Carla. "The Erotics of Talk: 'That Oldest Human Longing' in *Their Eyes Were Watching God*," in *American Literature* 67:1 (1995).

Kerr, John. *A Most Dangerous Method: the Story of Jung, Freud, and Sabina Spielrein* (New York, 1993).

Kloepfer, Deborah Kelly. *The Unspeakable Mother: Forbidden Discourse in Jean Rhys and H.D.* (Ithaca, 1989).

Koestenbaum, Wayne. *Double Talk: the Erotics of Male Literary Collaboration* (New York, 1989).

Kofman, Sarah. *The Enigma of Woman: Woman in Freud's Writings*, translated by Catherine Porter (Ithaca, 1985).

Krupat, Arnold. *Ethnocriticism: Ethnography, History, Literature* (Berkeley, 1992).

"Fiction and Fieldwork," in *The Nation*, 2–9 July 1988, pp.22–23.

Lambert, Angela. *1939: the Last Season of Peace* (London, 1989).

Lauretis, Teresa de. *Alice Doesn't: Feminism, Semiotics, Cinema* (Bloomington, 1984).

Technologies of Gender: Essays on Theory, Film, and Fiction (Bloomington, 1987).

"Habit Changes," in *differences* 6:2–3 (1994).

Levy, Julien. *Memoir of an Art Gallery* (New York, 1977). *Surrealism* (New York, 1995).

Lewis, David Levering. *When Harlem Was in Vogue* (New York, 1981).

Lionnet, Françoise. *Autobiographical Voices: Race, Gender, Self-Portraiture* (Ithaca, 1989).

Lowe, Sarah M. *Frida Kahlo* (New York, 1991).

"Essay," in *The Diary of Frida Kahlo: an Intimate Self-Portrait*, introduction by Carlos Fuentes, essay and commentaries by Sarah M. Lowe (New York, 1995).

Lunn, Eugene. *Marxism and Modernism: an Historical Study of Lukács, Brecht, Benjamin and Adorno* (London, 1985).

McDonogh, Gary (ed.). *The Florida Negro: a Federal Writer's Project Legacy* (Jackson, Miss., 1993).

McDowell, Deborah. "'Transferences: Black Feminist Discourse: the 'Practice' of 'Theory,'" in Diane Elam and Robyn Wiegman (eds.), *Feminism Beside Itself* (New York, 1995).

McGrath, William J. *Freud's Discovery of Psychoanalysis: The Politics of Hysteria* (Ithaca, 1986).

Mabille, Pierre. "Le Paradis," in *VVV* 4 (February 1944).

Mackey, Nathaniel. "Other: From Noun to Verb," in *Representations* 39 (Summer 1992).

Bibliography

Mani, Lata. "Multiple Mediations: Feminist Scholarship in the Age of Multinational Reception," in *Feminist Review* 35 (Summer 1990).

Marcus, George E. and Michael M. J. Fischer. *Anthropology as Cultural Critique: an Experimental Moment in the Human Sciences* (Chicago, 1986).

Martin, Biddy. *Woman and Modernity: the (Life)Styles of Lou Andreas-Salomé* (Ithaca, 1991).

Mascia-Lees, Frances E., Sharpe, Patricia, and Cohen, Colleen Ballerino. "The Postmodernist Turn in Anthropology: Cautions from a Feminist Perspective," in *Signs* 15:1 (1989).

Mead, Margaret. *Blackberry Winter: My Earlier Years* (New York, 1972).

Ruth Benedict (New York, 1974).

"Apprenticeship Under Boas," in Walter Goldschmidt (ed.), *the American Anthropologist, Memoir No. 89: the Anthropology of Franz Boas: Essays on the Centennial of His Birth* (New York, 1959).

Mead, Margaret (ed.). *Writings of Ruth Benedict: An Anthropologist at Work* (Boston, 1959).

Messerschmidt, Donald A. "On Anthropology 'at home,'" in Donald A. Messerschmidt (ed.), *Anthropologists at Home in North America: Methods and Issues in the Study of One's Own Society* (Cambridge, 1981).

Miller, Nancy K. *Getting Personal: Feminist Occasions and Other Autobiographical Acts* (New York, 1991).

Miller, Nina. "The Bonds of Free Love: Constructing the Female Bohemian Self," in *Genders* 11 (Fall 1991).

Mitford, Jessica. *Hons and Rebels* (London, 1978).

Modell, Judith. *Ruth Benedict: Patterns of a Life* (Philadelphia, 1983).

Modleski, Tania. "Doing Justice to the Subjects: Mimetic Art in a Multicultural Society: the Work of Anna Deveare Smith" (forthcoming, 1997).

Mohanty, Chandra Talpade. "Under Western Eyes: Feminist Scholarship and Colonial Discourses," in *Boundary* 2 12:3/13:1 (Spring/Fall 1984).

Moi, Toril. *Feminist Theory and Simone de Beauvoir* (Cambridge, Mass., 1990).

Moraga, Cherríe and Anzaldúa, Gloria (eds.). *This Bridge Called My Back: Writings by Radical Women of Color* (1981) (New York, 1983).

Morrison, Toni. *Beloved* (New York, 1987).

Murray, Janette. "Ella Deloria: a Biographical Sketch and Literary Analysis" (Dissertation: University of North Dakota, 1974).

Nadeau, Maurice. *The History of Surrealism* (1944), translated by Richard Howard (Cambridge, Mass., 1989).

Narayan, Kirin. "How Native is a 'Native' Anthropologist?," in *American Anthropologist* 95:3 (1993).

Newton, Judith and Stacey, Judith. "Learning Not to Curse, or, Feminist Predicaments in Cultural Criticism by Men: Our Movie Date with James Clifford and Stephen Greenblatt," in *Cultural Critique* (Winter 1992/93).

North, Michael. *The Dialect of Modernism* (New York, 1994).

Ogden, Christopher. *Life of the Party: the Biography of Pamela Digby Churchill Hayward Harriman* (Boston, 1994).

Osborne, Charles. *The Complete Operas of Richard Strauss* (North Pomfret, V., 1988).

Parsons, Elsie Clews (ed.). *American Indian Life* (Lincoln: Neb., 1991).

Prakash, Gyan. "Science 'Gone Native' in Colonial India," in *Representations* 40 (Fall 1992).

Pratt, Mary Louise. " 'YO SOY LA MALINCHE': Chicana Writers and the Poetics of Ethnonationalism," in *Callaloo* 16:4 (1993).

Probyn, Elspeth. "Moving Selves and Stationary Others: Ethnography's Ontological Dilemma," in Elspeth Probyn, *Sexing the Self: Gendered Positions in Cultural Studies* (New York, 1993).

Pryse, Marjorie and Spillers, Hortense J., eds. *Conjuring: Black Women, Fiction, and Literary Tradition* (Bloomington, 1985).

Raynaud, Claudine. " 'Rubbing a Paragraph With a Soft Cloth'? Muted Voices and Editorial Constraints in *Dust Tracks on a Road*," in Sidonie Smith and Julia Watson (eds.), *De/Colonizing the Subject* (Minneapolis, 1992).

Rice, Julian. *Deer Women and Elk Men: the Lakota Narratives of Ella Deloria* (Albuquerque, 1992).

Lakota Storytelling: Black Elk, Ella Deloria, and Frank Fools Crow (New York, 1989).

Rose, Peter. "Problems in Conveying the Meaning of Ethnicity: the Insider/Outsider Debate," in Peter Rose, *Mainstreams and Margins: Jews, Blacks, and Other Americans* (New Brunswick, 1983).

Roustang, François. *Dire Mastery: Discipleship from Freud to Lacan*, translated by Ned Lukacher (Baltimore, 1982).

Rubin, Gayle. "The Traffic in Women: Notes on the 'Political Economy' of Sex," in Ilene J. Philipson and Karen V. Hansen (eds.), *Women, Class, and the Feminist Imagination: A Socialist–Feminist Reader*, (Philadelphia, 1990).

Rubin, Gayle and Butler, Judith, "Sexual Traffic," in *differences* 6:2–3 (1994).

Rubin, William S. *Dada, Surrealism, and Their Heritage* (New York, 1982).

Said, Edward W. *Culture and Imperialism*. (New York, 1993).

The World, the Text, and the Critic (Cambridge, Mass., 1983).

"Representing the Colonized: Anthropology's Interlocutors," in *Critical Inquiry* 15 (Winter 1989).

Salisbury, Stephan. "In Dr. Freud's Collection," *The New York Times*, 9/29/89.

Sapir, Edward. "A Symposium of the Exotic," in *Dial* 73 (1922).

Sawin, Martica. "El Surrealismo etnográfico y la América indígena," in *El Surrealismo entre viejo y nuevo mundo* (Centro Atlantico de Arte Moderno, 1990).

Schaefer, Claudia. *Textured Lives: Women, Art, and Representation in Modern Mexico* (Tucson, 1992).

Sedgwick, Eve Kosofsky. *Between Men: English Literature and Male Homosocial Desire* (New York, 1985).

Showalter, Elaine. *The Female Malady: Women, Madness, and English Culture, 1830–1980* (New York, 1985).

Bibliography

Silver, Brenda R. "Mis-fits: The Monstrous Union of Virginia Woolf and
    Marilyn Monroe," in *Discourse* 16:1 (1993).
    "Textual Criticism as Feminist Practice: Or, Who's Afraid of Virginia
    Woolf Part II," in George Bornstein (ed.), *Representing Modernist
    Texts: Editing as Interpretation* (Ann Arbor, 1991).
Smith, Paul. "H.D.'s Flaws," in *Iowa Review* 16 (1986).
    "H.D.'s Identity," in *Women's Studies* 10 (1984).
Spivak, Gayatri Chakravorty. "Acting Bits/Identity Talk," in *Critical
    Inquiry* 18 (Summer 1992).
    "Can the Subaltern Speak?," in Lawrence Grossberg and Cary Nelson
    (eds.), *Marxism and the Interpretation of Culture* (Urbana, 1988).
    "Displacement and the Discourse of Woman," in Mark Krupnick (ed.),
    Displacement: Derrida and After (Bloomington, 1983).
    "Who Claims Alterity?" in Barbara Kruger and Phil Mariani (eds.),
    Remaking History (Seattle, 1989).
Stadler, Quandra Prettyman. "Learning What She Wanted: Zora Neale
    Hurston '28," in *Barnard College Alumnae Magazine* (Winter 1979).
Stepto, Robert B. "I Rose and Found My Voice: Narration, Authentica-
    tion, and Authorial Control in Four Slave Narratives," in Robert B.
    Steps, *From Behind the Veil: a Study of Afro-America Narrative* (Urbana,
    1991).
Stewart, Susan. *Crimes of Writing: Problems in the Containment of Represen-
    tation* (Oxford, 1991).
Stich, Sidra. *Anxious Visions: Surrealist Art* (New York, 1990).
Stocking, George W., Jr. *Race, Culture, and Evolution: Essays in the History
    of Anthropology* (New York, 1968).
    "The Ethnographic Sensibility of the 1920s and the Dualism of the
    Anthropological Tradition," in George W. Stocking, Jr. (ed.),
    Romantic Motives: Essays on Anthropological Sensibility (Madison,
    1989).
    "Ideas and Institutions in American Anthropology: Thoughts Toward
    a History of the Inter-War Years," in George W. Stocking, Jr., *Selected
    Papers from "The American Anthropologist," 1921–45* (Washington,
    1976).
Stocking, George W., Jr., ed. *A Franz Boas Reader: the Shaping of American
    Anthropology, 1883–1911* (New York, 1974).
Suleiman, Susan Rubin. *Subversive Intent: Gender, Politics, and the Avant-
    Garde* (Cambridge, Mass., 1990).
    "The Bird Superior Meets the Bride of the Wind: Leonora Carrington
    and Max Ernst," in Whitney Chadwick and Isabelle de Courtivron
    (eds.), *Significant Others: Creativity and Intimate Partnership* (London,
    1993).
Theweleit, Klaus. *Object–Choice (All You Need is Love ...)* (1990), tran-
    slated by Malcolm R. Green (London, 1994).
Tibol, Raquel. *Frida Kahlo: an Open Life*, translated by Elinor Randall
    (Albuquerque, 1993).
Time magazine. "Bomb Beribboned" (unsigned review), 14 November
    1938.
Toor, Frances. *A Treasury of Mexican Folkways* (New York, 1947).

Trinh T. Minh-Ha. *When the Moon Waxes Red: Representation, Gender, and Cultural Politics* (New York, 1991).

Woman, Native, Other: Writing Postcoloniality and Feminism (Bloomington, 1989).

Trotsky, Leon. "Leon Trotsky to André Breton," in *Partisan Review* 6:2 (Winter 1939).

Tucker, Herbert. "Dramatic Monologue and the Overhearing of Lyric," in Patricia Parker and Chaviva Hosek (eds.), *Lyric Poetry: Beyond New Criticism* (Ithaca, 1985).

Visweswaran, Kamala. *Fictions of Feminist Ethnography* (Minneapolis, 1994).

"Defining Feminist Ethnography," in *Inscriptions* 3–4 (1988).

Vizenor, Gerald. *Manifest Manners: Postindian Warriors of Survivance* (Hanover, N.H., 1994).

Walker, Alice. *In Search of Our Mothers' Gardens* (New York, 1983).

Wall, Cheryl (ed.). *Changing Our Own Words: Essay on Criticism, Theory, and Writing by Black Women* (New Brunswick, N.J., 1989).

Wallace, Michele. *Invisibility Blues: from Pop to Theory* (London, 1990).

Washington, Mary Helen. "Foreword," to Zora Neale Hurston, *Their Eyes Were Watching God* (New York, 1990).

"'I Love the Way Janie Crawford Left her Husbands': Emergent Female Hero," in Henry Louis Gates, Jr. and K. A. Appiah (eds.), *Zora Neale Hurston: Critical Perspectives Past and Present* (New York, 1993).

Watt, Donald (ed.). *Aldous Huxley: the Critical Heritage* (Boston, 1975).

Wharton, Edith. *The Age of Innocence* (New York, 1948).

Whitfield, Stephen J. *A Death in the Delta: the Story of Emmett Till* (New York, 1988).

Williams, Raymond. *Keywords: a Vocabulary of Culture and Society*, revised edition (Oxford, 1984).

The Politics of Modernism: Against the New Conformists, edited by Tony Pinkney (London, 1989).

Wolfe, Bertram. "Rise of Another Rivera," in *Vogue* (November 1938).

Woolf, Virginia. *A Room of One's Own* (New York, 1957).

Index

Index

Index

Matta Echaurren, Roberto, 42, 87
Mauss, Marcel, 43, 187
Mead, Margaret, 102
Mégnen, Jeanne, 87, 88, 92
Michigan, University of, 28
Miller, Lee, 85
Miller, Nina, 24
Mitford, Jessica, 78
Modleski, Tania, 30
Mohanty, Chandra Talpade, 5
Momaday, N. Scott, 126
Moraga, Cherríe, 226n12
Morrison, Toni, 153–55
Moses and Monotheism (Freud), 14,
    158–60, 170, 171–73, 179
Moses, Man of the Mountain
    (Hurston), 140, 148, 150, 158
Mules and Men (Hurston), 10, 102,
    105–6, 108, 109, 114, 115, 121–23,
    135, 136–39
Murray, Janette, 134
My Dress Hangs There (aka *My Dress
    Was There Hanging*) (Kahlo),
    53–54
*My Grandparents, My Parents and I
    (Family Tree)* (Kahlo), 60–61

NAACP, 102
Nadeau, Maurice, 43
Nadja (Breton), 50, 51, 58, 81, 82, 97,
    98
Narayan, Kirin, 2, 39
National Autonomous University of
    Mexico, 58
"Negro's Americanism, The"
    (Herskovits), 102–4, 110
New Directions, 44
New Negro, The (ed. Locke), 102
North, Michael, 212n24

Oberlin College, 125
Obeyesekere, Gananath, 220n3
Ogden, Christopher, 75, 87
Opportunity, 116–17
Oval Lady, The (Carrington), 74

"Paradis, Le" (Mabille), 88–89
Parisot, Henri, 81
Parsons, Elsie Clews, 110
Partisan Review, 41
Pascal, Blaise, 93
"'Pet Negro' System, The"
    (Hurston), 99
Picasso, Pablo, 46, 64–68
Poe, Edgar Allan, 174
Polizzotti, Mark, 57
Pound, Ezra, 24
Prakash, Gyan, 12, 199n23
Prassinos, Gisèle, 42
"Preface" to *Mules and Men* (Boas),
    105–7
Probyn, Elspeth, 54
Pryse, Marjorie, 121–22

Read, Herbert, 77
Reichard, Gladys, 101
Retamar, Roberto Fernández, 152
Revenge on Culture (Lee Miller), 85
Rice, Julian, 125, 129, 216n4
Rieman, Donald, 33
"Rise of Another Rivera" (Wolfe),
    51–52
Riviere, Joan, 161
Rivera, Diego, 26, 40, 41, 48, 52, 53,
    54, 60, 61, 66, 68, 78
Rose, Peter, 13
Roustang, François, 160, 170
Rubin, Gayle, 15, 27, 28, 29, 30, 31,
    180, 185–86, 187
Rubin, William S., 71

Sachs, Hanns, 165, 178
Said, Edward W., 23, 27, 31, 45
Salomé, Lou Andreas, 160
Sapir, Edward, 103, 111–12
Schaefer, Claudia, 55
Schiaparelli, Elsa, 52
Schlegel, Caroline, 49
Sedgwick, Eve Kosofsky, 225n2
*Self-Portrait (Dedicated to Leon
    Trotsky)* (aka *Between the
    Curtains*) (Kahlo), 48, 52, 66–68